Practical Ext JS 4

Prabhu Sunderaraman

Apress

Practical Ext JS 4

ISBN-13 (pbk): 978-1-4302-6073-8

ISBN-13 (electronic): 978-1-4302-6074-5

President and Publisher: Paul Manning
Lead Editor: Ben Renow-Clarke
Development Editor: Tom Welsh
Technical Reviewer: Massimo Nardone
Editorial Board: Steve Anglin, Mark Beckner, Ewan Buckingham, Gary Cornell, Louise Corrigan, Morgan Ertel, Jonathan Gennick, Jonathan Hassell, Robert Hutchinson, Michelle Lowman, James Markham, Matthew Moodie, Jeff Olson, Jeffrey Pepper, Douglas Pundick, Ben Renow-Clarke, Dominic Shakeshaft, Gwenan Spearing, Matt Wade, Tom Welsh
Coordinating Editor: Anamika Panchoo
Copy Editor: Angie Wood
Compositor: SPi Global
Indexer: SPi Global
Artist: SPi Global
Cover Designer: Anna Ishchenko

Distributed to the book trade worldwide by Springer Science+Business Media New York, 233 Spring Street, 6th Floor, New York, NY 10013. Phone 1-800-SPRINGER, fax (201) 348-4505, e-mail orders-ny@springer-sbm.com, or visit www.springeronline.com. Apress Media, LLC is a California LLC and the sole member (owner) is Springer Science + Business Media Finance Inc (SSBM Finance Inc). SSBM Finance Inc is a Delaware corporation.

For information on translations, please e-mail rights@apress.com, or visit www.apress.com.

Apress and friends of ED books may be purchased in bulk for academic, corporate, or promotional use. eBook versions and licenses are also available for most titles. For more information, reference our Special Bulk Sales–eBook Licensing web page at www.apress.com/bulk-sales.

Any source code or other supplementary materials referenced by the author in this text is available to readers at www.apress.com. For detailed information about how to locate your book's source code, go to www.apress.com/source-code/.

To my family

Contents at a Glance

Contents

About the Author

Prabhu Sunderaraman is a programmer, speaker, trainer, and writer who works with DuraSoft, in Chennai, in the southern part of India. He has more than 11 years of experience in working with a wide range of projects in various technologies. He has offered more than 300 corporate training sessions all over the world. Prabhu is a strong advocate of Test Driven Development and likes coding all the time. Prabhu is also the author of Spring 3.0 Black Book, and blogs actively at http://healthycoder.in. He enjoys reading and traveling and has been a passionate practitioner of KravMaga for several years.

About the Technical Reviewer

Massimo Nardone holds a Master of Science degree in Computing Science from the University of Salerno, Italy. He worked as a PCI QSA and Senior Lead IT Security/Cloud Architect for many years, and currently he leads the Security Consulting Team in Hewlett Packard Finland. With more than 19 years of work experience in SCADA, Cloud Computing, IT Infrastructure, Mobile, Security, and WWW technology for national and international projects, Massimo has worked as a Project Manager, Software Engineer, Research Engineer, Chief Security Architect, and Software Specialist. He worked as visiting lecturer and supervisor for exercises at the Networking Laboratory of the Helsinki University of Technology (Helsinki University of Technology TKK became a part of Aalto University) for the course of "Security of Communication Protocols." He holds four international patents (PKI, SIP, SAML and Proxy areas).

Acknowledgments

A number of people have helped me in shaping this book.

First of all, I have to thank all the developers I have interacted with during my talks and consulting assignments for the last 2 years. The discussions with them made me understand the concepts of Ext JS 4 better. Some of the comments contributed by readers of my blog posts offered good insights into the framework.

I would like to thank my technical reviewer Massimo Nardone, whose comments and troubleshooting, particularly in the code examples, have been really helpful in shaping this into a better book.

Writing a book is not easy. It eats up your time, as it involves a lot of focus. I would like to thank my manager and friend Siva at DuraSoft for being extremely accommodating and encouraging all through.

Lastly, I would like to thank the team at Apress for being thoroughly professional throughout. It was a pleasure working with you all.

Introduction

This book is a succinct guide to the Ext JS 4 framework written from a developer's perspective. My objective is that, after reading this book, you should be able to develop an Ext JS 4 application right away.

Who Should Read This Book?

This book is written for programmers who want to build rich Internet applications using the Ext JS 4 library. If you are working on a project using Ext JS 4, or are ready to get started with a new Ext JS 4 application, this book is for you, as it explains all the concepts in Ext JS 4 from a developer's point of view. Or if you are just interested in reading about Ext JS 4 and its features, this book should make it clear.

I have assumed a basic knowledge of HTML and JavaScript on the part of the reader. If you have been an OO programmer but have never been in the mainstream of JavaScript development, and now want to write rich web applications, then Ext JS 4 and this book are for you. However, this book should not be used as a primer on general web application development and JavaScript; it is more specialized than that.

How to Read This Book?

It's strongly recommended that you read the book in chapter order from the first to the last. Each chapter talks about a particular topic and will have examples built using the concepts covered in previous chapters. Hence skipping chapters may lead to confusion as you may well run into terms that were explained in the chapters you missed.

This book is not a comprehensive substitute for the Ext JS 4 API documentation. Ext JS 4 provides tons of classes and functions, and I don't have time and space to explain all of them. So you still need to refer to the documentation.

The concepts are explained in a pretty straightforward and succinct manner.

Contents overview

- **Chapter 1**, *Core JavaScript and JavaScript Frameworks* introduces you to the core language features of JavaScript such as function hoisting, the arguments keyword, JSON, etc., that will help you understand Ext JS 4 API better. It also introduces you to JavaScript frameworks in general and their significance in web development.

- **Chapter 2**, *Overview of Ext JS 4* gets you started with Ext JS 4 by setting up the environment and writing some basic code.

- **Chapter 3**, *Understanding Ext JS 4 API* explains the structure of the Ext JS 4 API. I show you how to use Ext JS 4 syntax to create custom classes and objects, and introduce features like inheritance, overriding, and mixins.

- **Chapter 4**, *Controls and Layout* covers the basic UI controls such as textbox, button, checkbox, etc. It also deals with basic form validations and form processing concepts. The chapter explains the layout controls and gives a detailed description of using layout controls like Border layout, Card layout, etc.

- **Chapter 5**, *Working with Data* dives into the data exchange and data handling capabilities of Ext JS 4. You will learn how to access server and HTML 5 resources and exchange JSON and XML data.

- **Chapter 6**, *Data Controls* delves deeper into data controls like grids, trees, list boxes, and charts.

- **Chapter 7**, *Drag and Drop* explains drag and drop behavior in Ext JS 4. You will learn the Drag and Drop API in detail and apply it to UI components like grids, trees, etc.

- **Chapter 8**, *Theming and Styling* introduces you to the concepts of styling and theming in Ext JS 4. You will see the usage of SASS and Compass with practical examples.

- **Chapter 9**, *MVC and Ext JS 4* covers MVC architecture in Ext JS 4 in detail. We'll build an application from scratch using the MVC architecture.

- **Chapter 10**, *Extending, Unit Testing, and Packaging* talks about extending Ext JS 4 by creating custom components and using them. You will learn how to unit test Ext JS 4 applications using the unit testing library Jasmine. This chapter covers how to package and deploy Ext JS 4 applications.

CHAPTER 1

■ ■ ■

Core JavaScript and JavaScript Frameworks

A lot of applications are being developed today using Ajax and HTML 5. Developing a rich web application can get really tedious, thanks to JavaScript. Building an application by writing JavaScript code that can be easily tested and maintained is not simple. It requires a great deal of coding discipline. Moreover we don't want to be doing repetitive tasks like validating our forms, sending Ajax requests, manipulating the DOM, drawing, etc., in all our applications. And that's the reason you have a number of JavaScript frameworks available today.

These JavaScript frameworks make life easier for web developers. They provide APIs that save time and effort in implementing the necessary behavior. These frameworks give us ready-made UI controls and reusable methods and properties that make developing applications a breeze.

This chapter talks about some of the popular JavaScript libraries and highlights the features of Ext JS 4. You'll also learn about some features of the JavaScript language that will help you prepare for working with Ext JS 4 API. The objective of this chapter is to introduce you to the kind of JavaScript code we need to write when working with Ext JS 4 API. The Ext JS 4 API is simple to understand, provided you have a good knowledge of the JavaScript language.

JavaScript Frameworks

Let's take a quick look at some JavaScript libraries that are widely used by developers. I'll just highlight the important aspects of these libraries, and not delve into them in detail.

- **Prototype**- One of the early JavaScript frameworks that made coding in JavaScript really simple, Prototype provides a set of utility functions to work with the DOM and Ajax. It doesn't offer ready-made UI components. Prototype is a nice little API that can be used for simple tasks like form validations, sending Ajax requests, DOM operations etc.

- **jQuery**- jQuery is a very popular JavaScript library that took JavaScript coding to the next level. It provides an easy-to-use API. The jQuery UI, which is built over the core of jQuery, gives us a lot of UI controls. You can extend it to suit your needs by creating plugins. But jQuery has some drawbacks; for instance its codebase can grow to be a monster when used alone. It's more convenient when used with frameworks like Backbone or KnockOut for greater modularity.

- **DOJO**- The DOJO toolkit brings an OO flavor to JavaScript. It's a complete toolkit with UI controls, utility functions, and theming support that can be used for building enterprise applications. DOJO, however has always been criticized for its lack of coherent documentation, and also for performance issues.

- **GWT**- Google Web Toolkit is actually a Java library that gets compiled to JavaScript. We develop a Java web application using GWT API, and it emits highly optimized JavaScript code that can be deployed to a web server. Naturally, the library is targeted at Java developers.

- **Angular JS**- This is an open source library from Google. It's popular for the Model-View-Controller (MVC) capabilities it offers. Angular JS gives you a template-based declarative solution for building web pages. Its main drawback is a steep learning curve, largely due to its poor documentation and code examples.

As a developer, I have used most of these JavaScript libraries in my applications. Libraries like jQuery and Prototype are well suited to smaller applications. If you're looking at developing an enterprise application that deals with graphs, data grids, communicating with a server, and exchanging lot of data, drag and drop behavior etc, Ext JS 4 is a pretty good candidate. Personally Ext JS 4 has impressed me a lot compared to other libraries. Here's a list of features in Ext JS 4 that make it more compelling to work with.

- **Object-Oriented flavor**- JavaScript has never been taken seriously as a programming language. We never learn JavaScript the way we have learned Java or C# or Ruby. Developers who come from an OO background find it difficult to shift to the functional style of coding; so JavaScript, as a functional programming language, poses adaptability issues for OO developers. Ext JS 4 lends an OO flavor to the JavaScript language. So developers who are accustomed to coding in OO languages will be in tune with the Ext JS 4 API.

- **Rich UI controls**- Ext JS 4 provides a rich set of UI components, like any other JavaScript library. The UI controls include different types of form components, and data components such as grid, tree, and charts. You have to write a few lines of code in JavaScript even to create a simple label or a textbox. The programmatic approach to using UI components paves the way for extending and customizing them.

- **Support for HTML 5**- HTML 5 provides a set of features like a new set of UI tags, multimedia capabilities without depending on third party plugins, data storage facilities, web sockets, web workers, Canvas API for drawing, GeoLocation, and working with history. The Ext JS 4 API supports HTML 5 tags, working with local storage and session storage, drawing, etc.

- **MVC architecture**- Modularity has always been an issue in JavaScript libraries. Maintenance is a nightmare in web applications developed using JavaScript, no matter what framework we use. Incorporating new behavior into existing code is a tedious task. Very few libraries in JavaScript take care of modularity. Ext JS 4 stands apart in this respect. One of the reasons for Ext JS 4's popularity is the support that it offers for implementing MVC. The complete code can be organized into folders and files following the MVC architecture. Making changes and testing becomes easier because of this.

- **Theming and Styling**- Creating stylesheets by writing vanilla CSS code for an entire application can be very frustrating: it's an uphill task. Ext JS 4 gives us themes that can be used in applications. You can modify those themes to suit your needs. But we don't have to write CSS code to do that. Ext JS 4 relies upon SASS (Syntactically Awesome StyleSheets) scripts for styling. The style sheets for the UI controls are available as SASS files which we can play with. The SASS scripts are then compiled to CSS files using a Ruby script called Compass. This makes styling our applications much easier.

- **Documentation**- Sencha maintains very good API documentation for all the versions. The documentation is very well organized and includes nice reference material, something I have missed while working with other JavaScript libraries. It has good code examples that illustrate the usage of many features.

- **Moving to the mobile version**- Many of my clients who have built web applications targeting desktop browsers also plan to build—or already building—mobile-friendly versions of the same applications. Building applications that can work seamlessly in a desktop, as well as on smart phones and tablets, requires a great deal of effort. Using Ext JS 4 in applications has an added advantage if you aim to develop a mobile version too. Sencha provides us with a popular JavaScript library called Sencha Touch for building mobile web applications. The structure of Sencha Touch API is very similar to Ext JS 4. The concepts, coding style and the patterns of these two libraries are almost the same. There are some differences and Sencha has been working to even out these two APIs with every release. Apart from the inherent complexities in developing mobile applications, developers working with Ext JS 4 can very quickly adopt Sencha Touch and create a mobile version.

Ext JS 4 is one of the very few frameworks where you develop the UI not using plain HTML but by writing JavaScript code. As mentioned earlier, even if you want to create a simple UI component like a Button you would have to write some lines of JavaScript code. You can imagine the number of lines of code you would need to create components like grid, trees and charts. So it's very important to be extremely comfortable with the core JavaScript language before you begin working with Ext JS 4.

If you want to understand Ext JS 4 API and master its use, it's important to understand certain aspects of JavaScript. These concepts are often ignored by OO developers who find they have to write JavaScript code. Let's run through these concepts in JavaScript which play an important role in understanding Ext JS 4 API.

■ **Note**   The next section talks about some core JavaScript concepts and their relevance to the code we'll write using Ext JS 4. If you are eager to get started coding with Ext JS 4, just jump ahead to Chapter 2. But bear in mind that reading this section will reinforce your awareness of the JavaScript features you need to be happy with before using Ext JS 4. It will also give you a feel for the style of code that you'll be writing in Ext JS 4.

JavaScript Language Features

JavaScript is a functional, interpreted, and dynamically typed language. It's case-sensitive and a lot of its programming constructs—like the `for` and `while` loops, `if-else`, `switch-case` statements etc.—are very similar to their equivalents in C and Java.

In this first chapter, it would be hopeless to try to describe all the features of JavaScript. Instead, I shall focus on those that will get you started with Ext JS 4 quickly.

Let's begin with the `arguments` keyword.

The Arguments Keyword

The `arguments` keyword is an implicit parameter available to functions in JavaScript. It's an array that is used to access the function's parameter list, which basically says you don't really have to formally declare arguments for a function, but you can still access the values passed, using the 'arguments'.

Say you have a method to calculate the sum of all the values passed to a method. You can write it as shown in Listing 1-1.

Listing 1-1. The arguments keyword

```
function sum(){
 var sum = 0;
 for(var i=0;i<arguments.length;i++){
   sum += arguments[i];
 }
 console.log(sum);
}
add(1,2,3); //Prints 5
add(10,20,30,40,50); //Prints 150
add(100,12); //Prints 112
```

You can see that the `arguments` keyword is a built-in array parameter that can be used to access the parameters passed when the function is invoked.

Use of Arguments in Ext JS 4

Ext JS 4 API has many functions defined to accept a number of arguments, but you do not always invoke them by passing all the arguments. For example, here is a code snippet where I handle the `itemclick` event for a data grid. Both lines are valid; the difference lies in the number of arguments you pass to the function.

```
Ext.getCmp("mygrid").on("itemclick",function(src,record){...});
Ext.getCmp("mygrid").on("itemclick",function(src,record,index){...});
```

You can call a base class method from the derived class method in Ext JS 4 by writing `this.callParent(arguments);` notice the use of the `arguments` keyword. You will learn more about creating classes in Chapter 3.

Functions

In JavaScript functions are first class citizens, like classes in OO languages.

You can define a function in the traditional way like this.

```
function eat(){ console.log("Eating"); }
```

You can invoke the `eat()` function even before you define it, as shown here.

```
eat();//Prints Eating
function eat(){ console.log("Eating"); }
```

Though JavaScript is an interpreted language, function definitions are run first, irrespective of where they are placed in the code. So you can invoke a function even before you define it like the `eat()` function call.

You can also assign a function to a variable like this:

```
var eat = function(){ console.log("Eating"); }
```

Though eat is defined to be a variable, you can still invoke it like a normal function call: eat(). But what you have to watch out for is that you cannot invoke the eat() function before defining the variable. The following code will throw an error if the function is declared as an expression.

```
eat();//Uncaught TypeError: Property 'eat' of object [object DOMWindow] is not a function
var eat = function(){ console.log("Eating"); }
```

So what's the use of assigning a function to a variable? You can pass the eat variable as an argument to other functions, as shown in Listing 1-2.

Listing 1-2. Functions as arguments

```
function work(arg){
  arg();
}
work(eat);
work(function(){console.log("Coding");});
```

As shown in Listing 1-2, the work() function accepts an argument which can be a reference to another function. We can then invoke the passed function using the arg() call. A function that accepts another function as an argument is commonly referred as a *Higher-order function*.

Use of Higher-Order Functions in Ext JS 4

In Ext JS 4 you have plenty of functions that accept other functions as arguments. For example, the function that's called after the DOM is loaded is:

```
Ext.onReady(function(){
  ...
});
```

Ext.onReady() is a higher order function.. You'll learn about this in detail in Chapter 2.

Classes in JavaScript

As you have seen, JavaScript is a functional language. It doesn't have classes like those in OO languages. You can treat functions as classes, and create objects, by using the new keyword. You can create function objects that you can manipulate and pass around like objects. This feature can be used to write traditional OO code.

Say you want to create a class with variables and methods in JavaScript. Instantiate it just as you would in C# or Java. Let's create a class Person with name and age attributes and an eat() method as shown in Listing 1-3.

Listing 1-3. Person class

```
function Person(theName,theAge){
    this.name = theName; //public variable
    this.age = theAge;
    this.eat = function(){
       console.log(this.name + " is eating");
    }
  }
```

If you now want to create an object of class Person and invoke its eat() method, you can use the new keyword just as in other OO languages.

```
var p1 = new Person("Sam",23);
p1.eat(); //Prints Sam is eating
console.log(p1.age); // Prints 23
```

The new keyword creates an object from the Person function and returns a reference to the object. Notice the use of this keyword in the Person class. The this keyword binds a variable to the object that is created. You can treat this keyword like a public variable.

Use of Classes in Ext JS 4

The UI components in Ext JS 4 are available as classes. So if you want to create a button, you actually create an object of Button class like this.

```
var button = new Ext.button.Button();
```

Now you know how a Button class would be defined in Ext JS 4. It's just a function. I'll discuss this in detail in Chapter 4.

JSON

One of the most popular and widely-used features of JavaScript is the JavaScript Object Notation (JSON). It's used to represent a JavaScript object. It's also used as a data format like XML. Here's a JSON object.

```
var myBook = {
 title : "Practical Ext JS4",
 author:"Prabhu Sunderaraman",
 publisher : "APress",
 price : 49.99,
 formats : ["e-book","paperback"],
 order : function(){
   console.log("Ordering " + this.title + " in Amazon");
 }
};
```

The myBook variable is a JSON object with some properties. The formats is an array and order() is a function.

Use of JSON in Ext JS 4

Ext JS 4 uses JSON heavily. The properties of the UI components that you create in Ext JS 4 are specified in JSON format. Here is some code that creates a button in Ext JS 4.

```
var btn = new Ext.button.Button({
  text : "Click",
  id : "mybutton",
  handler : function(){
      console.log("Button clicked");
  }
});
```

As you can infer from the code, the button's attributes like text, handler, id are specified as properties of a JSON object.

Summary

In this chapter I discussed various JavaScript frameworks, zooming in to an overview of the features of Ext JS 4. Ext JS 4 provides an OO based API, support for the MVC architecture, creating custom themes, extending UI components, etc. I explained some of the core JavaScript features like arguments, JSON, higher order functions, classes etc., that are pretty important when working with Ext JS 4.

In the next chapter you will get started with Ext JS 4 by downloading and extracting it. You will get to understand the library structure, create a sample application and (at last) crack some code.

■ ■ ■

CHAPTER 2

Overview of Ext JS 4

Let's get started with Ext JS 4. In this chapter you'll learn Ext JS 4 from scratch. We'll install it, configure it, and churn out some code to get a feel for the API.

Downloading Ext JS 4

Getting started with Ext JS 4 is really easy. You can download the latest stable version of Ext JS 4 from http://www.sencha.com/products/extjs/download/. You have two options that you can choose for downloading.

- *Commercial trial version*: You can download a 45-day commercial evaluation version of Ext JS 4. You can buy commercial licenses for Ext JS 4, based on your project needs, from https://www.sencha.com/store/extjs/.

- *GPL version*: Ext JS 4 is available under the General Public License (GPL) version 3. You can use this for building open source projects. Note, however, that Ext JS 4 applications built using the GPLv3 license require the release of the source code.

Just visit http://www.sencha.com/products/extjs/license/ to read more about Ext JS 4 licensing options. No matter which version you choose, you'll get a zip file of the entire Ext JS 4 library.

The examples in this book were tested against version 4.2 of Ext JS 4.

Getting Started With Ext JS 4

Extracting the Ext JS 4 zip will give you the contents shown in Figure 2-1.

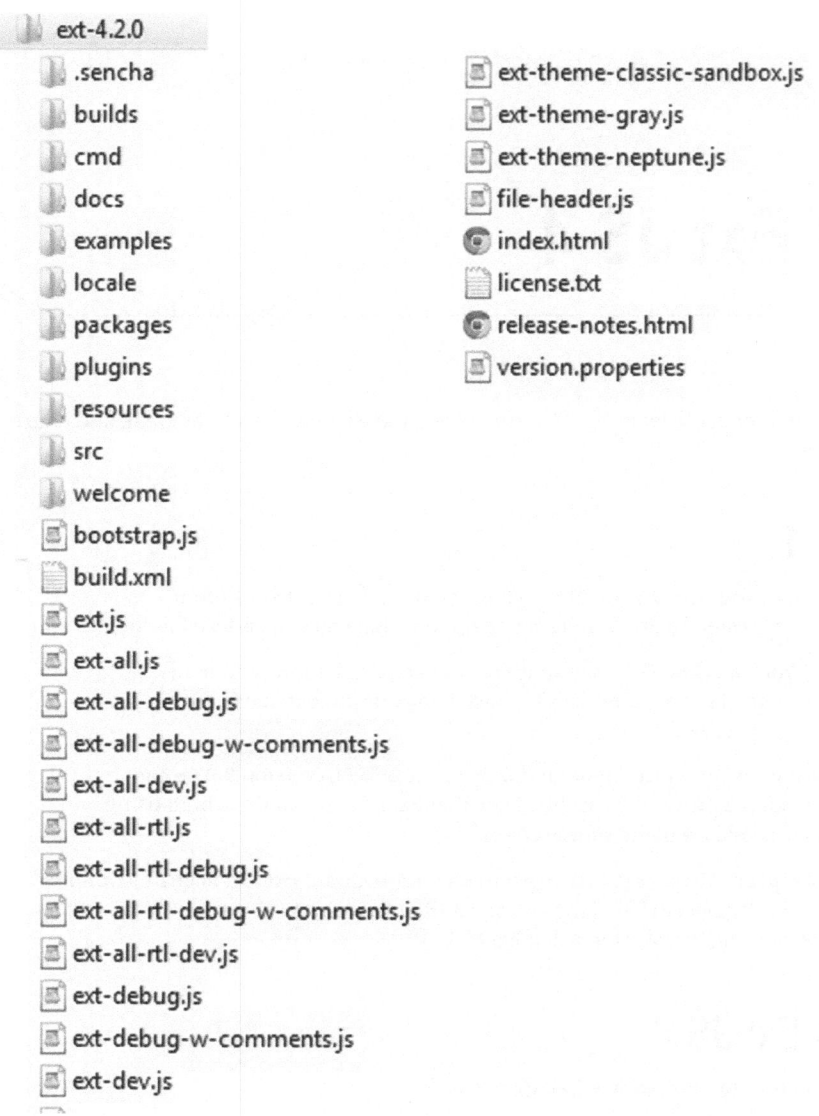

Figure 2-1. *Contents of the Ext JS 4 folder*

Let me give you a quick overview of the contents of the folder.

- The *resources* folder contains the standard set of themes that you can use in your application.

- The *src* folder contains the entire API organized into numerous JavaScript files.

- The *docs* folder contains the API documentation and guides.

- The *ext.js* file contains the core API.

- The *ext-all.js* file contains the complete API in a compressed or minified format. It's a large-sized file that is suitable for development purposes only.

- The *ext-all-dev.js* contains the complete API with comments.

- The *ext-all-debug-w-comments.js* contains the complete API with comments and console warnings. This file is meant to be used for development.

The Ext JS 4 zip file can be extracted to a web server's directory to access the documentation as a web application. I have a Microsoft Internet Information Services (IIS) server running on my Windows machine. I extracted the zip archive into the IIS root directory C:\inetpub\wwwroot folder. Figure 2-2 shows the index.html file, one of the documents loaded when you access it from a web browser.

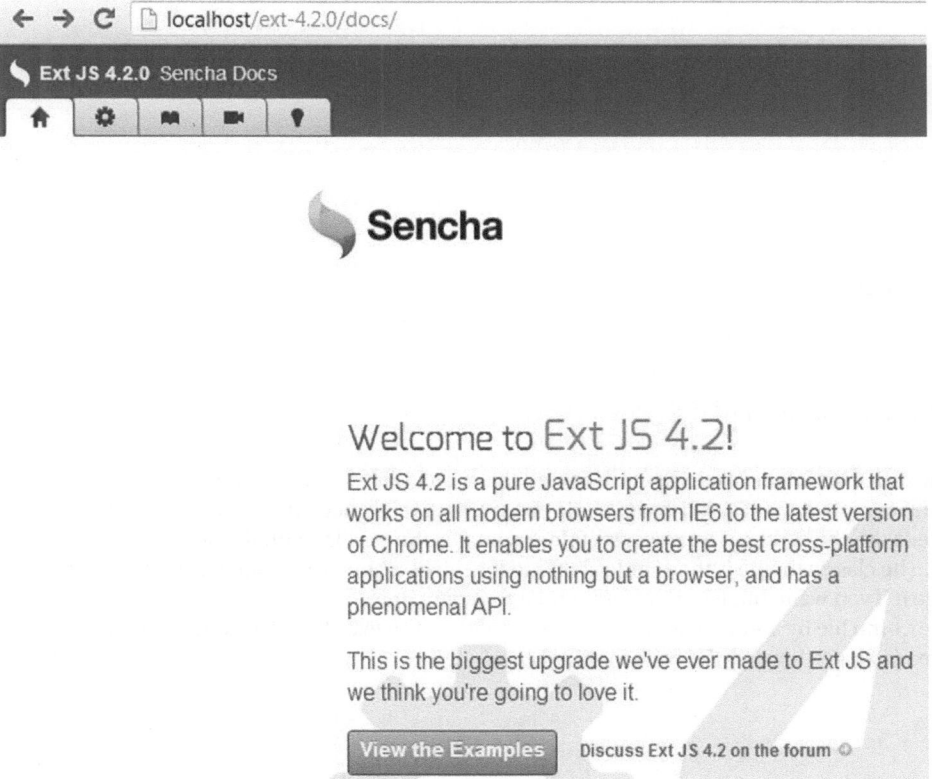

Figure 2-2. *Documentation*

IDE for Ext JS 4 Development

Sencha has a product known as Sencha Architect that can be used to design Ext JS 4 applications. Sencha Architect is not a full-fledged editor, but it is very useful to design the UI and then use the generated code in the main copy of the application.

You can use any simple JavaScript editor for working with Ext JS 4. The choice usually depends on the server side technology you decide to use while working with Ext JS 4 applications. If you're a Java developer, you can use Eclipse or Net Beans or IntelliJ IDEA. If you're a .NET developer, Visual Studio is all that you need. The same applies to Rails or Grails as well.

Ext JS 4 applications run on almost all major browsers. Chrome, Safari, or Firefox is generally preferred during development because of the debugging facilities they provide.

Let's create an Ext JS 4 application and crack some Ext JS 4 code.

Hello World With Ext JS 4

Let's create an Ext JS 4 application called *Chapter02*. We'll create a folder called *extjs* in Chapter02. The *extjs* folder will contain the Ext JS 4 library files that we need for developing the application. We'll copy the necessary resources from the Ext JS 4 folder that we've extracted earlier and put them in the *Chapter02/extjs* folder. The resources include the js files, css files, and the default set of images. You don't really have to call the folder extjs, though; it's just a convention. You can name it scripts or lib or resources, or anything that you feel is appropriate.

Let's create an index.html file and write some Ext JS 4 code in it. The structure of the *Chapter02* application is shown in Figure 2-3.

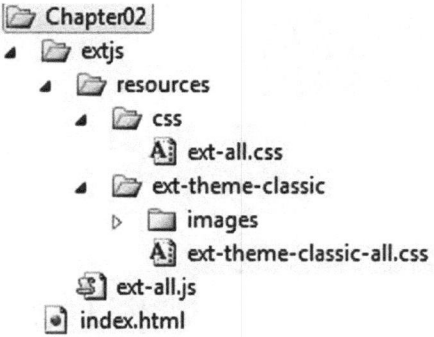

Figure 2-3. *Structure of Chapter02 application*

The application contains an *extjs* folder where we have copied the ext-all.js file from the Ext JS 4 library folder. The ext-all.js file contains the complete Ext JS 4 API code. While you may not really need the entire API in a project, this is adequate to get started with the coding. The *resources* folder contains the css files with the default theme folder ext-classic-theme. The classic theme is the standard theme that gives a bluish look and feel to the entire application. You can change it if you want, but let's not worry about that right now.

Let's play with the index.html file by adding references to the ext-all.css and ext-all.js files. And let's display a Hello world in an alert box. Listing 2-1 shows the code for index.html.

Listing 2-1. index.html File

```
<!DOCTYPE html>

<html>
<head>
    <link href="extjs/resources/css/ext-all.css" rel="stylesheet" type="text/css" />
    <script src="extjs/ext-all.js" type="text/javascript"></script>
    <script>
        Ext.onReady(function () {
            Ext.Msg.alert("Hello World","All set!!!");
        });
    </script>
</head>
<body>
</body>
</html>
```

Running index.html page in the browser will pop up a window with the title *Hello World*, as shown in Figure 2-4.

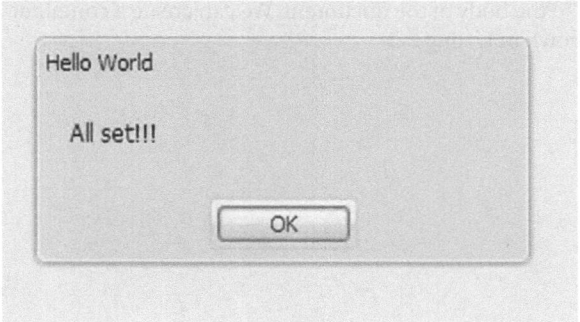

Figure 2-4. *index.html*

The starting point of the Ext JS4 application is an Ext.onReady() function. The onReady() function takes a function as an argument. The onReady() function is called when the document is loaded and DOM is ready. We've created a simple dialog box using Ext.Msg.alert() method.

If you want to display hello world in a label, let's modify the onReady() method in Listing 2-1 as shown below. We can create an object of the Label class provided by Ext JS 4 as shown below.

```
Ext.onReady(function () {
  Ext.create("Ext.form.Label", {
    text: "Hello World",
    renderTo: Ext.getBody()
  });
});
```

We create an object of the class Ext.form.Label and render it to the document body. If you have to display a *Hello World* button, we'll create an object of the Ext.Button class and render it to the document body as shown below.

```
Ext.onReady(function () {
  Ext.create("Ext.Button",{
    text : "Hello World",
    renderTo : Ext.getBody()
  });
});
```

One noteworthy aspect of Ext JS 4 code is its object-oriented approach. All the UI components are available as classes, and we just need to create instances of the classes and render them.

Let's add an event handler to the button we created. Clicking the button will pop up a message as shown in Listing 2-2.

Listing 2-2. Button With the Click Event Handler

```
Ext.create("Ext.Button",{
  text : "Hello World",
  handler : function(){
    Ext.Msg.alert("You clicked the hello world button");
  },
  renderTo : Ext.getBody()
});
```

Now, let's create a textbox and a button and render them to the body of the document. We can create a container such as a panel and add textbox and button components as shown in Listing 2-3.

Listing 2-3. Panel With a Textbox and Button

```
Ext.create("Ext.Panel",{
  title : "Hello World Panel",
  items : [
            Ext.create("Ext.form.field.Text",{
              fieldLabel : "Name"
            }),
            Ext.create("Ext.Button",{
              text : "Click"
            })
  ],
  renderTo : Ext.getBody()
});
```

The Ext.Panel class has an array property called items. The items array holds the list of components that need to be added to the panel. The output of Listing 2-3 is shown in Figure 2-5.

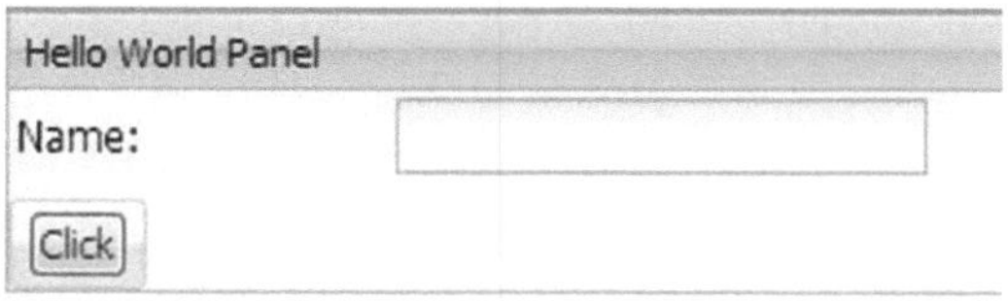

Figure 2-5. *Panel with a textbox and a button*

If you want to display the value of the textbox, when the button is clicked, let's modify the code in Listing 2-3 and add an id to the textbox and access it like this.

```
Ext.create("Ext.form.field.Text",{
 fieldLabel : "Name",
 id:"nametext"
}),
Ext.create("Ext.Button",{
 text : "Click",
 handler : function(){
   Ext.Msg.alert(Ext.getCmp("nametext").getValue());
 }
})
```

We've used the Ext.getCmp() method to access the UI component by specifying the id. You can then invoke the getValue() method on the text box to fetch the value.

I hope this short introductory chapter has given you a basic feeling for Ext JS 4 coding style. The intent is to get you started with some Ext JS 4 code without really worrying about the syntax. You'll learn more about the API in the subsequent chapters. As we delve deeper into the API, you'll find various different options available for creating even a simple component like a button.

At this point if you are able to view an Ext JS 4 textbox and button in your browser you're good to go to the next chapter.

Summary

In this chapter you got started working with Ext JS 4. We extracted the Ext JS 4 library and created a simple Ext JS 4 application by copying the necessary CSS and JavaScript files. `Ext.onReady()` is the starting point in an Ext JS 4 application. All the UI components are available as classes. You saw how to create simple UI components such as a textbox, a button, and a label. I introduced you to adding simple event handlers to components such as buttons. I also discussed container components like Panel where you can add child components as items.

In the next chapter you'll learn about the structure and syntax of the Ext JS 4 API.

CHAPTER 3

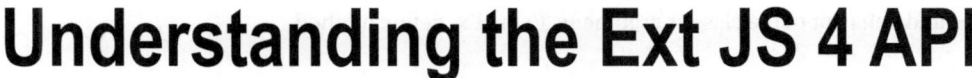

Understanding the Ext JS 4 API

Ext JS 4 is one of the few JavaScript libraries whose API has been designed specifically for developers with experience in working with object-oriented (OO) languages. The library is organized into packages and classes, making it easy for any OO programmer to understand.

In this chapter, you'll find out about the structure of Ext JS 4 API. And you'll learn how to write OO code using Ext JS 4.

Structure of the API

The Ext JS 4 API documentation can be found at `http://docs.sencha.com/extjs/4.2.0/#!/api`.

The Ext JS 4 API is grouped into packages like those in Java. Every package contains a collection of classes, whose names begin with the letters **Ext**. Examples of class names are Ext.JSON, Ext.chart.series.Pie. You can think of Ext as a root namespace name for all the classes, though technically Ext is a JavaScript object that houses all other classes in Ext JS 4. You can think of Ext as being defined thus:

```
var Ext = {};
```

The general format of any class name is

```
Ext.packageName.optionalSubPackageName.ClassName
```

All class names begin with an uppercase character. Package names begin with a lowercase character. The names follow the "CamelCase" naming convention, where words are run together with no intervening spaces, and each word begins with an uppercase. Ext.Base is the base class for all the classes in Ext JS 4.

The packages are stored in folders with the same name as the package, and the classes are stored in files with the same name as the class. Let's take the class Ext.chart.series.Pie. In this case you'll find the class Pie defined in Pie.js file. The class Pie is present in chart and series packages. You'll have the Pie.js file stored in the series folder. The series folder will be present in the chart folder. Figure 3-1 shows the folder structure Ext.chart.series.Pie class.

Figure 3-1. *Pie.js stored in chart/series folder*

Developing an Ext JS 4 application involves not only using the built-in classes but also defining your own classes by using the constructs of an OO language. Let's discuss the features involved in creating custom classes.

Classes and Objects

You can define a new class in Ext JS 4 using the `Ext.define` method. You pass in the class name and the object where you define the attributes and behavior of the class as arguments to the Ext.define method.

```
Ext.define("Book",{});
```

If you have worked with Ext JS 3 or the earlier versions, you will notice that the `Ext.define` method incorporates the functionalities of using Ext.reg, Ext.ns, and Ext.extend methods.

You can create an object of the Book class using **Ext.create** method as shown here.

```
Ext.create("Book");
```

You can specify a fully qualified class name with a root namespace and package names included as shown below.

```
Ext.define("DuraSoft.tech.extjs4.Book",{});
```

In traditional OO languages the **new** keyword is used to create objects. You can use new to create objects in Ext JS 4 also.

```
var book1 = new DuraSoft.tech.extjs4.Book();
```

The `Ext.create("classname")` method dynamically loads all the JavaScript files that the classname is dependent on before creating an instance, whereas this is not possible when you use the new keyword. You'll learn about loading dependent files later in this chapter.

We'll use Ext.create for creating objects in our code examples in this book.

Constructor

Constructor is the first function that's called when an object is created. You can define constructors in our classes using the special property **constructor**. The constructor property is wired to a function that gets invoked when an object is created using Ext.create.

```
Ext.define("DuraSoft.tech.extjs4.Book",{
 constructor : function(){
   console.log("Book created");
}
});
```

The second argument of the Ext.define method is an object that has a *constructor* property.

On creating an object of class DuraSoft.tech.extjs4.Book the constructor gets invoked and you'll see *Book created* printed on the console.

You can define properties of the class and initialize them in constructors.

Property

Let's define our Book class with two properties *title* and *price*. These two properties will be initialized in our constructors.

```
Ext.define("DuraSoft.tech.extjs4.Book",{
 title : "",
 price : -1,
 constructor : function(title,price){
  this.title = title;
  this.price = price;
  }
});
```

The two properties are initialized using the *this* keyword, which makes them visible to the objects of the class. You can instantiate the Book class and initialize it as shown below.

```
var xml = Ext.create("DuraSoft.tech.extjs4.Book","XML",12.00);
console.log(xml.title);
console.log(xml.price);
```

You can access title and price properties using the object reference. The above code snippet prints XML and 12.00 in the console.

A class may have a number of attributes. It becomes tedious to define and initialize them one after the other using the constructor. It'll be better if we can define the attributes with default values and initialize only the required ones.

Config

Ext JS 4 provides a config section for every class where you can list the attributes of the class with default values. The object can be created by initializing the attributes in which you are interested.

```
Ext.define("DuraSoft.tech.extjs4.Book",{
 config : {
  title : "",
  price : -1,
  authors: []
},
constructor :  function(cfg){
 this.initConfig(cfg);
}
});
```

In the code snippet above, we've defined a Book class with title, price, and authors listed in the *config* section. The config section is initialized in the constructor by calling the *initConfig* method. The *initConfig* method that is present in *Ext.Base* class initializes the configuration object. You can create an object of the Book class as shown below.

```
var xml = Ext.create("DuraSoft.tech.extjs4.Book",{
  title : "XML for beginners", authors : ["Sam","Kim"]
});
```

We've created the Book object by initializing the `title` and `authors` attributes. As mentioned earlier, it's not mandatory to initialize these attributes while creating the instance. The variables declared in the config section have the *getter/setter* methods generated automatically. In the above example where xml is a reference to the Book object, you can access the properties as shown below.

```
console.log(xml.getTitle());
xml.setPrice(12.00);
console.log(xml.getAuthors()[0]);
```

■ **Note**   In OO languages the getter and setter methods are usually known as accessor methods. They are used to access a variable. Ext JS 4 follows the Java convention of generating the getter and setter methods. If you have a variable called age, the accessor methods for it will be getAge() and setAge(age). The getAge method will return the value of age and the setAge method will modify the value of the age.

You can override the getter/setter methods if you want to take more control of the class. For example, say you want the price of the Book to have a minimum value of 5.00. You can perform this validation in the overridden setPrice method as shown in Listing 3-1.

Listing 3-1. Validating the Book Price

```
Ext.define("DuraSoft.tech.extjs4.Book", {
          config: {
              title: "",
              price: 5,
              authors: []
          },
          constructor: function (cfg) {
              this.initConfig(cfg);
          },
          setPrice: function (priceVal) {
              if (priceVal < 5)
                  console.log("Invalid value for price " + priceVal);
              else
                  this.price = priceVal;
          }
});
var xml = Ext.create("DuraSoft.tech.extjs4.Book",{
 title : "XML", authors : ["Sam","Kim"]
});

xml.setPrice(3);
console.log(xml.getPrice());
xml.setPrice(30);
console.log(xml.getPrice());
```

In Listing 3-1 the setPrice method has been overridden with the validation check. The output of the code will be

---

```
Invalid value of price 3
30
```

The config generates an apply method for every attribute automatically as well. The apply method is called internally by the setter method. In Listing 3-1, you can override the *applyPrice* method to implement the validation rule as shown in Listing 3-2.

Listing 3-2. Overriding the applyPrice Method

```
Ext.define("DuraSoft.tech.extjs4.Book", {
    config: {
        title: "",
        price: 5,
        authors: []
    },
    constructor: function (cfg) {
        this.initConfig(cfg);
    },
    applyPrice: function (priceVal) {
        if (priceVal < 5)
            console.log("Invalid value for price " + priceVal);
        else
            this.price = priceVal;
        return this.price;
    }
});
```

Methods

You can define custom methods in classes as shown below.

```
Ext.define("DuraSoft.tech.extjs4.Book",{
    config : {
 title : "", price: 0
    },
    constructor : function(cfg){
      this.initConfig(cfg);
    },
    read: function(){
 console.log("Reading " +  this.getTitle());
    }
});
```

The Book class has a read function that can be accessed using the object reference.

```
var xml =  Ext.create("DuraSoft.tech.extjs4.Book",{
 title : "XML", price:12.00
});
xml.read(); //Prints Reading XML
```

You can also change the behavior of the read method by extending the Book class and overriding it. We'll discuss it when we cover inheritance later in this chapter.

Static Members

Ext JS 4 provides a **statics** property where you can list static variables and methods. The static members can be accessed using the class name, as in OO languages.

```
Ext.define("DuraSoft.tech.extjs4.Book",{
 statics : {
   numberOfBooks: 0,
   getNumberOfBooks: function(){
    return this.numberOfBooks;
   }
 },
 constructor : function(){
   this.statics().numberOfBooks++;
 }
});
```

In the code snippet above, the Book class has two static properties *numberOfBooks* and *getNumberOfBooks* which is a function. In the constructor of the class, we can increment the numberOfBooks variable.

We can create an object of this class and access the static members as shown below.

```
Ext.create("DuraSoft.tech.extjs4.Book");
Ext.create("DuraSoft.tech.extjs4.Book");
console.log(DuraSoft.tech.extjs4.Book.getNumberOfBooks());
```

You can access the numberOfBooks property also using the class name.

```
console.log(DuraSoft.tech.extjs4.Book.numberOfBooks);
```

In OO languages like Java and C#, you have a *getClass()* or a *getType()* method to access the underlying class. Ext JS 4 provides a keyword called self similar to that. You can use self on the object to access its class as shown below.

```
Ext.define("DuraSoft.tech.extjs4.Book",{
 statics : {
   numberOfBooks: 0,
   getNumberOfBooks: function(){
    return this.numberOfBooks;
   }
 },
 constructor : function(){
   console.log("Constructor of " + this.self.getName() + " called");
   this.self.numberOfBooks++;
 }
});
```

In the constructor we've used *this.self* to access the static member numberOfBooks. You can also notice the call to the getName() function. When a Book instance is created the output of the code will be

```
Constructor of DuraSoft.tech.extjs4.Book called
```

Ext JS 4 provides support for inheritance.

Inheritance

We have an **extend** keyword that can be used to inherit a class in Ext JS 4. Let's create an *Employee* class and a *Manager* class that inherits the Employee class.

```
Ext.define("Employee",{
 config : {
     employeeid : "",
           name : "",
           salary : 0
       },
       constructor : function(cfg){
    this.initConfig(cfg);
       },
       work : function(){
    console.log(this.getName() + "  is working");
       }
});
```

```
Ext.define("Manager",{
 extend : "Employee",
 config : {
             level : 1
       }
});
```

The Manager class inherits the Employee class using the extend keyword. The configuration properties and the work function in the Employee class are available to the Manager class.

We can create a Manager object and invoke the work function as shown below.

```
var mgr = Ext.create("Manager",{
 employeeid:"DS123",  name: "Sam", level: 4
});
mgr.work(); //Prints Sam is working
```

We can override the Employee's work function in Manager's class.

```
Ext.define("Manager",{
 extend : "Employee",

 //...

     work : function(){
    console.log(this.getName() + " is in a meeting");
       }
});
```

We can call the base class work function using this.callParent()

```
Ext.define("Manager",{
        extend : "Employee",

            //...

            work : function(){
            this.callParent();
                console.log(this.getName() + " is in a meeting");
              }
        });
```

The arguments passed to the Manager's work function can be supplied to the Employee's work function by using the *arguments* keyword in JavaScript as shown below.

```
this.callParent(arguments);
You can extend a class and override the constructor as shown below. You can invoke the base class
constructor using this.callParent method.
Ext.define("Manager",{
    extend : "Employee",
    constructor : function(cfg){
      this.callParent(arguments);
   }
});
```

You can override the constructor of the base class whenever you inherit generic classes like Employee, Manager, etc. However, you have to be careful when you inherit UI classes. The constructor of the UI component classes have a set of operations like initializing events, plugins, etc.. Inheriting a UI component class and overriding the constructor is not a recommended practice. The UI component classes provide a method called initComponent(), which is used to initialize the component. This initComponent method is usually invoked from the constructor. The general practice is to override the initComponent method in the derived class. Say you want to create a custom Button, then you can do that as shown below.

```
Ext.define("MyButton",{
  extend : "Ext.button.Button",
  initComponent : function(){
     //Your code goes here
  }
});
```

You'll learn more about creating custom components in Chapter 10.

Multiple inheritance is not supported in Ext JS 4. We have mixins for multiple inheritance similar to interfaces in Java and C#.

Mixins

Mixins help you to mix the behavior of different classes into your class. Your class can have the functionalities of any number of classes mixed together. It's somewhat similar to interfaces in Java where a class can implement any number of interfaces.

Let's create two classes, Aquatic and Terrestrial, with swim and walk functions, respectively.

```
Ext.define("Aquatic",{
    swim : function(){
      console.log("Swimming");
    }
});

Ext.define("Terrestrial",{
    walk : function(){
      console.log("Walking");
    }
});
```

We'll create a class Reptile that can walk as well as swim. The Reptile class is created by mixing Aquatic and Terrestrial together.

```
Ext.define("Reptile",{
 mixins : ["Aquatic","Terrestrial"]
});
```

A Reptile instance can invoke the walk and swim functions.

```
var reptile = Ext.create("Reptile");
reptile.swim();
reptile.walk();
```

We have discussed the basic OO concepts in Ext JS 4. Let's learn few other features in the class system in Ext JS 4.

Alias

You can define an alias name for the classes. The alias name is mainly used when you create custom components. You can use the *alias* property in the definition of the class as shown below.

```
Ext.define("DuraSoft.tech.extjs4.Book", {
        alias : "Book",
});

Ext.create("Book");
```

There are certain conventions involved in creating these alias names. For example, alias names for custom components begin with the prefix **widget**, whereas alias names for custom proxy classes begin with **proxy**. We'll discuss this in detail later in this chapter.

Singleton

Ext JS 4 provides a way to create singleton classes. Singleton is a popular design pattern in OO languages where a class configured to be singleton has only one instance throughout the application.

You can configure a class to be singleton by setting the property **singleton** to be true. When a class in Ext JS 4 is configured as singleton, an instance is automatically created. This kind of behavior, where an instance is automatically created for a singleton class, is not a standard practice in OO languages.

```
Ext.define("Company", {
    singleton : true,
    config: {
        title: "Ace Inc.,",
    },
    getNumberOfEmployees: function () {
            return 154;
    }
});
console.log(Company.title);
console.log(Company.getNumberOfEmployees());
```

In the code above, Company class is defined to be singleton, and an instance of the class is automatically created. However, you will access the members of the class using the class name as if they were static members.

If you try to create an instance of the class var c1 = Ext.create("Company");, then you'll get a class instantiation error.

■ **Note**   Singleton pattern is a popular design pattern in OO languages that talks about maintaining one and only one instance of a class. A Singleton class is a class that can be instantiated only once. You can design your class to be singleton and can create an object of the class.

In Ext JS 4 you actually define a singleton object and not a class. You don't have to define a singleton class and create an instance later. You automatically get a singleton instance create when you write
Ext.define("classname",{singleton:true})

Loading Dependencies

Ext JS 4 introduces the concept of dynamic loading of the dependent JavaScript files. You can specify the classes that your code is dependent on and the appropriate class files are loaded dynamically.

The heart of this dynamic loading of dependent JavaScript files is the **Ext.Loader** class. This class is responsible for loading the dependent files either synchronously or asynchronously. You can specify the classes to be loaded explicity by using Ext.Loader.require method.

Say your class uses the Ext.button.Button class, you can load the Button class explictly by using Ext.Loader. require or the shortcut Ext.require method.

```
Ext.Loader.require("Ext.button.Button");
```

(or)

```
Ext.require("Ext.button.Button");
```

Ext.require loads the Button.js file and recursively the Button's dependent files as well.

There's another way of specifying the loading information by using the *requires* property in a class, as shown below.

```
Ext.define("MyPanel",{
 requires : ["Ext.button.Button"]
});
```

In the above code the dependent files will be loaded before creating an instance of MyPanel class.

Sometimes you may not mandatorily require the dependent files for creating an object of your class. You can use the *uses* property in this case, as shown below.

```
Ext.define("MyPanel",{
 uses : ["Ext.button.Button"]
});
```

We've discussed various concepts involved in working with classes and objects in Ext JS 4. When you define a class, what's going on behind the screens? Let's discuss Ext.Class in detail to understand the details.

Ext.Class

You've seen that Ext.define is used for defining a new class. Internally Ext.define calls **Ext.ClassManager.create** method. Ext.ClassManager.create creates an instance of **Ext.Class**. So when you define a new class using Ext.define, you're actually creating an object of the class, Ext.Class.

The following code where you create a Book class using Ext.Class is equivalent to whatever you've been learning using Ext.define method.

```
var Book = new Ext.Class({
    config: {
        title: "",
        price: 5
    },
    constructor: function (cfg) {
        this.initConfig(cfg);
    },
    read: function () {
        console.log("Reading " + this.getTitle());
    }
});

var ajax = Ext.create("Book", { title: "AJAX",price:12.00 });
ajax.read();
```

We've created an instance of Ext.Class and assigned to a variable called *Book*, which is treated as the class name. You can create the instance of the Book class using the standard Ext.create method.

Ext.Class is also responsible for running what is commonly referred as *'pre' and 'post' processors*, such as config, extend, mixings, requires, etc., while creating a class.

We've discussed the core OO features of Ext JS 4. Let's move on to an overview of the Ext JS 4 API.

The Ext JS 4 API

The Ext JS 4 API (as you will have noticed) is organized into various packages. The package nomenclature is very similar to that of Java.

Table 3-1 shows some of the core packages in Ext JS 4.

Table 3-1. *Core Packages in Ext JS 4*

Package	Description
Ext.form.field	Contains the classes that represent form elements like textbox, checkbox, etc.
Ext.data	Contains classes like Store, Model, or Proxy that deal with fetching and playing with data.
Ext.layout.container	Deals with various layout components like Table, Accordion, Card, Border, etc.
Ext.grid	Used for working with data grids
Ext.tree	Used for displaying tree components
Ext.chart	Provides classes to develop charts like Pie, Bar, Line, etc.
Ext.menu	Contains classes used for creating menus
Ext.toolbar	Provides classes for creating toolbars
Ext.dd	Contains classes that implement drag and drop

Apart from the core packages, there are a number of utility classes in the *Ext namespace*. Here is a list of utility classes.

- Ext.Ajax
    - Used for sending Ajax requests.
- Ext.Json
    - Used for encoding and decoding JSON data.
- Ext.XTemplate
    - Used for creating UI templates that can be applied on data.
- Ext.Array
    - Contains functions for working with arrays.
- Ext.ComponentQuery
    - Provides functions to query the UI components.
- Ext.Date
    - Contains date related functions.

The Ext namespace, which is nothing but a class, provides a number of commonly used functions. Listed below is a set of commonly used functions in Ext class.

- onReady()

  - Used to wire up a function that is called after the DOM tree is ready and dependent files are loaded.

- application()

  - Creates an instance of Ext.app.Application after the DOM is ready. You'll use it when we discuss MVC architecture.

- getCmp()

  - Most commonly used method to access the components based on their id.

- query()

  - Used to query the DOM tree based on selector expressions.

- apply()

  - Used for copying the configuration data to an object

The Ext class also provides properties like *is[BrowserType]* like isIE6, isChrome, isGecko, etc. for browser-related information.

Summary

In this chapter I discussed the Ext JS 4 API and explained the OO concepts. The Ext JS 4 API is organized into packages and classes similar to Java.Ext is the root object that includes the complete API. You can define classes by using Ext.define method and create objects using Ext.create method. The classes can have properties, config attributes, methods, constructor, and static members. You can inherit a class by using extend attribute. You can inherit more classes by using mixins. Ext.Loader enables dynamic loading of the dependent JavaScript files. I gave you an overview of some of the packages and classes in Ext JS 4.

In the next chapter you'll learn about using UI controls and the layout components.

CHAPTER 4

Controls and Layout

Ext JS 4 provides a suite of UI controls that are used in applications. The UI controls include simple form controls like text boxes, buttons, layout containers like accordion, table, and so on. In this chapter we'll discuss the UI controls and layout containers.

Just like OO UI frameworks such as Swing for Java and WinForms for .NET, EXT JS 4 provides a well-defined hierarchy of UI components starting with a base class that establishes a common set of properties and functionalities to all the components. Let's start exploring the UI components in Ext JS 4 by looking at the Ext.Component class.

Ext.Component

The Ext.Component class serves as the base class for all the UI components in Ext JS 4. Ext.Component inherits the Ext.AbstractComponent class. It provides the common behavior and properties for all the UI components. The common functions include the basic creation, destruction, and rendering of the components. You can instantiate this class as shown below, though you'll use it very rarely in the raw format.

```
Ext.create("Ext.Component", {
    html: "Raw Component",
    renderTo : Ext.getBody()
});
```

The above code displays a text *Raw Component* in the page. It generates the following HTML snippet.

```
<div id="component-1099 class="x-component x-component-default">Raw Component</div>
```

The Ext.Component generates a <div> tag with an automatically generated id and a default CSS class. You'll learn about the CSS classes in *Theming and Styling* chapter.

All the components used in a page can be accessed through a singleton object Ext.ComponentManager. Ext.ComponentManager serves as a registry of all the components. You can access all the components by using the all property as Ext.ComponentManager.all.

You can access the individual components based on their id by using the get method as Ext.ComponentManager.get("id of the component"). We'll discuss more about the id attribute later in this section.

It's important to understand the common configuration attributes and methods of the Ext.Component class before you start working with the UI controls that are just derived classes of Ext.Component.

Configuration attributes of Ext.Component

Ext.Component class provides a large number of configuration attributes. You can get the complete list of the attributes from `http://docs.sencha.com/extjs/4.2.0/#!/api/Ext.Component`.

Let's discuss some of the configuration attributes of the Ext.Component class. These attributes are available to all the UI controls that you'll use.

id

Every component has an automatically generated unique id assigned to it. You can use *Ext.getCmp()* method to access the component by specifying the id. You can assign your own id for the component as well.

```
Ext.create("Ext.Component",{
 id : "mycomp1"
});
```

You can use Ext.getCmp as shown below

```
Ext.getCmp("mycomp1");
```

It's generally not recommended to define your own id, because as the application grows and you start adding components dynamically it may lead to duplication issues.

itemId

You can mark the component with an itemId instead of an id. The component that has itemId assigned to it can be accessed using that itemId through its parent component. Say, you have a Panel that has a component with an itemId. You can access the component using the itemId by invoking the method getComponent() on the Panel.

```
var panel1 = Ext.create("Ext.panel.Panel",{
 // ...
 items : [
 Ext.create("Ext.Component",{
 html : "Raw Component inside panel",
 itemId : "rawcomp1"
})
]
// ...
     });
```

```
panel1.getComponent("rawcomp1")
```

The itemId property is preferred to the id as you don't have to worry about the complications that arise due to duplicate id.

autoEl

The autoEl attribute is used to specify a custom HTML element that will encapsulate the the component. This attribute is usually used when we create custom components. You'll learn this in detail in Chapter 10. Here's a component that generates a hyperlink element using autoEl attribute.

```
Ext.create("Ext.Component", {
      renderTo: Ext.getBody(),
      autoEl: {
          html: "Link",
          href: "#",
          tag: "a"
      }
});
```

The code snippet will generate the following HTML snippet.

```
<a class="x-component x-component-default" href="#" id="component-1009">Link</a>
```

listeners

The listeners attribute is used to wire up the events with their handlers. listeners is a simple object that contains the list of all events along with their event handler functions.

```
listeners : {
        eventname1 : function(...) { ... },
        eventname2 : function(...){ ... },
   ...
}
```

renderTo

The component is rendered to the specified HTML element. If a component is added to a container, it's then the container's job to render the components. You can use renderTo as shown below.

```
renderTo : Ext.getBody() //renders to the body element
renderTo : Ext.get("content") //renders to the HTML element with the id "content"
```

hidden, disabled

The hidden and disabled attributes are used to specify visibility and whether the component is disabled or not, respectively. The default value for these attributes is false.

tpl, data

The components have a tpl property that's used to configure the UI template for the Component. The data attribute supplies data to be applied to the template. You'll learn about Templates in detail later in this chapter.

Let's discuss some of the methods in Component class.

Methods in Ext.Component

up

This method is used to navigate to the ancestors of the component that matches the expression passed as an argument. For example, if you have a component, say *cmp1*, calling **cmp1.up("panel")** walks up the container and returns the panel component that's a parent or grandparent or any ancestor. This method returns the immediate parent if the argument is ignored.

enable, disable

These are two commonly used methods that are used to enable and disable the components. Here's how you can use them on a component say comp1.

```
comp1.enable()
comp1.disable()
```

show, hide

These are two commonly used methods that are used to show and hide the components. Here's how you can use them on a component say comp1.

```
comp1.hide()
comp1.show()
```

destroy

The destroy method destroys the component. It removes the reference to the element in the DOM tree.

on, un

The listeners attribute is used to statically register the events and handler functions. The *on* method is used to dynamically do that. The on method accepts the name of the event, the event handler function and the scope or context of the executing handler function as arguments.

```
comp1.on("eventName",function(){...},scope)
```

```
mycombobox1.on("change",function(){...},this)
```

In the code snippet above, you've registered the change event on the combobox object. The scope 'this' refers to the context object where the handler function gets executed. The scope is an optional parameter.

The un method is used to remove the event handler for the specified event.

```
comp1.un("eventName",function(){...},scope)
```

You have to specify the same event handler function and scope used in the on method.

addEvents, fireEvent

The Component class provides methods addEvents and fireEvent for adding events and firing the event respectively. These two methods are mainly used when you create custom components with custom events. You can call addEvents on a component comp by writing `comp.addEvents('eventname1','eventname2' ...)`. You can invoke the fireEvent like `comp.fireEvent('eventname')`.

You'll learn more about these functions in Chapter 10 when we discuss creating custom components.

Now let's discuss the events in the Component class.

Events in Ext.Component

The Component class provides a number of lifecycle events. These are raised when the component is created, activated, rendered, destroyed, and so on. All these events can be handled by registering them using the listeners attribute or using the on method. Most of these lifecycle events are actually defined in the Ext.AbstractComponent class. Table 4-1 describes some of the events.

Table 4-1. *Events in a Component*

Event	Description
Added	Raised when the component is added to the container
Removed	Raised when the component is removed from the container
beforerender	Raised before rendering the component on to the HTML element
render	Raised after the component is rendered to the HTML element
afterrender	Raised after completion of the component rendering
beforedestroy	Raised before calling destroying the component or before calling destroy method
destroy	Raised after destroy or after calling the destroy method
beforeactivate	Raised before a component is activated. This is mainly used in accordions and tab panels.
activate	Raised after a component is activated
beforedeactivate	Raised before a component is deactivated
deactivate	Raised after a component is deactivated
beforeshow	Raised before calling the show method on the component
show	Raised after calling the show method on the component
beforehide	Raised before calling the hide method on the component
hide	Raised after calling the hide method on the component

Listing 4-1 shows the code snippet where you create a component and add to a Panel. The component has some of these events handled.

Listing 4-1. Events in Component

```
var pnl = Ext.create("Ext.panel.Panel", {
        items: [
            Ext.create("Ext.Component", {
                html: "Raw Component",
                itemId : "rawcomp1",
                listeners: {
                    activate: function () {
                        console.log("activate")
                    },
                    added: function () {
                        console.log("added")
                    },
                    afterrender: function () {
                                console.log("afterrender")
                    },
                    beforeactivate: function () {
                                console.log("beforeactivate")
                    },
                    beforedeactivate: function () {
                                console.log("beforedeactivate")
                    },
                    beforerender: function () {
                                console.log("beforerender")
                    },
                    beforeshow: function () {
                                console.log("beforeshow")
                    },
                    beforedestroy: function () {
                                console.log("beforedestroy")
                    },
                    destroy: function () {
                                console.log("destroy")
                        },
                    render: function () {
                                console.log("render")
                        },

                show: function () {
                                console.log("show")
                    },
                beforehide: function () {
                                console.log("beforehide")
                    },
                hide: function () {
                                console.log("hide")
                },
                enable: function () {
                                console.log("enable")
                    },
```

```
                    disable: function () {
                            console.log("disable")
                    },
                    removed: function () {
                            console.log("removed")
                    }
            }
        })
    ],
    renderTo: Ext.getBody()
        });

        console.log("******Calling disable")
        pnl.getComponent("rawcomp1").disable();
        console.log("******Calling enable")
        pnl.getComponent("rawcomp1").enable();
        console.log("******Calling hide")
        pnl.getComponent("rawcomp1").hide();
        console.log("******Calling show")
        pnl.getComponent("rawcomp1").show();
        console.log("******Calling destroy")
        pnl.getComponent("rawcomp1").destroy();
```

In Listing 4-1 we've registered the events using the listeners block. After rendering the component, we call methods like enable, disable, show, hide, or destroy to understand the event handling sequence. Here's the output of this code.

```
added
beforerender
render
afterrender
******Calling disable
disable
******Calling enable
enable
******Calling hide
beforehide
hide
******Calling show
beforeshow
show
******Calling destroy
beforedestroy
removed
```

destroy Another important aspect of the components in Ext JS 4 is *xtype*. Let's take a look at xtype in detail.

xtype

In Ext JS 4 every UI component class has an alias name or a short name known as '*xtype.*' Using xtype in our code offers some advantages. Let's discuss them by creating a Panel with a textbox and a button as shown below.

```
Ext.create("Ext.panel.Panel",{
  items : [
 Ext.create("Ext.form.field.Text",{
   fieldLabel : "Name"
 }),
 Ext.create("Ext.Button",{
   text : "Submit"
 })
 ]
});
```

Let's move the creation of textbox and button out of the Panel as shown below.

```
var nameText = Ext.create("Ext.form.field.Text",{
    fieldLabel : "Name"
});
var submitButton = Ext.create("Ext.Button",{
    text : "Submit"
});
```

The Panel will refer to the nameText and submitButton variables in the items collection.

```
Ext.create("Ext.Panel",{
 items : [
  nameText,submitButton
 ]
});
```

We've stored the textbox and button objects in separate variables and reused them inside the Panel. There are some disadvantages to writing code in this fashion, although it is useful to segregate the container and the individual components.

`Ext.create("Ext.form.field.Text")` creates a text box and holds it in the DOM tree. It occupies memory even if we don't render it on to the screen. Suppose we don't add the nameText variable in the Panel, it would remain in the DOM tree occupying memory. In an application, we want to instantiate UI components only when required and not create them at will. At the same time we want the component creation code maintained separately.

Using the fully qualified class name like *Ext.form.field.Text* everywhere is a tedious task, particularly when we create custom components. It would be better if we can use the xtype of these UI components. Let's rewrite the example as shown below.

```
var nameText = {
    xtype : "textfield",
    fieldLabel : "Name"
};
var submitButton = {
    xtype : "button",
    text : "Submit"
};
```

```
Ext.create("Ext.panel.Panel",{
    renderTo : Ext.getBody(),
    items : [
      nameText,submitButton
    ]
});
```

The nameText and submitButton are plain JavaScript objects. They have an additional xtype property with values textfield and button, respectively. The actual text box and button objects are created when they get added to the Panel and rendered to the body. This not only makes the code simpler but also provides us the lazy instantiation facility, thereby improving the performance.

As we discussed earlier, Ext.Component is inherited by a number of classes. Table 4-2 shows the list of subclasses of Ext.Component.

Table 4-2. *Subclasses of Ext.Component*

Class	Description
Ext.container.AbstractContainer	Base class for the container controls
Ext.button.Button	The button control
Ext.form.Label	The standard label element
Ext.form.field.Base	Base class for all the field components like textfield
Ext.draw.Component	Represents the surface on which you can draw shapes

One of the important subclasses of Ext.Component is Ext.container.AbstractContainer. This class is inherited by Ext.container.Container that serves as the base class for all the container clases like the Panel. Let's discuss the Ext.container.Container class in detail.

Ext.container.Container

Ext.container.Container class is the base class for all the container-based components in Ext JS 4. It provides the common behavior and properties for all the UI containers. The common functions include the addition, udpation, and removal of the components. You can instantiate this class as shown below, though you'll use it very rarely in the raw format.

```
Ext.create("Ext.container.Container", {
    html : "Raw Container",
    renderTo: Ext.getBody()
});
```

In the code snippet above, we've created an instance of Container class. This instance is empty as we've not added any components to it. The code displays a text Raw Container in the page. It generates the following HTML snippet.

```
<div id="container-1009" class="x-container x-container-default">Raw Container
<div id="container-1009-clearEl" class="x-clear" role="presentation"></div>
</div>
```

It's necessary to understand the common configuration attributes and methods of the Container class before you start working with the UI controls that are just derived classes of Container.

Configuration Attributes of Ext.container.Container

Let's discuss some of the configuration attributes of the Container class.

items

The items attribute refers to the collection of components that you'll add to the container. A Container class with a textbox and button component added to it using items is shown below.

```
Ext.create("Ext.container.Container",{
    items : [
             Ext.create("Ext.form.field.Text",{...}),
             Ext.create("Ext.button.Button",{...})
    ]
});
```

layout

This attribute is used to configure the layout for the container, so that the components may be arranged in a particular fashion. You'll learn more about the layout later in this chapter.

defaults

The defaults attribute is used to specify a set of default properties for all the items in the container. It helps you avoid duplication of code. If you want all the items in the container to have a specific width and height, then you can configure that using defaults as shown below.

```
Ext.create("Ext.container.Container",{
        defaults : {
        width:100,height:150
        },
        items : [
            ...
        ]
});
```

Some Methods in Container class.Methods of Ext.container.Container
add

The add method is used to dynamically add components into the container. When the components are added dynamically using the add method the container rearranges itself automatically. You can pass component or an array of components as argument to the add method.

```
var container1 = Ext.create("Ext.container.Container",{
 ...
});
var item1 = Ext.create("Ext.Component",{...});
container1.add(item1);
```

doLayout

doLayout method triggers the container to recalculate the layout and refresh itself.

down

This method, similar to the up method in Component class, is used to navigate to the descendants of the container that matches the expression passed as an argument. For example if you have a container, say *container1*, that has a button calling `container1.down("button")` walks down the container and returns the button component that's a child or grandchild or any descendant.

remove

The remove method is used to remove the components from the container. You can invoke remove method by passing the component or id of the component to be removed as argument.

```
var container1 = Ext.create("Ext.container.Container",{
  ...
});
var item1 = Ext.create("Ext.Component",{...});
container1.add(item1);
container1.remove(item1);
```

Let's discuss some of the events in Container class.

Events of Ext.container.Container

Table 4-3 shows the events in the Container class.

Table 4-3. *Events in Container class*

Event	Description
beforeadd	Fired before adding an item to the container
Add	Fired after an item is added
beforeremove	Fired before removing an item from the container
remove	Fired after removing an item from the container

Listing 4-2 shows the code snippet where you create a component and add to a Container. The Container has these events handled.

Listing 4-2. Events in Container

```
var container = Ext.create("Ext.container.Container", {
    html: "Default Container",
    listeners: {
        beforeadd: function () {
            console.log("beforeadd");
        },
        add: function () {
            console.log("add");
        },
        beforeremove: function () {
            console.log("beforeremove");
        },
        remove: function () {
            console.log("remove");
        }
    }
});

console.log("***Adding comp1");
container.add({
    xtype: "component", html: "Raw",id:"comp1"
});

console.log("***Removing comp1");
container.remove("comp1");
```

In Listing 4-2 we've registered the events using the listeners block. Here's the output of this code.

```
***Adding comp1
beforeadd
add
***Removing comp1
beforeremove
remove
```

`Ext.container.Container` is inherited by several classes that you'll commonly use. Table 4-4 shows the subclasses of Container class.

Table 4-4. *Subclass of Ext.container.Container*

Class	Description
Ext.container.Viewport	Represents the viewable area
Ext.panel.AbstractPanel	Base class for all the panel based containers
Ext.toolbar.Toolbar	Represents a toolbar

We've discussed the basics of the Component and Container classes. All the UI controls in Ext JS 4 are subclasses of these two classes. Let's discuss these UI controls.

Container Controls

Ext.panel.Panel

Ext.panel.Panel with the xtype *'panel'* is the root container class for several container classes. It's probably the most commonly used container class. You can create a Panel as shown below.

```
Ext.create("Ext.panel.Panel",{
    title : "Sample Panel",
    items : [
        ...
    ]
});
```

Ext.panel.Panel is inherited by a number of classes shown in Table 4-5.

Table 4-5. *Panel Controls*

Class	Description
Ext.form.Panel	Represents a form
Ext.menu.Menu	Represents a menu
Ext.window.Window	Represents a floatable, draggable window component
Ext.tab.Panel	Represents a tabbed container

Ext.window.Window

Window represents a floatable, draggable, resizable panel. Windows can be configured to be modal. You can create a Window as shown in Listing 4-3.

Listing 4-3. Window

```
var win = Ext.create("Ext.window.Window", {
  title: "Find and Replace",
  modal: true,
  items: [
   {
     xtype: "textfield",
     fieldLabel: "Find what"
   }
  ],
  buttons: [
   {
     text: "Find next"
   },
   {
     text: "Cancel"
   }
  ]
});
win.show();
```

43

In Listing 4-3 we've created a Window object with a textbox and two buttons using the items and buttons properties, respectively. Invoking the show method on the window object will show the window as shown in Figure 4-1.

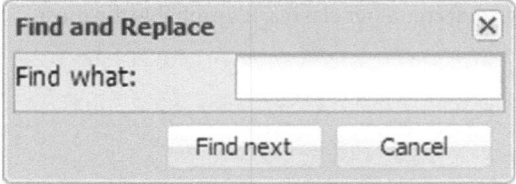

Figure 4-1. *A Window component*

The window will be a modal one masking the background completely as you've configured the modal property to be true.

Ext.menu.Menu

Ext.menu.Menu is the container that's used to display menus. Menu is made up of Ext.menu.Item controls. A menu can be shown as a standalone control or can be added as a child. A standalone menu can be created as shown in Listing 4-4.

Listing 4-4. Menu

```
var editMenu = Ext.create('Ext.menu.Menu', {
  items: [
    {
      text: 'Undo'
    },
    {
      text: 'Cut'
    },
    {
      text: 'Copy'
    },
    {
      text: "Paste"
    }
  ]
});
editMenu.show();
```

The menu is made of menu items. The default xtype of each menu item is a panel, and it has a text property that can be used to configure the text. You'll get the menu displayed as shown in Figure 4-2.

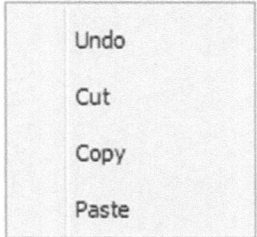

Figure 4-2. *Menu component*

You can add the menu as a child item as well. Let's add the menu to a Button using its menu attribute as shown below.

```
Ext.create("Ext.button.Button",{
    text : "Edit",
    menu : editMenu
});
```

You'll get an Edit button with the menu as shown in Figure 4-3.

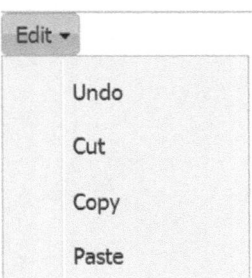

Figure 4-3. *Menu added to a Button*

Ext.tab.Panel

This class is used to create tabbed containers. It can be interpreted as a panel with the child items following a card layout. A tab panel has a tab bar represented by the Ex.tab.Bar class that can be positioned at the top, bottom, left, or right. Each tab in the panel is an object of the Ext.tab.Tab class. You can create a tab panel as shown in Listing 4-5.

Listing 4-5. Tab Panel

```
Ext.create('Ext.tab.Panel', {
  renderTo: Ext.getBody(),
  title: "Documentation",
  plain: false,
  height : 200,
  tabPosition: "bottom",
```

```
  items: [
    {
      title: 'Home',
      html : "Welcome to Ext JS 4"
    },
    {
      title: 'API',
      html : "API docs"
    },
    {
      title: 'Guides',
      html : "Standard guides"
    }
  ]
});
```

The tab panel has three tabs. The tab panel is configured to be plain, with no background for the tab bar. You'll get the tab panel as shown in Figure 4-4.

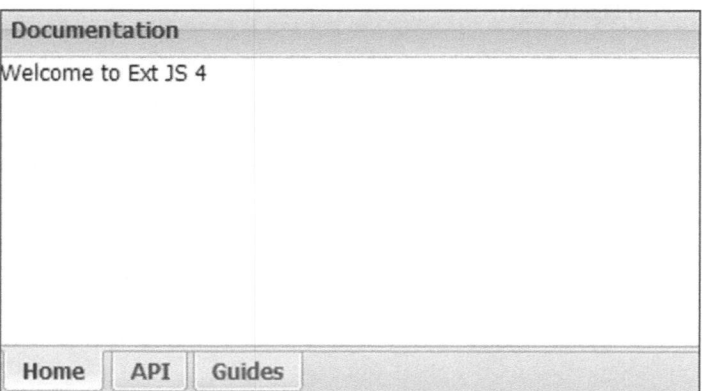

Figure 4-4. *Tabbed Pane*

Ext.form.Panel

Form panel class serves as the container for forms. You can add the controls in Ext.form.field package to the form panel class. The form panel provides support for processing form, validation, and so forth.

Ext.form and *Ext.form.field* are the packages that supply us the form controls. The list of commonly used UI controls along with their xtype is shown in Table 4-6.

Table 4-6. *Form Controls*

Class	xtype
Ext.form.field.Text	textfield
Ext.form.field.TextArea	textarea
Ext.form.field.Checkbox	checkbox
Ext.form.field.ComboBox	combobox
Ext.form.field.Radio	radio
Ext.form.field.Date	datefield
Ext.form.field.Number	numberfield
Ext.form.Label	label
Ext.form.RadioGroup	radiogroup
Ext.form.CheckboxGroup	checkboxgroup
Ext.form.FieldSet	fieldset

Let's create a form using some of these controls. We'll develop a page as shown in the Figure 4-5.

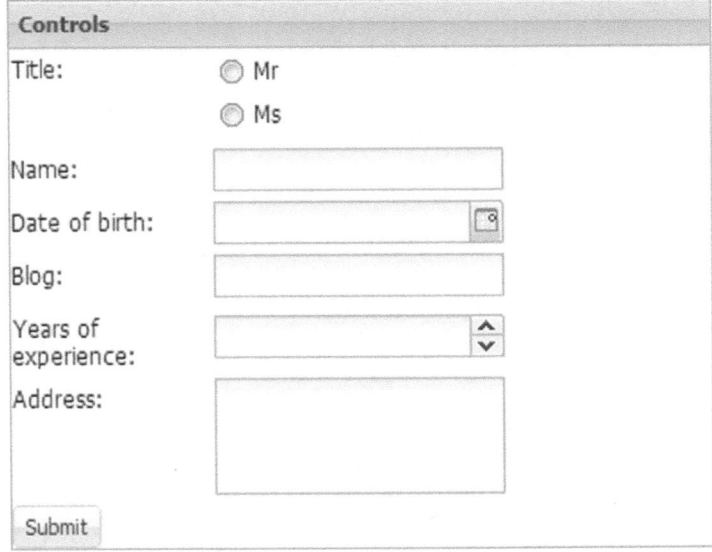

Figure 4-5. *A Form panel*

The controls form has a radio group, date field, number field, text area, and a button. Listing 4-6 shows the code for the form control.

Listing 4-6. Form Panel

```
Ext.create("Ext.form.Panel",
              {
  title : "Controls",
  items : [
   {
    xtype : "radiogroup",
    fieldLabel : "Title",
    vertical:true,columns:1,
    items : [
               {boxLabel:"Mr",name:"title"},
                      {boxLabel:"Ms",name:"title"}
    ]
   },
   {
    xtype : "textfield",
    fieldLabel : "Name"
   },
   {
    xtype : "datefield",
    fieldLabel : "Date of birth"
   },
   {
    xtype : "textfield",
    fieldLabel : "Blog"
   }
   {
    xtype : "numberfield",
    fieldLabel : "Years of experience",
    minValue : 5,
    maxValue : 15
   },
   {
    xtype : "textarea",
    fieldLabel : "Address"
   },
   {
    xtype : "button",
    text : "Submit"
   }
   ],
});
```

The form controls can be wired up with basic validation rules. For instance, the common validation properties of the text based controls are allowBlank, maxLength, minLength, and so on. In the form we created, we can apply the validation rules to Listing 4-6 as shown below.

```
{
 xtype : "textfield",
 fieldLabel : "Name",
 allowBlank : false,
 maxLength : 50,
 msgTarget : "side"
},
{
      xtype : "datefield",
 fieldLabel : "Date of birth",
 msgTarget : "side"
}
```

The name textfield has validation rules used. The msgTarget displays the error message by the side of the textfield when the validation fails. The default value is qtip where the error message is displayed as a quick tip as shown in Figure 4-6.

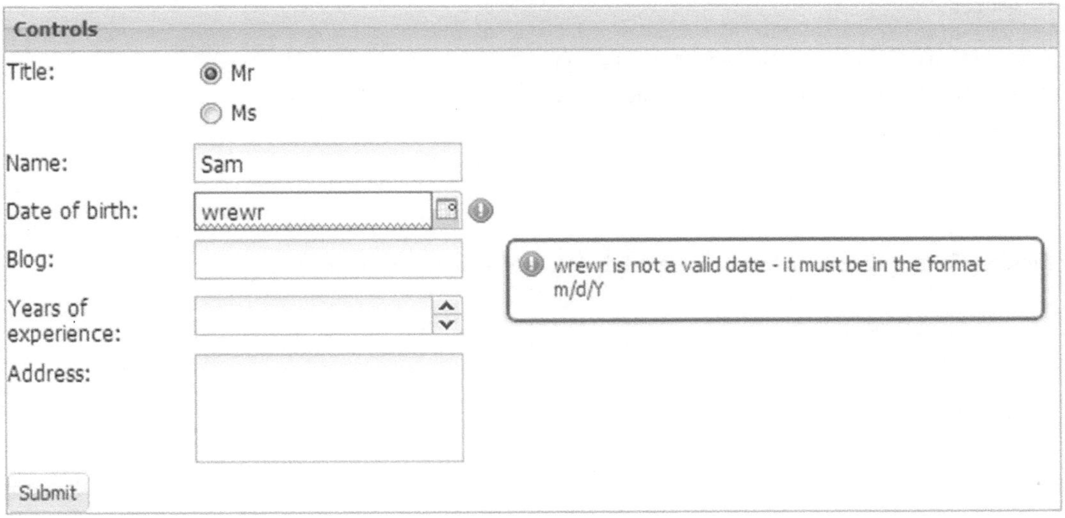

Figure 4-6. *Form panel with validation rules*

Another useful property called vtype can be used for using built-in validation rules like e-mail, URL, and so forth. The blog text field we have used in our example can be configured to have a validation type as shown here.

```
{
  xtype : "textfield",
  fieldLabel : "Blog",
  vtype : "url"
}
```

The blog field will display an error message as shown in Figure 4-7.

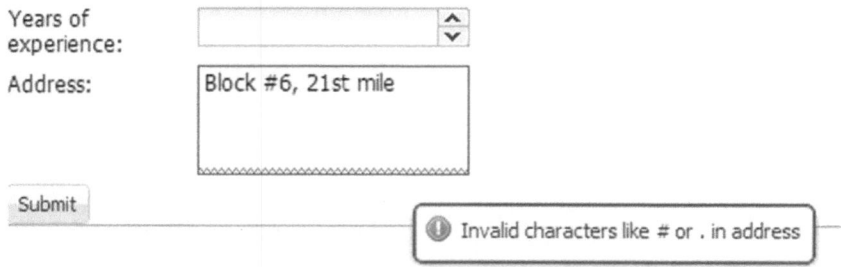

Figure 4-7. *Text field with url vtype*

We can also register our own validation functions using validator property. The validator function is passed in the value of the field. It returns the error message or true based on the outcome of validation. The address field with a custom validator is shown below.

```
{
 xtype : "textarea",
 fieldLabel : "Address",
 validator : function(val){
  if(val.indexOf("#") != -1 || val.indexOf(".") != -1)
   return "Invalid characters like # or . in address";
  return true;
 }

}
```

The error message for the address field when the validation fails is shown in Figure 4-8.

Figure 4-8. *Text area with custom validation function*

The FormPanel has a submit() method that can be used to submit the form to the server. The form values are submitted to the server using AJAX by default. The server URL can be specified using the url property. The submit button's click event can be handled to submit the form. The form will be submitted only when there are no validation errors. The FormPanel's submit method can be invoked as shown in Listing 4-7.

Listing 4-7. FormPanel With a submit

```
Ext.create("Ext.form.Panel",
              {
   title : "Controls",
```

```
  url : "someUrl",
 items : [
  {
   xtype : "datefield",
   fieldLabel : "Date of Birth",
   name : "dob"
  },
  {
   xtype : "textfield",
   fieldLabel : "Blog",
   name : "blog"
  }
  {
    xtype : "button",
    text : "Submit",
    listeners : {
           "click" : function(src){
            src.up("form").submit();
            }
      }
   }
 ]
});
```

The click listener for the button navigates to the form using the up() method. The form is automatically submitted to the configured url attribute. The form data is passed to the server using the name property of the elements. The server resource can access the form elements using their respective names.

The submit method can optionally accept an Ext.form.action.Action object as parameter with AJAX callback functions.

```
src.up("form").submit({
success :  function(form,action){
        alert("Successfully submitted");
      },
   failure : function(form,action){
     console.log(action.failureType);
     console.log(action.result);
alert(action.response.status + ", " + action.response.statusText);
     }
  });
```

The success and failure callback functions are invoked after the form submission. We can disable AJAX and opt for a normal form submission instead using the standardSubmit property. Inside the FormPanel we can set standardSubmit property to be true.

Ext.toolbar.Toolbar

This container class is used to create toolbars. The toolbar is composed of various child controls. The default component that is added to a toolbar is a button. You can add items declaratively to a toolbar and also dynamically using the add() method present in the Toolbar class. You can also add the following toolbar-related items to a toolbar apart from the regular collection of controls like textfield, label, and so on.

Ext.toolbar.TextItem (tbtext)

This class is used to render a simple text in a toolbar. You can use it as shown below.

```
{xtype:"tbtext", text:"Sample text"}
```

Ext.toolbar.Separator (tbseparator)

This class adds a vertical separator bar in the toolbar. You can use it as shown below.

```
{xtype:"tbseparator"}
```

You can use a Separator with a "-" hyphen symbol instead of configuring it using xtype.

Ext.toolbar.Spacer (tbspacer)

This class adds a default 2px space in the toolbar. You can use it as shown below.

```
{xtype:"tbspacer"}
```

You can use a Spacer with a " " blank space instead of configuring it using xtype.

Ext.toolbar.Fill (tbfill)

This class right justifies the items to be added after adding this item. You can use it as shown below.

```
{xtype:"tbfill"}
```

You can use a Fill with a "➤" right arrow instead of configuring it using xtype.

Ext.toolbar.Paging (pagingtoolbar)

This class is used to display a paging bar when you use data components like grid panel. We'll discuss this topic in Chapter 6 on data controls.

Let's create a panel with a toolbar at the bottom as shown in Figure 4-9.

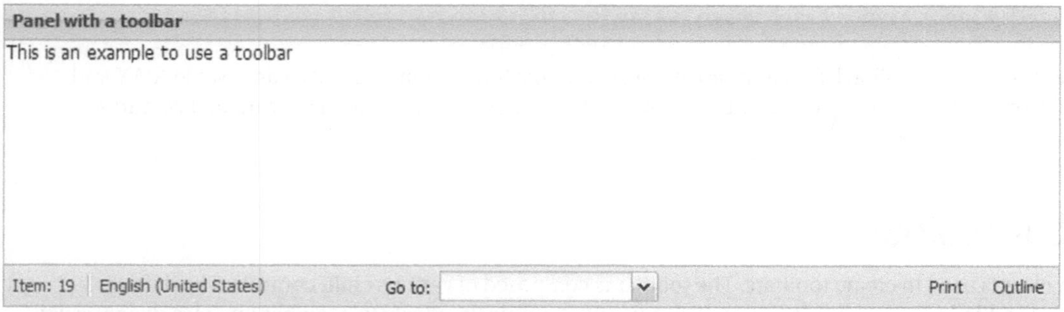

Figure 4-9. *Panel with a toolbar*

The toolbar contains text items, combobox, and buttons. Listing 4-8 shows the code snippet for creating a toolbar.

Listing 4-8. Panel With a toolbar

```
Ext.create("Ext.panel.Panel", {
    renderTo: Ext.getBody(),
    title: "Panel with a toolbar",
    html : "This is an example to use a toolbar",
    dockedItems: [
      {
        xtype: "toolbar",
        dock: "bottom",
        items: [
            {
              xtype: "tbtext",
              text: "Item: 19"
            },
            "-",
            {
              xtype: "tbtext",
              text: "English (United States)"
            },
            " ",
            {
              xtype : "combo",
              fieldLabel : "Go to",
              labelAlign : "right",
            },
            "➤",
            {
              text: "Print",
            },
            " ",
            {
              text: "Outline",
            }
        ]
      }
    ]
});
```

The toolbar is docked to the bottom of the toolbar. The toolbar has the spacer, separator, and tbfill items added using the shortcut notations. The combobox is intentionally empty.

Ext.container.Viewport

All the containers that we have discussed lack the capability to resize themselves when the browser window is resized. You've a specialized container for this purpose called Viewport. ViewPort is present in Ext.Container package and it represents the viewable browser area. Items added to the Viewport automatically get resized when the browser window is resized. Viewport is usually created as the root container of an application. Viewport is a container defined with an Auto layout by default, and it can be changed according to our requirement. We can create a Viewport with border layout as shown below.

```
Ext.create("Ext.container.Viewport",{
 layout : "border",
 items : [
  ..
]
});
```

Ext JS4 provides a number of layout controls that can be used to design our applications. Let's discuss these layout controls.

Layout Controls

All the container classes arrange their items in a specific fashion based on the layout you provide. A container with a table layout arranges the items in a tabular format, the one with a vbox layout arranges the components vertically. Ext.layout.Layout is the base class for all the layout classes. Layout class is inherited by the Ext.layout.container. Container that serves as the base class for all layout controls.

The *Ext.layout.container* package provides the different layout controls that are used to arrange our components. Table 4-7 shows the list of layout controls with a brief description.

Table 4-7. *Layout controls*

Class	xtype	Description
Absolute	absolute	Used to arrange the components by specifying the x- and y-coordinates.
Accordion	accordion	Denotes the accordion style
Anchor	anchor	Arrange the components relative to their container's position.
Border	border	Split the entire page into different regions. It's usually used to design an entire page in the application.
Card	card	The container's items are treated as a pack of cards and only one of them is shown at any point of time.
Form	form	The components are rendered one after the other as a typical form.
Table	table	Arrange the components in a tabular fashion.
HBox	hbox	Arrange the components horizontally.
VBox	vbox	Arrange the components vertically.
Fit	fit	The components of the container with fit layout is arranged to fit the entire area of the container.

The general configuration required for using any layout is given below.

```
Ext.create("container",{
 layout :  {
  type : "xtype of any layout control",
  //propertiesOfTheLayoutControl
 }

});
```

If you don't have any additional properties of the layout to be configured, the layout configuration is

```
Ext.create("container",{
 layout : "xtype of any layout control"
});
```

Let's discuss the various layout components.

Auto Layout

The default layout for the containers in Ext JS4 is Auto layout. This layout manager automatically renders the components in a container.

Fit Layout

The fit layout arranges the contents of the container to occupy the space completely. It fits the items to the container's size. Fit layout is usually used on containers that have a single item. Fit layout is the base class for the Card layout that we'll discuss later in this section. Let's add a text field to a Panel with a fit layout as shown below.

```
Ext.create("Ext.panel.Panel",{
 layout :  "fit",
       height:200,width:200,
       title : "Fit layout panel",
       items : [
                 {
                        xtype : "textfield",
                        fieldLabel : "Email"
                  }
       ]
});
```

The panel has a textfield that will be fit into the container to occupy the complete space as shown in Figure 4-10.

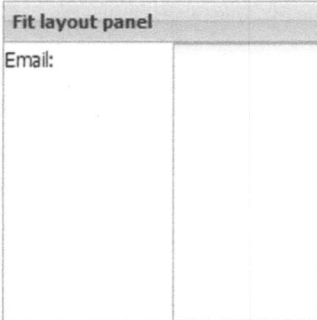

Figure 4-10. *Panel with Fit layout*

Anchor Layout

The anchor layout manager arranges the items of a container relative to the size of the container. Whenever the container is resized, the anchor layout manager rearranges the items relative to the new size of the container. You can configure an anchor property to the child items. You can configure the width and height values in percentage and the offset values in the anchor property as shown below.

```
anchor : "width% height%"
(or)
anchor : "offsetWidth offsetHeight"
```

You can also mix these two options by specifying an offset value and a percentage. Here's a simple panel that has a text field and a button and configured with an anchor layout. The items are configured with anchor attributes. Whenever you click the button, the width and height of the panel are increased by 5px. Here's the code for that.

```
var pnl = Ext.create('Ext.panel.Panel', {
        layout: "anchor",
        height: 200, width: 200,
        title: "Anchor layout panel",
        items: [
            {
                xtype: "textfield",
                fieldLabel: "Name",
                anchor : "90% 15%"
            },
            {
                xtype: "button",
                text: "Resize",
                anchor : "-80 -145",
                listeners: {
                    click: function () {
                        pnl.setWidth(pnl.getWidth() + 5);
                        pnl.setHeight(pnl.getHeight() + 5);
                    }
                }
            }
```

```
        }
    ],
    renderTo: Ext.getBody()
});
```

By clicking on the resize button continuously, you'll find out that the size of the textfield and button increase proportionately.

Box Layout

Ext.layout.container.Box serves as the base class for VBox and HBox layouts. VBox and HBox stand for vertical box and horizontal box, respectively.

A Panel with three buttons (A, B, and C) using a VBox layout is shown below. The buttons are arranged vertically in the center of the panel as shown in Figure 4-11.

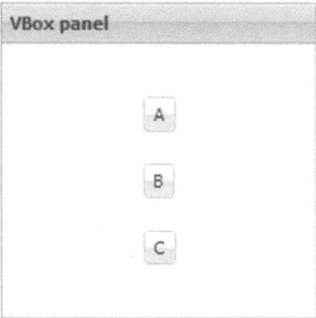

Figure 4-11. *Panel with a VBox layout*

The pack and align properties of the VBox layout are used for positioning the buttons inside the container. Listing 4-9 shows how to do that.

Listing 4-9. VBox Layout

```
Ext.create("Ext.panel.Panel", {
    height: 200, width: 200,
    title : "VBox panel",
    layout : {
type : "vbox",
pack : "center",
align : "center"
    },
    defaults : {xtype : "button",margin:"10"},
    items : [
{text : "A"},
{text : "B"},
{text : "C"},
            ],
    renderTo : Ext.getBody()
});
```

The code in Listing 4-9 can be modified to use the hbox layout. The layout configuration can be modified as shown below.

```
layout : {
          type : "hbox",
          pack : "center",
          align : "middle"
            }
```

The panel will look as shown in Figure 4-12.

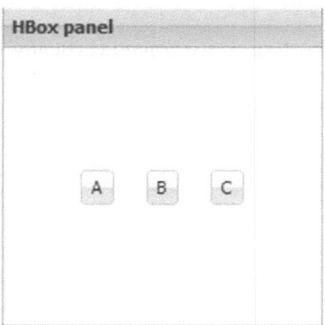

Figure 4-12. *Panel with HBox layout*

Accordion Layout

Accordion layout is an extension of VBox layout. It arranges a set of panels vertically with collapse and expandable features. Listing 4-10 shows the code snippet of a panel that uses the accordion layout.

Listing 4-10. Accordion Layout

```
Ext.create("Ext.panel.Panel", {
   height: 300, width: 300,
   title: "Accordion layout ",
   layout: {
             type : "accordion",
             multi : true
           },
   items: [
     {
   title: "Inbox",
               html : "Inbox contents"
           },
           {
               title: "Outbox",
               html: "Outbox contents"
           },
           {
```

```
                title: "Sent Items",
                html: "Sent Items"
            }
        ],
    renderTo: Ext.getBody()
});
```

The accordion layout is configured with a multi attribute which enables viewing multiple panels. The code throws up the output as shown in Figure 4-13.

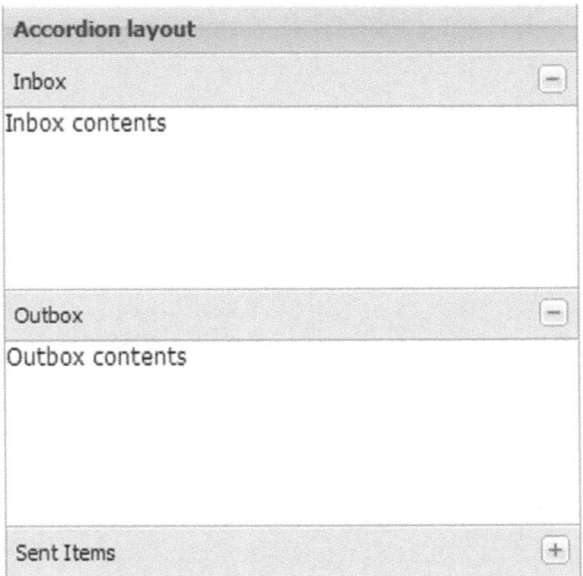

Figure 4-13. *Panel with Accordion layout*

Table Layout

Table layout is used to render a HTML table element. It has all the properties of a table, the most commonly used being the columns attribute. Listing 4-11 shows the code snippet of a panel that uses a table layout.

Listing 4-11. Table Layout

```
Ext.create("Ext.panel.Panel", {
    height: 200, width: 200,
    title: "Table layout ",
    layout: {
            type: "table",
            columns: 2
        },
```

```
defaults: {
            xtype: "button",
            margin: "10"
        },
    items: [
            {
                text: "A"
            },
            {
                text: "B"
            },
            {
                text: "C"
            },
            {
                text: "D"
            },
            {
                text: "E"
            },
            {
                text: "F"
            }
    ],
    renderTo: Ext.getBody()
});
```

You'll get an output as shown in Figure 4-14.

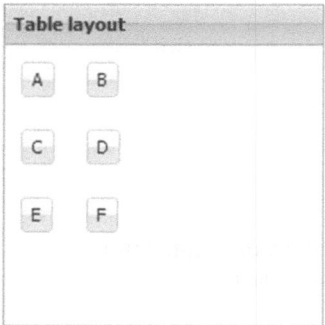

Figure 4-14. *Panel with a Table layout*

Column Layout

Column layout arranges the container in separate columns starting from left to right. Each item in the container that uses column layout is configured with a columnWidth attribute. The sum of the values of columnWidth attributes of all the items need to be equal to the total width of the container. You can provide the values of columnWidth in percentage or a concrete value. The percentage value is provided as a decimal number where the total columnWidth equals 1.

Let's create a panel with column layout as shown in Figure 4-15.

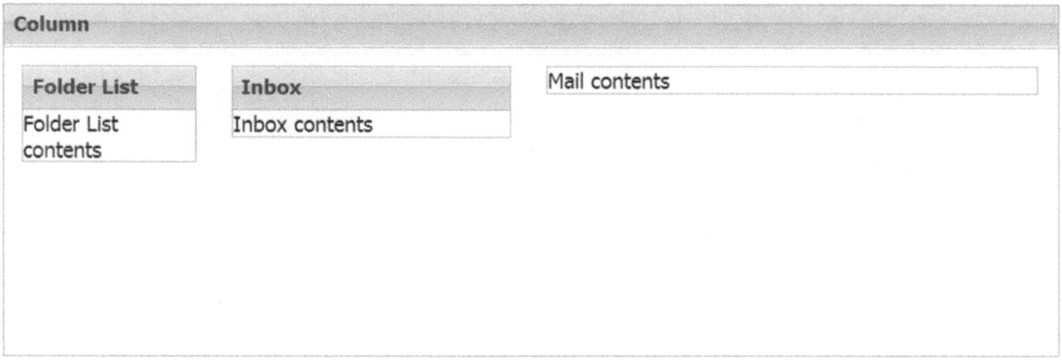

Figure 4-15. *Panel with a Column layout*

Listing 4-12 shows the code for that.

Listing 4-12. Column Layout

```
Ext.create('Ext.panel.Panel', {
  title: 'Column',
  width: 600, height: 200,
  layout: 'column',
  defaults : {margin : "10"},
  items: [
    {
      title : "Folder List",
      html : "Folder List contents",
      columnWidth : 0.20
    },
    {
      title: "Inbox",
      html: "Inbox contents",
      columnWidth : 0.30
    },
    {
      html: "Mail contents",
      columnWidth: 0.50
    }
  ],
  renderTo: Ext.getBody()
});
```

Border Layout

Border layout is usually the master layout in an Ext JS 4 application. You can design a master layout with regions like header, footer, and menus. In Ext JS 4, which is predominantly used for building single-page applications, border layout is used to design the entire layout of the page. The Ext JS 4 API documentation page, shown in Figure 4-16, is a good example of the use of border layout.

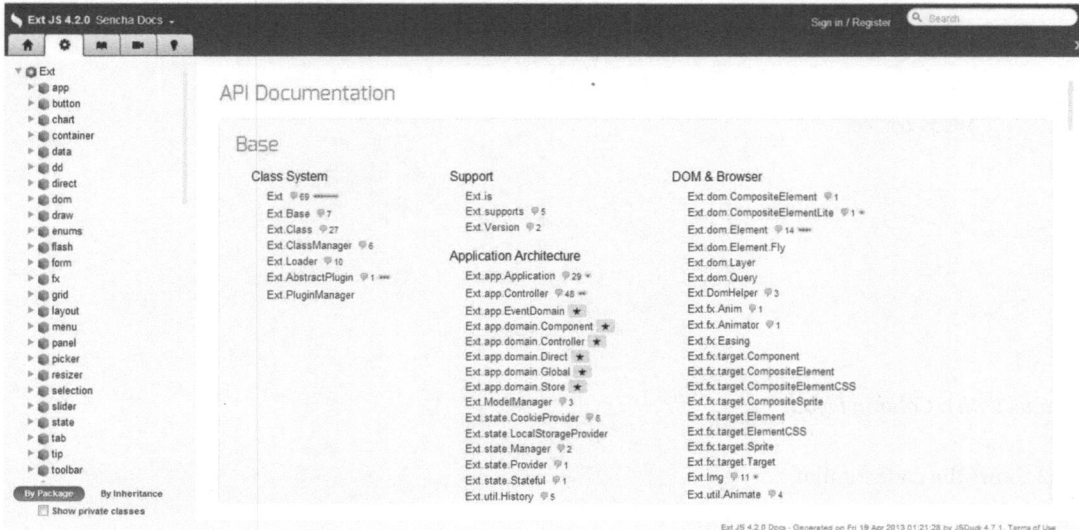

Figure 4-16. *A page that uses Border layout*

The border layout splits the page into different regions like north, south, east, west, and center. The center region has to be mandatorily configured while the other regions are optional. For example, in the figure above, you can say that the page has three regions, a header with a menu bar in the north, the list of classes in a tree format in the east, and the main content in the center.

Let's create a simple example of using Border layout. We'll create a panel that uses border layout as shown in Figure 4-17.

Figure 4-17. *A panel with a Border layout*

Listing 4-13 shows the code snippet for a panel with Border layout.

Listing 4-13. Border Layout

```
Ext.create("Ext.panel.Panel",{
    layout : "border",padding:30,id:"main",height:500,width:400,
    items : [
                {
                  xtype : "panel",
                  html : "Top ",
                  region : "north"
                },
                {
                  xtype : "panel",
                  html : "Main contents",
                  region : "center"
                },
                {
                  xtype : "panel",
                  html : "Side bar",
                  collapsible : false,
                  split : true,
                  region : "west"
                }
    ],
    renderTo : Ext.getBody()
});
```

The Panel is split into north, west, and center regions. In this example each region has a panel configured in it. The west region has optional properties like collapsible, split, and so forth, configured to be able to hide and resize the region dynamically.

Card Layout

You have a Panel with a number of child components and only one child control needs to be shown at a time. The Panel can use a card layout for this purpose. Card layout, when used on a container, treats its items as a collection of cards and shows only one item at any point of time.

Card layout has an important property called *activeItem* that holds the information about the item that has to be displayed. This property has to be manipulated to change the item to be shown. Listing 4-14 shows the code snippet for using card layout.

Listing 4-14. Card Layout

```
Ext.create("Ext.panel.Panel",{
    layout : "card",padding:30,id:"main",
    items : [
      {
        xtype : "panel",
        title : "Screen 1",
        items : [
```

```
                    {
                      xtype : "button",
                      text : "go to screen 2",
                      handler : function(){
                        Ext.getCmp("main").getLayout().setActiveItem(1);
                      }
                    }
                  ]
              },
              {
                xtype : "panel",
                title : "Screen 2",
                items : [
                    {
                      xtype : "button",
                      text : "go to screen 3",
                      handler : function(){
                        Ext.getCmp("main").getLayout().setActiveItem(2);
                      }
                    }
                  ]
              },
              {
                xtype : "panel",
                title : "Screen 3"
              }
            ],
          renderTo : Ext.getBody()
});
```

The main Panel uses the card layout. It has three panel children. The Screen1 and Screen2 panels have a button when clicked change the active item of the card layout. The setActiveItem method on the Card Layout class accepts a number that represents the index of the controls as the parameter. The setActiveItem can accept the id of the control as a parameter as well. If Screen 2 panel's id is "screen2", we can the change the active item by

```
Ext.getCmp("mainpanel").getLayout().setActiveItem("screen2")
```

We can also pass the component as the parameter like this:

Ext.getCmp("mainpanel").getLayout().setActiveItem(Ext.create("Ext.Button",{...})). This can be used if you create a new object and set it as an active item, instead of creating it beforehand and not showing it. Figure 4-18 shows the output of the code in Listing 4-14. You'll get Screen 1 panel, and when you click the "Got to Screen 2" button, you'll get Screen2. Clicking on "Go to Screen 3" button will give you the Screen 3. Please note that only one screen is showed at any point of time in card layout.

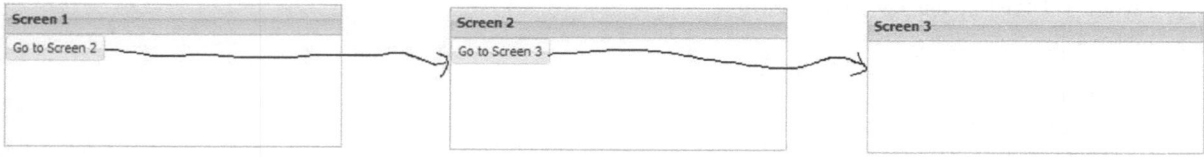

Figure 4-18. *Output of Card layout example*

One of the advantages of using Ext JS 4 as we discussed earlier is the support for writing modularized code. In the card layout code snippet shows in Listing 4-10 you can bring in some modularity by organizing the items of the main panel into individual classes. Listing 4-15 shows a modularized version of using card layout.

Listing 4-15. Modularized Version of Card Layout

```
Ext.define("Screen1",{
    extend : "Ext.panel.Panel",
    xtype : "screen1",
    title : "Screen 1",
    items : [
       {
         xtype : "button",
         text : "Go to Screen 2",
         handler : function(){
           Ext.getCmp("viewport").getLayout().setActiveItem(1);
         }
       }
    ]
});

Ext.define("Screen2",{
    extend : "Ext.panel.Panel",
    xtype : "screen2",
    title : "Screen 2",
    items : [
       {
         xtype : "button",
         text : "Go to Screen 3",
         handler : function(){
           Ext.getCmp("viewport").getLayout().setActiveItem(2);
         }
       }
    ]
});

Ext.define("Screen3",{
    extend : "Ext.panel.Panel",
    xtype : "screen3",
    title : "Screen 3"
});

Ext.onReady(function(){
    Ext.create("Ext.container.Viewport",{
      layout : "card",padding:30,id:"viewport",
      items : [
        {
          xtype : "screen1",
          id : "screen1"
        },
```

```
      {
        xtype : "screen2",
        id : "screen2"
      },
      {
        xtype : "screen3",
        id : "screen3"
      }
    ],
    renderTo : Ext.getBody()
  });
}
);
```

In the example above, we've defined three new classes Screen1, Screen2, and Screen3. These classes inherit Ext.panel.Panel and have screen1, screen2, and screen3 as xtypes, respectively. The main container, a Viewport with card layout, contains the instances of these classes. The Screen1 and Screen2 classes have simple buttons with their handlers taking care of the navigation to the next item. The best place to write the handler logic is a Controller class. We'll discuss the controller classes in our MVC chapter.

Summary

In this chapter I discussed the controls and layout of Ext JS 4. All UI controls inherit from Ext.Component class. Ext.Component provides several properties, methods, and events. The Ext.container.Container class serves as the base class for all the container controls like Panel, Viewport, and Toolbars. The form panel represents the standard HTML form with functionalities like validations, processing and so on. You can add the field controls to the form panel. Ext.layout.Layout is the base class for all the layout components. Border Layout defines the master layout of an application and Card layout is used to show one item at any point of time.

In the next chapter you'll learn the data handling mechanisms in Ext JS 4. I'll discuss the Ext.data package in detail and take a look at the core concepts of fetching, saving, and updating data from various data sources.

CHAPTER 5

■ ■ ■

Working with Data

Data handling techniques in applications have evolved over the years. You have the traditional set up of posting the form data to the server and loading a new page with data as response. With the advent of AJAX, you can send the request and load raw data as response. You can process the response data and display it in the page without the need to refresh it. AJAX became a de facto standard mechanism for communicating with the server. The data that you exchange with the server in AJAX can be in different formats like XML and JSON. This data can be cached in the client side in the data storage capabilities provided by HTML 5. The data that you exchange can be in a linear or hierarchical format depending on the complexity.

Ext JS 4 provides sophisticated components that indirectly send an AJAX request to the server, receive the data, process them, and display the output. These components provide the following functionalities.

- *Fetch the data from the data source*

- *Write the changes back to the data source*

- *Sort and filter the data*

- *Support various data formats like XML and JSON*

- *Integrate with RESTful services*

- *Support for HTML 5 data storage*

In this chapter you'll learn the various data handling mechanisms provided by Ext JS 4. Let's take a close look at the Ext.data package that is used for working with data.

Ext.data package

The Ext.data package provides all the classes that are responsible for loading, parsing and saving the data. The classes take care of fetching the data from the data source, parsing the data to the required format, writing the data back to the source, saving the data in the client, sorting, filtering, and querying the data.

Table 5-1 shows the basic set of classes that you will use in Ext.data package and its sub packages.

Table 5-1. *Classes in Ext.data and Its Sub-Packages*

Class	Description
Ext.data.Connection	Establishes the connection to the server, sends the requests, and gives you the response
Ext.data.Request	Encapsulates the request data sent to the server
Ext.data.Model	Represents the object or a record or a row.
Ext.data.Field	Represents the fields or columns in a row
Ext.data.validations	Provides a set of validation functions
Ext.data.association.Association	Represents the association relationships between Model classes
Ext.data.Store	Represents the data store that contains a collection of records or Model objects
Ext.data.proxy.Proxy	The class that is used to fetch data from a data source
Ext.data.reader.Reader	The class that's used to read the data and convert it to a Model format
Ext.data.writer.Writer	Write data back to the data source.

Each of the above mentioned classes serves as the base class for a numerous other classes that we'll discuss with you in the rest of the chapter. The three most widely used classes in Ext.data packages are the Model, Store, and Proxy classes that you'll learn in detail in this chapter.

At the outset, let's start with the basic set of classes.

Ext.data.Connection, Ext.data.Request

This class encapsulates the request sending mechanisms to the server. You can create an instance of this class and call its request function. The request function takes in an instance of Ext.data.Request as an argument. Let's say you've a books.txt file with the following data.

books.txt
Zend Framework
Beginning F#

Pro Hadoop Here's how you use the Connection and the Request classes to send request to books.txt and load the data.

```
Ext.create("Ext.data.Connection").request(
    Ext.create("Ext.data.Request",{
        url: "books.txt",
        success: function (xhr) {
            console.log(xhr.responseText);
        },
        failure : function(xhr){
            console.log("Error: " + xhr.statusText);
        }
    }
));
```

You can create an instance of Connection class and call its request method by passing a Request object to it. The Request object is supplied with the url attribute and callback functions success and failure. The success or failure functions will be called asynchronously by passing the *XmlHttpRequest* instance, depending on the response.

There's a much easier way of sending Ajax requests by using the Ext.Ajax class.. Ext.Ajax class itself is a singleton instance of Ext.Connection. You can rewrite the above code using Ext.Ajax as shown in Listing 5-1.

Listing 5-1. Ext.Ajax

```
Ext.Ajax.request(
        {
            url: "books.txt",
            success: function (xhr) {
                console.log(xhr.responseText);
            },
            failure : function(xhr){
                console.log("Error: " + xhr.statusText);
            }
        }
);
```

Since Ext.Ajax is an instance of Connection class, you can call the request method directly by passing the configuration object.

The Connection and Request classes are used indirectly by the proxy classes that you'll learn later in this chapter.

In a typical scenario, a Store class uses a Proxy to fetch data from the source. The reader parses the data and converts it to the format defined by a Model. The Store contains a collection of Model objects. The store uses a Writer to write the changes in the data, back to the source.

Let's discuss the Model class in detail..

Ext.data.Model

A Model class represents data models. It is used to define the format of data under consideration. It's similar to a record or row in a table. You can define a Model by giving it a name and listing the fields that the Model is composed of.

Let's define a Model class called Country with fields like name, capital, and population members as shown below.

```
Ext.define("Country", {
        extend: "Ext.data.Model",
        fields : ["name","capital","population"]
});
```

We've defined a class "Country" that inherits Ext.data.Model. It has the fields attribute to list the fields of the class. A Model instance can be created using the standard Ext.create method.

The Country class can be instantiated like this.

```
Ext.create("Country", {name: "France", capital: "Paris", population: 65436552});
```

You can access the values of the Country object using the get() and set() methods defined the Model class. The code below shows the usage of get() and set() methods.

```
var fr = Ext.create("Country", { name: "France", population: 65436552});
console.log(fr.get("name"));
fr.set("capital", "Paris");
```

Every Model class is internally defined with a field called "id" that serves as a primary key. The getId() method in the Model class can be used to access the id value. In the code above the id value is not initialized for the Model instance. Let's create a Country object initializing its id value as shown below.

```
var fr = Ext.create("Country", { id: "101", name: "France", capital: "Paris", population: 3248768787 });
console.log(fr.getId()); //Prints 101
```

If you want to configure any other field to serve as an id, idProperty can be used. Let's define the Country Model where you configure the idProperty to be name as shown below.

```
Ext.define("Country", {
    extend: "Ext.data.Model",
    fields : ["name","capital","population"],
    idProperty : "name"
});

var fr = Ext.create("Country", { name: "France", capital: "Paris", population: 65436552 });
console.log(fr.getId()); //Prints France
```

Invoking getId() will now output the name of the country as it's been configured as the idProperty. The purpose of having an id in a Model class is to pave way for performing operations like, search, and so on. You can invoke these operations only when you have the Model configured with a Proxy.

Let's take up a simple example of using a Model with a Proxy, though we'll discuss Proxy classes in detail later in the chapter. In this example we'll define the Model Country, wired up with a Proxy. The Proxy that we'll use is an in-memory Proxy, The in-memory proxy supplies the data for the Country in JSON format as shown in Listing 5-2.

Listing 5-2. Country Model

```
Ext.define("Country", {
    extend: "Ext.data.Model",
    fields: ["name", "capital", "population"],
    idProperty: "name",
    proxy: {
        type: "memory",
        data: {
            country: {
                name: "France",
                capital: "Paris",
                population: 65436552
                }
        },
        reader: {
            type : "json",
            root : "country"
        }
    }
});
```

In Listing 5-2 we've specified the data for the Model in JSON format. We've wired up a reader that parses the JSON formatted data.

You can load the Country object by using the id property, as shown below.

```
Country.load("France", {
            success: function (record) {
                console.log(record.get("capital"));     //Prints Paris
                console.log(record.get("population")); //Prints 65436552
            }
});
```

The **load** method accepts the id, which is the name of the country in our case, and a callback function as parameters. We've used a success callback function in this example. The load method invokes the proxy that fetches the contents corresponding to the id and hands over a Model object to the success callback.

Ext.data.Field

The fields of the model are instantiated to `Ext.data.Field` objects. In our Country class shown in Listing 5-2, the Country model will have three instances of Field class. The Field class has few useful properties to specify the data types, set default values, extract values from the data and assign it and so on. The Country class definition with the use of these additional field properties is shown below.

```
Ext.define("Country", {
    extend: "Ext.data.Model",
    fields: [
      {name: "name", type: "string"},
      "capital",
      {name: "population", type: "number", mapping: "country_population"},
      {name: "continent", type: "string",defaultValue:"Europe"},
    ]
});
```

Ext.data.validations

Model class provides a facility to configure the validation rules. `Ext.data.validations` class is used to configure the different validation rules. There are different validators like `length`, `presence`, `exclusion`, `inclusion`, `format`, and `email`. These validators are actually simple methods of Ext.data.validations class. Let's define a Model with few validation rules for the fields as shown in Listing 5-3.

Listing 5-3. Model with Validations

```
Ext.define("Book", {
    extend: "Ext.data.Model",
    fields: ["title", "author", "ISBN", "price"],
    validations: [
        { type: "presence", field: "title" },
        { type: "length", field: "author", max: 20, min: 3 },
        { type: "format", field: "ISBN",
matcher: /ISBN(?:-13)?:?\x20*(?=.{17}$)97(?:8|9)([ -])\d{1,5}\1\d{1,7}\1\d{1,6}\1\d$/ },
        {type:"inclusion",field:"price",list:["$20","$25","$30","$35"]}
    ]
});
```

The Book model is configured with the validations attribute. The title, author and price fields are configured with presence, length and inclusion validation types. The ISBN property is configured with a regular expression.

Let's create an instance of Book class and validate it by calling the validate() method.

```
var b1 = Ext.create("Book", { title: "Practical XYZ", ISBN: "ISBN: 978-3-5028-4391-71",price:"$45" });
var errors = b1.validate();
```

Calling the validate() method runs the validation rules on the fields and returns back an instance of Ext.data.Errors class. You can loop through the errors collection and display the error messages as shown below. The code prints the field name and the error message corresponding to the field, in the console.

```
errors.each(function (item) {
            console.log(item.field + " " +item.message);
 });
```

The output is

```
author is the wrong length
ISBN is the wrong format
price is not included in the list of acceptable values
```

If you need more control of the validation, you can always override the validate method in your Model class and construct an Ext.data.Errors object with custom error messages.

You can create custom validation rules by extending the Ext.data.validations singleton object. Say you want to create a validation rule called priceRange and check if the price value is between the permissible range like this.

```
{type:"priceRange" max:50,min:5,message:"must be between 5 and 50"}
```

Here's how you define a priceRange validator.

```
Ext.data.validations.priceRange = function (config, value) {
    var max = config.max;
    var min = config.min;
    return value < max && value > min;
};
```

All you need to do is attach a custom function in Ext.data.validations. This function accepts the configuration object and the value that is assigned to the field. You can access the max and min values from the configuration object, compare it with the value and return a Boolean output.

Ext.data.association.Association

A Model class in Ext JS 4 can be associated with other Model classes. This concept is pretty similar to the foreign key relationships in databases. Model classes can have the following association relationships with each other.

- hasMany

  - Represents an One-to-Many relationship

- hasOne

  - Represents an One-to-One relationship

- belongsTo

  - Represents a Many-to-One relationship

Let's understand associations with an example. We'll define four Model classes: *Country, CountryDetails, Continent, and City*. The associations between these classes are defined below.

- Country has many Cities

- Many Countries belong to a Continent

Each Country's information is present in a CountryDetails object. We'll define an in-memory proxy with JSON formatted data. The Continent, City, and CountryDetails classes are defined in Listing 5-4.

Listing 5-4. Continent, City, and CountryDetails Model Classes

```
Ext.define("Continent", {
    extend: "Ext.data.Model",
    fields: ["name"]
});
Ext.define("City", {
    extend: "Ext.data.Model",
    fields: ["name"]
});
Ext.define("CountryDetails", {
    extend: "Ext.data.Model",
    fields: ["id","population"],
});
```

The Country class that is related to these three classes along with the data is shown in Listing 5-5.

Listing 5-5. Country Model

```
Ext.define("Country", {
        extend: "Ext.data.Model",
        idProperty : "name",
        fields: ["name", "capital"],
        hasMany: [{ name: "cities", model: "City"}],
        hasOne:  [{model:"CountryDetails"}],
        belongsTo: [{ model: "Continent"}],
        proxy : {
            type : "memory",
            data : {
                    country : {
                        name : "France",
                        capital : "Paris",
```

```
                    countrydetails : {
                        id : "cd101",
                        population : 65436552
                    },
                    cities : [
                        {name:"Lyon"},{name:"Avignon"}
                    ],
                    continent : {
                        name : "Europe"
                    }
                }
            },
            reader : {
                type : "json",
                root : "country"
            }
        }
    });
```

Listing 5-5 shows the code snippet where the Country class has the hasOne, belongsTo, and hasMany associations with CountryDetails, Continent, and City classes, respectively. The proxy class has the data configured in JSON format. You can load the country based on the name that's configured to be the id of the Country and access the associated objects as shown below.

```
Country.load("France",{
                    success : function(record){
                        var continent = record.getContinent();
                        console.log(continent.get("name"));
                        var countryDetails = record.getCountryDetails();
                        console.log(countryDetails.get("population"));
                        var cities = record.cities();
                        cities.each(function(city){
                            console.log(city.get("name"));
                        });
                    }
            });
```

The output of the code is

```
Europe
65436552
Lyon
Avignon
```

The interesting parts in the code above are the getContinent(), getCountryDetails() and cities() methods that are automatically generated for the associations.

The hasOne and belongsTo associations have getter and setter methods generated.

The hasMany association has a method generated with the configured name property. In this case, a method called cities() generated which is a collection of City instances.

A Model instance just represents a single record. A Store is a collection of Model instances. Let's discuss the Ext.data.Store class and it's concepts in detail, in this section.

Ext.data.Store

The Ext.data.Store class represents a data store that contains a collection of Model instances. Just like the way you wire-up a Model with a proxy, you can wire-up a store with a proxy. A Store can be populated with data that's fetched from the data source using a Proxy. Another important aspect of a Store is the facility to sort, filter and search the underlying data.

Let's create a simple Store, populate it with data, and learn the basic operations that you can perform on it. We'll not bring in a Proxy or a Reader in this example and populate the Store explicitly.

Let's define a Model class called '**Book**' and create a book store as shown in Listing 5-6.

Listing 5-6. A Simple Store

```
Ext.define("Book", {
     extend : "Ext.data.Model",
     fields : ["title","author","price"]
});

var bookStore = Ext.create("Ext.data.Store", {
     model : "Book"
});
```

The bookstore is created by wiring the Book using the model property. You can create a Store without needing to explicitly define a Model as shown here.

```
var bookStore = Ext.create("Ext.data.Store", {
          fields: ["title","author","price"]
 });
```

You can also define the BookStore as a new class that extends Store like this.

```
Ext.define("BookStore",{
    extend : "Ext.data.Store",
    fields : ["title","author","price"]
});
```

We'll revisit this approach of defining a Store class when you learn MVC in Chapter 9.

The bookstore defined in Listing 5-6 is empty without any data now. Let's add some records to the bookStore using the **add method** in the Store class.

```
bookStore.add({ title: "Zend Framework", author: "Zend", price: 49.99 });
bookStore.add({ title: "Beginning F#", author: "Robert Pickering", price: 44.99 });
bookStore.add({ title: "Pro Hadoop", author: "Jason Venner", price: 39.99 });
```

You can iterate through the records in the Store using the **each method**.

```
bookStore.each(function (book) {
          console.log(book.get("title") + ", " + book.get("author"));
});
```

The each function prints the title and author of the book objects in bookStore. If you want to sort the bookStore by ascending order of title and before printing the contents, we can use the **sort method** as shown below.

```
bookStore.sort("title", "ASC");
```

You can provide multiple sorting rules by passing an array of sorters. Each sorter is an object of **Ext.util.Sorter** class. You can sort the bookStore by descending order of price and ascending order of title as shown here.

```
bookStore.sort([
    { property: "price", direction: "DESC" },
    { property: "title", direction: "ASC" }
]);
```

The Store class provides methods like **filter** and **filterBy** to filter the records based on some criteria. Say you want to filter the store by its price, here's how to do that.

```
bookStore.filter("price", 49.99);
```

You can provide custom criteria for filter functions by using the filterBy method as shown below.

```
bookStore.filterBy(function (record) {
                    return record.get("price") > 40.00;
});
```

You pass a callback function as an argument to the filterBy method. This function is invoked for every record in the store and, based on your filtering logic, the function returns a boolean value. The record is filtered out if the function returns a false and stays back otherwise.

After the filters are applied to the Store, the sorting operations will operate on those filtered records only. So you can clear the filters anytime by calling the clearFilter **method** on the store as

```
bookStore.clearFilter();
```

Filtering a Store makes changes to the underlying collection of data. The UI controls that are wired to the Store will update themselves when a store is filtered.

The Store class provides search functionalities in the form of find and query methods. You can query a store based on a property. The findRecord method returns the record against the condition. If you have to find the record in a store based on the title, you can do so by writing

```
var record = bookStore.findRecord("title", "Pro Hadoop");
console.log(record.get("author")); // Prints Jason Venner
```

If you need to find all the records against a custom validation condition, you can use the queryBy method. The queryBy method is very similar to the filterBy method that we discussed earlier, the only difference being the return value. The queryBy method returns a collection of records, while filterBy doesn't return anything. Say you want to get all the books with a price greater than $40, here's how you do that.

```
var books = bookStore.queryBy(function (record) {
                    return record.get("price") > 40;
});
```

```
books.each(function (book) {
                console.log(book.get("title"));
});
```

You created a Store and added Model instances by using the add method and played with sorting, filtering and searching options.

You can also create a store by specifying the data inline as shown in Listing 5-7.

Listing 5-7. Store with Inline Data

```
var bookStore = Ext.create("Ext.data.Store", {
        model: "Book",
        data: [
                { title: "Zend Framework", author: "Zend", price: 49.99 },
                { title: "Beginning F#", author: "Robert Pickering", price: 44.99 },
                { title: "Pro Hadoop", author: "Jason Venner", price: 39.99 }
        ]
});
```

Each item in the data is automatically converted to a Model object and added to the Store object. In a typical scenario, you would leave the job of loading the data to the Proxy class and the Store will be wired up with the Proxy. We'll discuss this topic later in the chapter.

In most of the scenarios, you'll create a Store that will load data from the data source using a Proxy and a Reader will parse the data and convert it to the Model format. There are different types of Reader classes available based on the data formats like Xml or Json or Array. Instead of creating a Store object and configuring with a particular reader, Ext JS 4 provides some helper store classes. These store classes accept all the configuration options of the corresponding reader classes. Table 5-2 shows the list of these store classes.

Table 5-2. *Different Types of Store*

Class	Description
ArrayStore	This class is used if the data is a simple array collection.
JsonStore	Used when the data is in JSON format
JsonPStore	Used to hold JSON formatted data loaded from different domains. This class uses the JsonPProxy class.
XmlStore	You've an XML formatted data that needs to be loaded into a Store and XmlStore comes in here. We'll discuss the use of XML data later in the chapter.
TreeStore	Mainly used in tree control, this class is used to load hierarchical data. We'll discuss in this the Chapter 6.
DirectStore	Ext Direct is a specification that paves way for communication of Ext JS 4 clients with the server platforms. For example if your Ext JS 4 code needs to talk to the Java objects on the server, Java implementation of Ext Direct can be used. The DirectStore class uses a Direct Proxy class to talk to the server and exchange JSON data.

Events in Store

Ext.data.Store class provides events that may be of good use in realtime applications. Events like **load, beforeload, update, datachanged, write,** and so on are pretty useful.

Since the Store loads the data asynchronously from the data source using a proxy, a **load** event can be handled to find out the state of the Store after the data has been loaded.

Whenever you make changes to the records in the store, the **update** event is raised. The **datachanged** event is raised when you add or remove records to the store. The **write** event is raised after you write the changes in the data through a proxy.

Here's a code snippet for handling some events of a Store. We'll first define a store with the **autoLoad** property set to false.

```
var bookStore = Ext.create("Ext.data.Store", {
    fields: ["title", "author", "price"],
    data: [
            { title: "Zend Framework", author: "Zend", price: 49.99 },
            { title: "Beginning F#", author: "Robert Pickering", price: 44.99 },
            { title: "Pro Hadoop", author: "Jason Venner", price: 39.99 }
    ],
    autoLoad : false
});
```

Let's register the load, updated and datachanged events.

```
bookStore.on("load", function (src) {
    console.log("loaded " + src.getCount());
});
bookStore.load();
bookStore.on("update", function (src, record) {
    console.log("updated " + record.get("title"));
});
bookStore.on("datachanged", function (src) {
    console.log("datachanged " + src.getCount());
});
bookStore.add({ title: "Pro Spring Security",author:"Carlo Scarioni",price:49.99 });
bookStore.getAt(0).set("price", 50.00);
```

The output of the above code is

```
loaded 3
datachanged 4
updated Zend Framework
```

When you call load method on the bookstore, load event handler is called and *loaded 3* is displayed in the console. After adding a new book to the store, datachanged event handler is called and you can see *datachanged 4* in the console. After updating the price of the book at 0th position, updated event handler is invoked and you get *updated Zend Framework* in the console.

We've discussed Store class so far. Let's get introduced to Reader classes before we venture into Proxy classes.

Ext.data.Reader

Ext.data.reader.Reader class parses the data into the format specified by the Model class. The data can be a simple array or JSON/XML formatted. A Reader class is used in conjunction with the Proxy class. There are three types of Reader classes one for each format of data, **Ext.data.reader.Json**, **Ext.data.reader.Xml** and **Ext.data.reader.Array**.

The general mechanism of using a reader is

```
reader : {
        type :  "array" or "json" or "xml"
        //properties like root, record
}
```

You can specify the type of the reader and some of the properties like root or record that'll help the reader look for the exact information in the data that is provided to it. Let's understand the use of different readers with simple examples.

Let's create a book store and populate it with data. To begin with, the data is supplied as an array. Listing 5-8 shows how to supply the array to a store.

Listing 5-8. Array Reader

```
var bookStore = Ext.create("Ext.data.Store", {
        fields: ["title", "author", "price"],
        data: [
                ["Zend Framework", "Zend", 49.99],
                ["Beginning F#", "Robert Pickering", 44.99],
                ["Pro Hadoop", "Jason Venner", 39.99]
        ],
        proxy: {
            type: "memory",
            reader: {
                type : "array"
            }
        }
});
```

In the code above you'll notice that the reader is configured to be an Array. The data property contains the array of records. The Array reader class maps the array items into a Model instance and loads it to the Store.

If you want to specify the data in JSON format, you can use the JSON reader. Though we've used JSON reader when we discussed Model associations, let's revisit it.

```
var bookStore = Ext.create("Ext.data.Store", {
        fields: ["title", "author", "price"],
        data: {
        library: [
          { title: "Zend Framework", author: "Zend", price: 49.99 },
          { title: "Beginning F#", author: "Robert Pickering", price: 44.99 },
          { title: "Pro Hadoop", author: "Jason Venner", price: 39.99 }
        ]
        },
```

```
      proxy: {
         type : "memory",
         reader: {
                     type : "json",
                     root : "library"
                 }
      }
});
```

The data contains a JSON array called library. You'll notice that library is configured to be the root property in the JSON reader class.

Let's create a book store where the data is in XML format. We'll create a simple XML file that contains a list of books. Our Store will load this XML file using an AJAX proxy that we'll learn later in detail, and use an Xml reader to parse it.

The **books.xml** file is shown below.

```
<?xml version="1.0" encoding="utf-8" ?>
<Books>
  <Book>
    <Title>Zend Framework</Title>
    272103_1_EnZend</Author>
    <Price>44.99</Price>
  </Book>
  <Book>
    <Title>Beginning F#</Title>
    272103_1_EnRobert Pickering</Author>
    <Price>49.99</Price>
  </Book>
  <Book>
    <Title>Pro Hadoop</Title>
    272103_1_EnJason Venner</Author>
    <Price>39.99</Price>
  </Book>
</Books>
```

The root element of the XML document is Books. The Books element contains Book elements. Let's create the Store that loads this books.xml.

```
var bookStore = Ext.create("Ext.data.Store", {
      fields: [
          { name: "title", mapping: "Title" },
          { name: "author", mapping: "Author" },
          { name: "price", mapping: "Price",type:"number" }
      ],
      autoLoad: true,
      proxy: {
          type: "ajax",
          url: "books.xml",
```

```
        reader: {
            type: "xml",
            record: "Book",
            root : "Books"
        }
    }
});
```

We've configured the proxy to be an Ajax proxy and the url attribute configured as books.xml. The reader is Xml reader, which has the root property configured as Books. The Book element is configured as the record property. Reader parses each Book element into a record. You'll also notice the mapping property used in the fields property. The lowercase title field is mapped to the Title element in the XML data.

Let's discuss Proxy classes in detail.

Ext.data.proxy.Proxy

Ext.data.proxy.Proxy is the class that deals with communication and exchange of data with the data sources. This class is similar to our classic proxy classes like stubs and skeletons used in distributed computing. Proxy classes are used by Stores usually for performing the CRUD (Create-Retrieve-Update-Delete) operations on the data. As a developer you may not really need to create or interact with the proxy classes directly.

You only have to declare the type of proxy that needs to be used and these proxy classes will perform their job.

The Proxy class has three main configuration attributes as shown in Table 5-3.

Table 5-3. *Configuration Attributes of Proxy Class*

Config	Description
model	The model property denotes the Model class that Proxy deals with.
reader	The reader property specifies the Reader object to be used for parsing data to Model format.
writer	The writer property specifies the Writer object to be used while writing to the resource.

The Proxy class has four important methods that indicate the operations that can be performed. Table 5-4 shows the methods in Proxy class.

Table 5-4. *Methods of Proxy Class*

Method	Description
read	Denotes the Read operation
create	Denotes the Create operation
update	Denotes the Update operation
destroy	Denotes the Destroy operation

The four methods accept an **Ext.data.Operation** object and a callback function that's called after completion of the operation as arguments.

The Proxy class serves as the base class for a number of proxy classes. Table 5-5 below shows the list of proxy classes with a short description.

Table 5-5. *Proxy Classes*

Class	Description
Ext.data.proxy.Ajax	Used to communicate with a server resource using Ajax.
Ext.data.proxy.Rest	Used to communicate with RESTful services. An extension of Ajax Proxy class.
Ext.data.proxy.JsonP	Used for cross-domain communication.
Ext.data.proxy.Direct	The direct communication with the server resource using Ext Direct mechanism.
Ext.data.proxy.Memory	An in-memory proxy where the data is specified inline.
Ext.data.proxy.LocalStorage	Used to communicate with HTML 5 local storage.
Ext.data.proxy.SessionStorage	Used to communicate with HTML 5 session storage.

We've already discussed the usage of Memory Proxy where you provide inline data.
Let's discuss the most commonly used proxy, Ajax Proxy.

Ajax Proxy

Ext.data.proxy.Ajax is used to send AJAX requests to the server. Let's understand the Ajax proxy class by using it in a raw format.

Say you want to load a file that has the following JSON data.

```
{
        "countriesInEurope" : [
                {"name":"Spain","capital":"Madrid"},
                {"name":"France","capital":"Paris"},
                {"name":"UK","capital":"London"},
                {"name":"Denmark","capital":"Copenhagen"}
        ]
}
```

The file has a JSON array called *countriesInEurope*. Let's save this file as *countries.txt*. We'll define a model and use an Ajax proxy to load this file.

The Country model is defined as shown below.

```
Ext.define("Country", {
      extend : "Ext.data.Model",
      fields : ["name","capital"]
});
```

Let's create an Ajax proxy instance as shown in Listing 5-9.

Listing 5-9. Ajax proxy

```
var ajaxProxy = Ext.create("Ext.data.proxy.Ajax", {
                   url: "countries.txt",
                   model: "Country",
```

```
                reader: {
                    type: "json",
                    root: "countriesInEurope"
                }
});
```

In Listing 5.9 countries.txt is configured using the url attribute of the Ajax proxy. We've wired up a Json reader object with the proxy. The root property of the reader object is mapped to the JSON array, 'countriesInEurope.'

You can call the `read()` method on the ajaxProxy object. As discussed earlier, the read method accepts an instance of `Ext.data.Operation` and a callback function as arguments.

Let's create an Operation object and pass it to the Proxy's read method.

```
var readOperation = Ext.create("Ext.data.Operation", {
                    action: "read"
});
ajaxProxy.read(readOperation, function (src) {
                    var records = src.getRecords();
                    for (var i = 0; i < records.length; i++) {
                        console.log(records[i].get("name"));
                    }
});
```

The Operation class instance has an action property that can hold values **"read" or "create" or "update" or "destroy"**.

Invoking the read function on the Ajax proxy object by passing the operation instance, triggers an AJAX request to countries.txt. The callback function is called finally where you display the records.

You can invoke update, create, and destroy methods on the Proxy class similarly to the read method. You have to keep changing the action attribute of the Operation instance accordingly.

Let's create an Operation instance and try to invoke the update method of the Proxy class as shown in Listing 5-10.

Listing 5-10. Update operation

```
var updateOperation = Ext.create("Ext.data.Operation", {
                    action: "update"
});
ajaxProxy.update(updateOperation, function (src) {
                    console.log("****Error****");
                    console.log(src.getError().status);
                    console.log(src.getError().statusText);
});
```

When you run the code in Listing 5.10, you'll see the following displayed in the console.

```
POST http://<server>/countries.txt?_dc=1366974091183 405 (Method not allowed)
****Error****
405
Method not allowed
```

What's happening here is, when you invoke the update function, the proxy tries to send a POST request to countries.txt which is not allowed. You get a HTTP 405 error as a result. You'll get the same error if you try to invoke the create or destroy functions as well.

If you want to use different URLs for different operations, the api config attribute of Ajax proxy class comes to rescue. You can configure the AJAX proxy with the api attribute as shown in Listing 5-11.

Listing 5-11. Using api in Ajax Proxy

```
var ajaxProxy = Ext.create("Ext.data.proxy.Ajax", {
                    api: {
                        create  : '/countries/add',
                        read    : 'countries.txt',
                        update  : '/countries/update',
                        destroy : '/countries/remove'
                    },
                    model: "Country",
                    reader: {
                        type: "json",
                        root: "countriesInEurope"
                    }
});
```

The api attribute specifies the different URLs to be used for different operations. Countries.txt will be used for the read operation alone. For create, update and destroy different URLs have been provided based on your server side implementation.

Another useful attribute of the AJAX proxy class is extraParams property that you can use to pass request parameters to the server.

```
extraParams: {
                    param1 : "value1",
                    param2 : "value2"
            },
```

Ajax proxy class sends out an Ajax request to the configured url with a querystring parameter called **_dc** as shown below.

http://server/countries.txt?_dc=1367069476131

_dc stands for default cache. The _dc parameter is appended to the url with a unique value to disable browser cache. You can enable browser cache by setting the **noCache** attribute to false as shown below.

```
{ noCache : false}
```

You can change the name of the cache parameter by configuring the cacheString attribute as

```
{cacheString : "mycacheparam"}
```

We discussed the raw use of the Ajax Proxy and Operation objects. You may not have to use the proxy in a raw format like these. Let's try to inject the AJAX proxy with a store as shown in Listing 5-12.

Listing 5-12. Store with Ajax Proxy

```
Ext.define("Country", {
            extend : "Ext.data.Model",
            fields : ["name","capital"]
});
 var countryStore = Ext.create("Ext.data.Store",{
                model : "Country",
                proxy: {
                        type: "ajax",
                        api: {
                          create  : '/countries/add',
                          read    : 'countries.txt',
                          update  : '/countries/update',
                          destroy : '/countries/remove'
                        },
                        reader: {
                            type : "json",
                            root : "countriesInEurope"
                        }
                }
});
```

You can call the load function on the countyStore object that triggers the proxy's read() method internally.

```
countryStore.load(); //invokes proxy's read method
```

If you update an existing record in the store and call sync method, proxy's update() method will be triggered internally.

```
countryStore.getAt(3).set("name","Kingdom of Denmark");
countryStore.sync(); //invokes proxy's update method
```

If you add a new record to the store and call sync method, proxy's create() method will be triggered internally.

```
countryStore.add({name:"Portugal",capital:"Lisbon"});
countryStore.sync(); //invokes proxy's create method
```

If you remove a record from the store and call sync method, proxy's **destroy()** method will be triggered internally.

```
countryStore.removeAt(0);
countryStore.sync(); //invokes proxy's destroy method
```

As you've configured separate URLs for each of four methods using the api attribute, the corresponding URLs will be invoked automatically.

Ajax Proxy class has a number of param attributes that can be used to configure the default parameters that will be sent along with the request in query string. All these attributes are used in the server side for fetching or sorting or grouping or filtering records. Table 5-6 shows the name of the config attribute and the corresponding URL with query string.

Table 5-6. *Param Attributes in Ajax Proxy Class*

Attribute	URL	Description
filterParam	?filter=	The filters are passed using this parameter. Used when you load a store with a filter.
sortParam	?sort=	The sorters are passed using this parameter.
startParam	?start=	This parameter specifies the starting index of the set of records you want to load.
limitParam	?limit=	This parameter specifies the number of records you want to load. The default value is 25.
pageParam	?page=	The index of the page that starts with 0.
idParam	?id=	The id of the entity that you want to pass to the server.

REST proxy

Ext.data.proxy.Rest an extension of Ajax Proxy is the class that's used to communicate with the RESTful web services. The Rest proxy is a specialization of the Ajax proxy and it maps the four actions(create, read, update, and destroy) to RESTful HTTP verbs. Let's take a close look at Rest proxy.

Say you've a RESTful book store service with functions to *add a book, get the list of all books, remove a book,* and *update a book.* Let the endpoint of this book store be '**library**.'

You've Book Model and a Store classes configured with a Rest proxy as shown in Listing 5-13.

Listing 5-13. Model with Rest Proxy

```
Ext.define("Book", {
          extend : "Ext.data.Model",
          fields : ["id","title","author"],
          proxy:{
                    type : "rest",
                    url : "library"
          }
});
var bookStore = Ext.create("Ext.data.Store",{
                    model : "Book",
});
```

Book model has id, title and author fields. It's linked with the Rest proxy pointing to the RESTful service 'library.' Table 5-7 shows the URL that'll be invoked for different operations on the model and store.

Table 5-7. *Restful Operations*

Operation	URL	Request Payload	HTTP verb
bookstore.load()	/library	--	GET

var book1 = Ext.create("Book",{id:101,title: "Pro Hadoop",author:"Jason Venner"});
 	
 book1.save();
	/library/101	{"id":101,"title":"Pro Hadoop", "author":"Jason Venner"}	POST

book1.destroy();	/library/101	{"id":101,"title":"Pro Hadoop", "author":"Jason Venner"}	DELETE

book1.set("title", "Pro Hadoop v2");
 	
 book1.save();
	/library/101	{"id":101,"title":"Pro Hadoop v2", "author":"Jason Venner"}	PUT

The operations on the Rest Proxy map to a standard URL pattern as shown in Table 5-7. Let's say you have a RESTful service with different endpoints and the URL is different for each operation as shown in Table 5-8.

Table 5-8. *RESTful URLs*

Operation	URL	HTTP verb
bookstore.load()	/library/list	GET

var book1 = Ext.create("Book",{id:101,title:"Pro Hadoop", author:"Jason Venner"});
 	
 book1.save();
	/library/add/101	POST

book1.destroy();	/library/remove/101	DELETE

book1.set("title", "Pro Hadoop v2");
 	
 book1.save();
	/library/update/101	PUT

You can configure the api property of the Rest proxy as we discussed earlier. You can also customize the Rest proxy by extending the Rest class and overriding the `buildUrl()` method. The buildUrl() method returns the URL that will be invoked for any operation. Let's define a class say, BookProxy that extends Rest Proxy and override the buildUrl method. The Book class that uses the bookproxy is shown below.

```
Ext.define("Book", {
        extend : "Ext.data.Model",
        fields : ["id","title","author"],
        proxy:{
            type : "bookproxy",
            url : "library",
        }
}
```

Listing 5-14 shows the code snippet to define the book proxy class.

Listing 5-14. BookProxy Class

```
Ext.define("BookProxy",{
    extend : "Ext.data.proxy.Rest",
    alias : "proxy.bookproxy",
    buildUrl : function(req){
     var originalUrl = this.callParent(arguments);
     if(req.action == "read"){
      var urlParts = originalUrl.split("?");
      targetUrl = urlParts[0] + "/list?" + urlParts[1];
     }
     if(req.action == "create"){
      var urlParts = originalUrl.split("/");
      targetUrl = urlParts[0] + "/add/" + urlParts[1];
     }
     else if(req.action == "update"){
      var urlParts = originalUrl.split("/");
      targetUrl = urlParts[0] + "/update/" + urlParts[1];
     }
     else if(req.action == "destroy"){
      var urlParts = originalUrl.split("/");
      targetUrl = urlParts[0] + "/remove/" + urlParts[1];
     }

     return targetUrl;
    }
});
```

The BookProxy class has an `alias` attribute configured to be `proxy.bookproxy`. This alias name configuration paves way for using the class with the *type* as bookproxy.

The `buildUrl()` method accepts `Ext.data.Request` object as parameter. We check for the type of operation and generate a new URL.

For example if a new book instance with id 101 is created and `save()` method is called on it, the control goes to the `if(req.action == "create")`. The original URL will be library/101. Inside the if-block we construct the new URL library/add/101/. The splitting and concatenation code `var urlParts = originalUrl.split("/");targetUrl = urlParts[0] + "/add/" + urlParts[1];` generates the required URL.

Ext.data.Writer

Ext.data.writer.Writer is the class used by the proxy classes for formatting the request payload that's sent to the server. There are two types of Writer classes available.

- **Ext.data.writer.Json**

  - Used to format the data in JSON. This is the default writer class used by the proxy.

- **Ext.data.writer.Xml**

  - Used to format the data in XML.

Let's define the Book model with a Rest proxy and a Json writer and study the request payload as shown in Listing 5-16.

Listing 5-16. Model Class with a Writer

```
Ext.define("Book", {
        extend: "Ext.data.Model",
        fields: ["id", "title", "author"],
        proxy: {
            type: "rest",
            url: "library",
            writer: {
                type : "json",
                root : "book"
            }
        }
});
```

In the code snippet in Listing 5-16 we've used a Json Writer with a root property. Let's create a Book instance and call save method as shown below.

```
var book1 = Ext.create("Book", { id: 101, title: "Pro Hadoop", author: "Jason Venner" });
```

book1.save();Here's how the request payload will look for the above operation.

{"book":{"id":101,"title":"Pro Hadoop","author":"Jason Venner"}}

You can configure the XML writer for the Book like

```
writer: {
        type : "xml",
        documentRoot : "books",
        record : "book
}
```

The Writer is configured with a documentRoot property that specifies the root element. The record property configures every Model instance as a <book> element. Calling the save() method on the Book instance will generate a payload as shown below.

```
<books><book><id>101</id><title>Pro Hadoop</title>272103_1_EnJason Venner</author></book></books>
```

JsonP Proxy

Ext.data.proxy.JsonP class is used to send cross domain Ajax requests. If you want to send requests to a domain that's different from the source domain that sends the request, you'll use JsonP proxy class.

Let's say you're trying to send a request from **http://extjs4book/example1.html** to **http://yourapp/books** that happens to be your endpoint that'll output the list of books. Since the domains are different you have to send a JsonP request to the endpoint. Sending a JsonP request involves padding up the JSON response. Your endpoint will send a JSON response padded up using what we call a callback function. Say, your endpoint is supposed to return the following JSON output.

```
{
 "books" : [
   {"name":"Zend Framework"},
   {"name":"Beginning F#"},
   {"name":"Pro Hadoop"}
    ]

}
```

If the request comes from a different domain the endpoint will have to pad it up with a callback function which is `Ext.data.JsonP.callback1` in the case of Ext JS 4. The endpoint's output should throw the following output.

```
Ext.data.JsonP.callback1({
 "books" : [
   {"name":"Zend Framework"},
   {"name":"Beginning F#"},
   {"name":"Pro Hadoop"}
    ]

})
```

Let's create a bookstore with the following code that'll send out a JSONP request to **http://yourapp/books.**

```
var bookStore = Ext.create("Ext.data.Store", {
            fields: ["name"],
            autoLoad: true,
            proxy: {
                type: "jsonp",
                url: "http://yourapp/books",
                reader: {
                    type: "json",
                    root: "books"
                }
            }
});
```

When you run this code, the bookstore will automatically inject a script tag as shown below.

```
<script src="http://yourapp/books?_dc=1367069254328&page=1&start=0&limit=25&callback=Ext.data.JsonP.callback1">
</script>
```

LocalStorage and SessionStorage

One of the prominent features of HTML 5 is client-side data storage. Every application can save data in the browser's memory. There are multiple places where a data can be stored in HTML 5 like Local Storage, Session Storage, Web SQL, and IndexedDB. Each storage space has specific set of characteristics. Unlike cookies, whatever data you store in these holders will not be taken to the server automatically. They will remain in the client-side only. Many applications make use of these storage spaces to store information that otherwise will have to be fetched every time from the data source.

You can use vanilla HTML 5 API to work with these concepts. Ext JS 4 provides its' own abstraction over the HTML 5 API for working with Local Storage and Session Storage. It provides two proxy classes **Ext.data.proxy. LocalStorage and Ext.data.proxy.SessionStorage**. Let's discuss these two proxy classes in detail.

Local Storage and Session Storage let you store data in browser's memory. The data that you store in local storage will be available until you clear the browser cache explicitly. The data that you store in session storage will be lost once the browser window is closed. Ext JS 4's API makes working with local storage and session storage a breeze. The data that you want to store in these holders will be serialized and deserialized automatically. You can create a complex object and save it in local/session storage, retrieve it and operate on it effortlessly using the SessionStorage and LocalStorage proxy classes.

Let's define a model class, configure a data storage proxy and play with it. To begin with, let's define a Country model with name and capital fields. This model class will have a localstorage proxy as shown in Listing 5-17.

Listing 5-17. Local Storage Proxy

```
Ext.define("Country", {
        extend: "Ext.data.Model",
        fields: ["name", "capital"],
        proxy: {
            type : "localstorage",
            id : "name"
        }
});
```

Country model has been defined with a localstorage proxy. This proxy needs to be configured with an id property. This id property will be used to differentiate the model instances. Let's create a couple of Country instances and save them.

```
var india = Ext.create("Country", { name: "India", capital: "New Delhi" });
var us = Ext.create("Country", { name: "US", capital: "Washington" });
india.save();
us.save();
```

If you run this code in chrome, you can go to the resources section in JavaScript console. The snapshot of the local storage section is shown in Figure 5-1.

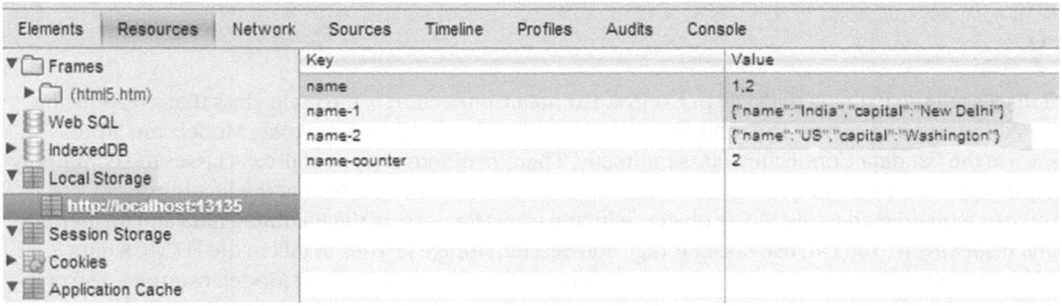

Figure 5-1.

91

The country instances have been serialized into JSON formatted string and stored in local storage. The LocalStorage proxy has created two more values to keep track of the number of instances present.

If you create a store and call load, these two instances will automatically be loaded from local storage.

```
var countryStore = Ext.create("Ext.data.Store",{
                model: "Country",
                autoLoad: true
});
```

If you want to add more country instances to the countryStore and synchronize it with the localstorage, here's what you do.

```
countryStore.add({name:"France",capital:"Paris"});
countryStore.add({name:"Spain",capital:"Madrid"});
countryStore.sync();
```

The sync() method synchronizes the store with the local storage. The local storage will now have four country objects: India, US, France, and Spain.

You can also use Country.load(...) by specifying the name of the country and load that instance from local storage.

In a nutshell, you use the sync() method on the store to update the data in the local storage. If you want to load data from the local storage, you can call the load() method. If you want to add data to the local storage, you can create a model instance and call save() method on it or add the model instance to the store and call sync() method on the store.

If you want to work with Session storage, the only change required in the above example is the proxy will now be sessionstorage instead of localstorage as shown below.

```
Ext.define("Country", {
            extend: "Ext.data.Model",
            fields: ["name", "capital"],
            proxy: {
                type : "sessionstorage",
                id : "name"
            }
});
```

Summary

In this chapter I discussed the Ext.data package in Ext JS 4. Ext.data.Connection is the main class that's responsible for Ajax communication with the server. The three main classes in Ext.data package are Proxy, Model, and Store. The Proxy classes use the Ext.data.Connection class indirectly. There're different types of proxy classes the commonly used being the Ajax proxy and Rest proxy. The Reader and Writer classes are used to format the incoming and outgoing data.You can wire up reader and writer objects with the proxy for parsing the incoming data and formatting the outgoing data, respectively. You can use LocalStorage and SessionStorage proxies to talk to the HTML 5 data storage. A Model class represents a record with columns or fields. A Store is a collection of Model instances. You can perform sorting, filtering, and searching operations on a Store.

In the next chapter you'll learn the data controls that work closely with the Ext.data package. I'll discuss the data controls like data grids, trees, comboboxes, and charts.

CHAPTER 6

■ ■ ■

Data Controls

Data binding is a facility provided by a number of UI frameworks. The data source is bound to the UI controls, which display the data in a predefined format. Ext JS 4 provides a rich set of controls that display the data fetched from different sources. The data source is wired to the UI controls that automatically process the data and display it in appropriate format. These controls update themselves whenever the data changes. The controls that are bound to the data sources usually include data grids, trees, and so on.

In this chapter you'll learn about various data controls provided by Ext JS 4. The list of data controls that Ext JS 4 provides is given below.

- ComboBox
- Grid
- Tree
- Chart

In Chapter 5 I discussed using the Store classes that the Ext.data package provides. These stores serve as input to the data controls. They can be wired up to the data controls so that these controls will automatically display the data in the store. In other words, if you have to work with data controls in Ext JS 4, you need to create stores and wire them up with the data controls. Figure 6-1 shows the data controls wired to the store.

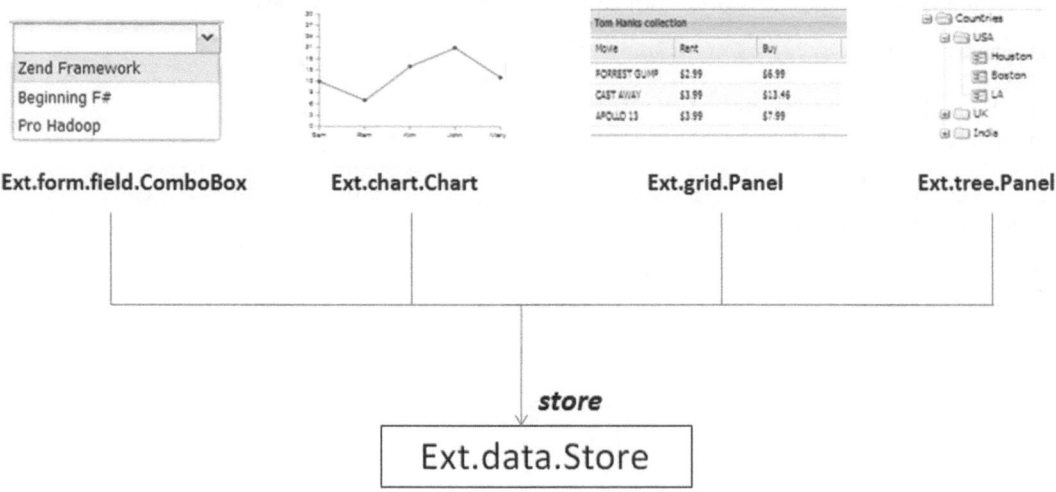

***Figure 6-1.** Data controls wired to the Store*

As shown in Figure 6-1 the combobox, grid, tree, and chart classes are associated with the Store class using the store attribute.

The data controls process the records in the Store instance and display the values in the required format. The controls have a standard HTML formatted template that is applied to the data. This template that generates the HTML output is specified as an object of the Ext.XTemplate class. Before we delve into the details of the data controls let's take a look at the XTemplate class.

Ext.XTemplate

Ext.XTemplate is the class that's used to define a HTML template that can be applied to data. You can define a HTML UI template that will result in HTML output when applied to the underlying data store. In other words XTemplate is a mechanism by which you can introduce raw HTML code in an Ext JS 4 application.

The syntax of creating an XTemplate instance may remind you of the XPath expressions that we use while creating XSL stylesheets. The XTemplate syntax provides options for iterating the data using *for-loops*, write if-else conditions, and so on.

Let's create a Store instance as shown below and create an XTemplate object to display the data in the Store.

```
var countryStore = Ext.create('Ext.data.Store', {
        fields: ["name","capital"],
        data: [
            { name: 'India', capital: "New Delhi" },
            { name: "USA", capital: "Washington" },
            { name: "UK", capital: "London" }
        ]
  });
```

Let's create an XTemplate instance as shown below.

```
var tpl = Ext.create("Ext.XTemplate",
            '<tpl for=".">',
                '<p>{data.name}, <i>{data.capital}</i></p><br/>',
            '</tpl>');
```

We've created a for loop in the XTemplate and display the name and capital in a paragraph element.

Let's apply the template to the countryStore and display the result in a Panel as shown below.

```
Ext.create("Ext.panel.Panel",{
            title : "Countries",
            html : tpl.apply(countryStore),
            renderTo : Ext.getBody()
});
```

Figure 6-2 shows the output of the code.

Figure 6-2. *XTemplate applied to the store*

Say you want to emphasize the country "the United States of America" by applying a different style. You can modify the XTemplate by introducing an if-else condition as shown below.

```
var tpl = Ext.create("Ext.XTemplate",
        '<tpl for=".">',
        '<tpl if="data.name == \'USA\'">',
          '<p style="text-decoration:underline">{data.name},  <i>{data.capital}</i></p><br/>',
        '<tpl else>',
          '<p>{data.name}, <i>{data.capital}</i></p><br/>',
      '</tpl>',
  '</tpl>');
```

Figure 6-3 shows the output of the code.

Figure 6-3. *XTemplate with if-else condition applied to the Store*

As you can see XTemplate is mainly used in rendering custom HTML output. You'll learn more about the use of XTemplate when I discuss creating custom components in Chapter 10.

Let's discuss the data controls in detail by delving into the ComboBox control.

ComboBox

The ComboBox component represents a dropdownlist. It's present in the Ext.form.field package. The xtype of the ComboBox component is *combobox* or *combo*.

Let's create an inline data store as shown below. You'll display the data in this store in a combobox.

```
var bookStore = Ext.create("Ext.data.Store", {
    fields: ["isbn","title", "author"],
    data: [
      { isbn: "1430219424", title: "Zend Framework", author: "Zend" },
      { isbn: "1430223898", title: "Beginning F#", author: "Robert Pickering" },
      { isbn: "1430219424", title: "Pro Hadoop", author: "Jason Venner" }
    ]
});
```

The store contains a list of books with ISBN, title, and author fields. Let's display the title of the books in the combobox.

```
Ext.create("Ext.form.field.ComboBox", {
    fieldLabel : "Book",
    store : bookStore,
    displayField : "title",
    valueField : "isbn"
});
```

The code above has the bookStore wired up to the store property. The displayField and valueField properties specify the value that is displayed in the combobox and the underlying value of the displayed item, respectively. You will get the combobox as shown in Figure 6-4. You can notice that the combobox is rendered with a textbox and a picker icon. Clicking on the picker icon will render the values as a dropdown list.

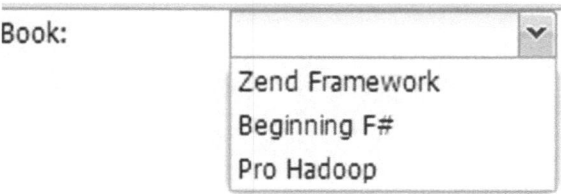

Figure 6-4. *Combobox that displays the title of the books*

You can create a combobox using the xtype like this.

```
{
        xtype   : "combo",
        store : bookStore,
        //...
}
```

The ComboBox class has a number of config attributes. Let's discuss some important attributes here.

editable

In the combobox that you just created, you can type in any text you want, as shown in Figure 6-5.

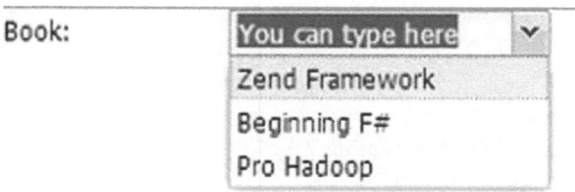

Figure 6-5. *Combobox with editable property set to true*

You can disable this by setting the editable property to false as shown below.

```
{
        xtype : "combobox",
        store : bookStore,
        editable : false,
        // ...
}
```

typeAhead, typeAheadDelay

These two properties provide the autocomplete feature for the combobox. When you set typeAhead property to true and key-in some text in the combobox, the combobox automatically searches the items and displays the remaining text. The typeAheadDelay specifies the delay in milliseconds in displaying the text. You can use these two properties as shown below. The default time delay is 250 milliseconds.

```
{
        xtype : "combobox",
        store : bookStore,
        typeAhead : true,
        typeAheadDelay : 100
        // ...
}
```

multiSelect, delimiter

The multiselect attribute enables you select multiple items in the combobox. The items are delimited by comma. You can change the delimiter using the delimiter attribute.

```
{
        xtype : "combobox",
        multiSelect : true,
        delimiter : ";"
        //...
}
```

In the code snippet above, we've given the delimiter as semicolon. You'll get the output shown in Figure 6-6.

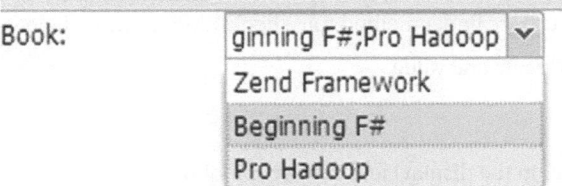

Figure 6-6. *Multiselect combobox with semicolon as delimiter*

queryMode, queryDelay, queryCaching

Say the combobox is configured with a store that loads data from the server. Whenever the user interacts with the combobox the combobox tries to send a request to the remote server and load the data. You can change this configuration by using the queryMode attribute. The queryMode attribute is configured as *remote* by default. You can change this to *'local'* in which case the data from the store is loaded without going to the remote server.

The queryDelay attribute specifies the delay time in milliseconds before querying for the data. The value is 500 milliseconds by default for remote mode and 10 milliseconds for the local mode.

You can cache the query that's used to load the records using queryCaching attribute, which is true by default. These attributes can be used as shown below.

```
{
        xtype : "combobox",
        Store : bookStore,
        queryMode :  "local",
        queryDelay : 5,
        queryCaching : false
}
```

Let's discuss some methods in the ComboBox class.

bindStore

The bindStore() method in combobox is used to dynamically configure a store. If you have a combobox object booksCMB and want to bind the bookStore to it, here's how you do that.

```
booksCMB.bindStore(bookStore);
```

collapse, expand

You can programmatically collapse and expand the picker in the combobox by calling the collapse() and expand() methods on it. You can call these methods on a combobox component booksCMB like this.

```
booksCMB.expand();
booksCMB.collapse();
```

findRecord, findRecordByDisplay, findRecordByValue

You know that Ext.data.Store class provides finder methods to access the records. Similarly, the ComboBox class provides finder methods to access the underlying Model instance. You can use the finder methods on a booksCMB as shown below.

- findRecord: Used to find the record based on the fieldname and value

    ```
    booksCMB.findRecord("title","Pro Hadoop")
    ```

- findRecordByDisplay: Used to find the record based on the displayField of the combobox

    ```
    booksCMB.findRecordByDisplay("Pro Hadoop")
    ```

- findRecordByValue: Used to find the record based on the valueField of the combobox

    ```
    booksCMB.findRecordByValue("1430219424")
    ```

ComboBox class provides a lot of events that can be useful in various scenarios. Let's take a look at some events here.

select

The select event is fired when you select an item in the combobox. You can handle the select event as shown below.

```
booksCMB.on("select",function(src,records){
  //YOUR LOGIC
});
```

change

The change event is fired when the value of the combobox field is changed either by selecting an item with a new value or by calling setValue() method. You can handle the change event as shown below.

```
booksCMB.on("change",function(src,newValue,oldValue){
  //YOUR LOGIC
});
```

Let's discuss the data grids provided by Ext JS 4 in detail.

Grid

Grid is one of the most commonly used controls in web applications. A grid is an effective way of showing large amounts of tabular data. Ext.grid.Panel class represents a grid component that's nothing but a supercharged, formatted table. The Grid panel is composed of columns and the data is supplied by a Store instance.

Let's create a movie store with three fields that you'll display in a grid as shown below.

```
var movieStore = Ext.create("Ext.data.Store", {
    fields: ["title", "rent", "buy"],
    data: [
        {title: "Forrest Gump", rent: 2.99,buy:6.99},
        {title: "Cast Away", rent: 3.99,buy:13.46},
        {title: "Apollo 13", rent: 3.99,buy:7.99}
    ]
});
```

Here's a simple grid that displays the items in the store.

```
Ext.create("Ext.grid.Panel", {
            store: movieStore,
            title : "Tom Hanks collection",
            width : 350,
            columns: [
                    {
                        text: 'Movie',
                         dataIndex: 'title',
                    },
```

```
                    {
                        text: 'Rent',
                        dataIndex: 'rent',
                    },
                    {
                        text: 'Buy',
                        dataIndex: 'buy',
                    }
                ]
        });
```

You'll get a grid as shown in Figure 6-7.

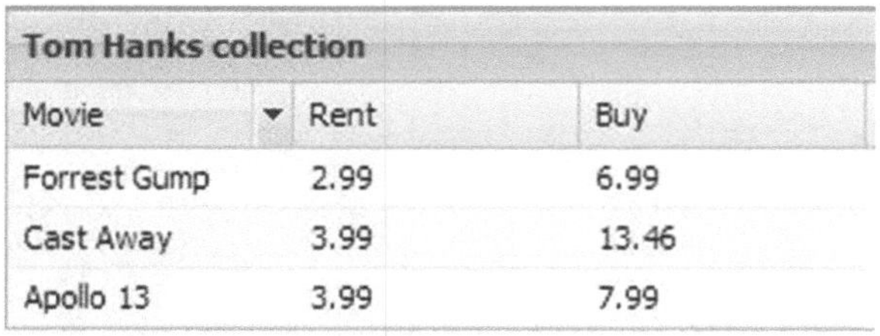

Tom Hanks collection		
Movie ▼	Rent	Buy
Forrest Gump	2.99	6.99
Cast Away	3.99	13.46
Apollo 13	3.99	7.99

Figure 6-7. *A simple Grid panel*

The two fundamental properties of a grid panel are the store and columns. You can dynamically set the store and columns using the reconfigure() method provided in the grid panel class. If you have a grid component, moviesGrid then you can call reconfigure() method as shown below.

```
moviesGrid.reconfigure(store,columns)
```

Calling the reconfigure() method fires a reconfigure event that can be handled as shown here.

```
moviesGrid.on("reconfigure",function(src,newStore,newColumns,oldStore){
    ...
});
```

The grid panel is composed of columns. Let's discuss the grid columns in detail.

Grid Columns

As you would have noticed in the grid example, the fundamental building block of the grid panel is columns, which is configured using the columns attribute. Each column is an instance of Ext.grid.column.Column class.

The Column class has a set of configuration attributes that's used to configure the columns. Table 6-1 shows some commonly used attributes of the Column class.

Table 6-1. *Attributes of the Ext.grid.column.Column class*

Attribute	Description
Text	The text to appear as a header
dataIndex	The field name whose value will be displayed in the column
Renderer	A function or a string that's used to customize the display
Sortable	A boolean attribute used to enable or disable sorting against a column
Resizable	A boolean attribute used to enable or disable resizing of columns
Editor	This object is used to configure the display of a column when it's in an editable mode
enableColumnHide	A boolean attribute used to enable or disable show/hide option of a column

We'll discuss the editor attribute in the plugins section. Here's the code snippet for the grid that uses these attributes.

```
Ext.create("Ext.grid.Panel", {
            store: movieStore,
            title: "Tom Hanks collection",
            width: 350,
            columns: [
                    {
                        text: 'Movie',
                        dataIndex: 'title',
                        resizable: false,
                        enableColumnHide: false,
                        renderer: Ext.util.Format.uppercase
                    },
                    {
                        text: 'Rent',
                        dataIndex: 'rent',
                        sortable: false,
                        renderer: Ext.util.Format.usMoney
                    },
                    {
                        text: 'Buy',
                        dataIndex: 'buy',
                        renderer: function (value) {
                          return "$" + value;
                        }
                    }
                ]
            });
```

The renderer() function for the title of the movie returns a built-in renderer called uppercase in Ext.util.Format class. The rent column is also formatted using a built-in renderer called usMoney. The buy column is formatted using a custom renderer function. You'll get the output as shown in Figure 6-8.

Tom Hanks collection		
Movie ▾	Rent	Buy
FORREST GUMP	$2.99	$6.99
CAST AWAY	$3.99	$13.46
APOLLO 13	$3.99	$7.99

Figure 6-8. *Grid panel with column attributes*

In the grid that you have created you can notice that the movie column cannot be resized and you cannot sort the grid by the rent column.

The Ext.grid.column.Column class serves as the base class for the number of other types of column. Table 6-2 shows the list of column classes.

Table 6-2. *Column Classes*

Class	xtype	Description
Ext.grid.column.Action	actioncolumn	Represents a column that renders a collection of icons each with a click handler. Usually used to perform operations like add, edit, delete, etc.
Ext.grid.column.Date	datecolumn	Used to render a date formatted column
Ext.grid.column.Number	numbercolumn	Used to render a number formatted column
Ext.grid.column.CheckColumn	checkcolumn	Represents a checkbox column
Ext.grid.column.Boolean	booleancolumn	Used to display a boolean value formatted column
Ext.grid.column.TemplateColumn	templatecolumn	Used to specify an XTemplate instance to format the data
Ext.grid.RowNumberer	rownumberer	Render row numbers

Here's an example of a grid that uses these columns. We need to modify our movie store with few more fields as shown below.

```
var movieStore = Ext.create("Ext.data.Store", {
        fields: [
               "title",
               "rent",
               "buy",
               {name:"dvdReleaseDate",type:"date",format:"MM/dd/YYYY"},
               "bluerayFormat",
                "wikipedia"
           ],
        data: [
             { title: "Forrest Gump", rent: 2.99, buy:6.99, dvdReleaseDate:"08/01/2001",
bluerayFormat:true, wikipedia:"http://en.wikipedia.org/wiki/Forrest_Gump"},
             { title: "Cast Away", rent: 3.99, buy:13.46, dvdReleaseDate:"02/15/2004",
bluerayFormat:false, wikipedia:"http://en.wikipedia.org/wiki/Cast_Away"},
```

```
            { title: "Apollo 13", rent: 3.99, buy:7.99, dvdReleaseDate:"12/23/2002",
bluerayFormat:true, wikipedia:"http://en.wikipedia.org/wiki/Apollo_13_(film)"}
            ]
        });
```

The movie store has few more fields now in addition to title, rent, and buy fields. The Grid panel that displays these items is shown below.

```
Ext.create("Ext.grid.Panel", {
            store: movieStore,
            height : 150,
            title : "Tom Hanks collection",
            columns: [
              {xtype : "rownumberer"},
              {
                 text: 'Movie',
                 dataIndex: 'title',
              },
              {
                 text: 'Rent',
                 dataIndex: 'rent',
                 xtype : "numbercolumn",
                 format : "0.00"
              },
              {
                 text: 'Buy',
                 dataIndex: 'buy',
                 xtype : "numbercolumn",
                 format : "0.00"
              },
              {
                 text : "Blue-ray",
                 dataIndex : "bluerayFormat",
                 xtype : 'booleancolumn',
                 trueText : "Available",
                 falseText : "Not available"
              },
              {
                 text: 'DVD release date',
                 dataIndex: 'dvdReleaseDate',
                 xtype : "datecolumn",
                 format : "M d, Y"
              },
              {
                 text : "Wiki",
                 xtype : "templatecolumn",
                 tpl : "<a href='{wikipedia}' target='_blank'>Read</a>"
              },
```

```
        {
            text: 'Add',
            xtype : "actioncolumn",
            items : [
                    {
                      tooltip:"Edit",
                      icon : "edit.jpg",
                      handler : function(grid,rowNum,colNum){
                        //Edit logic
                      }
                    },
                    {
                      tooltip:"Delete",
                      icon : "delete.jpg",
                      handler : function(grid,rowNum,colNum){
                          //Delete logic
                      }
                    }
            },
        ]
    });
```

You'll get the output as shown in Figure 6-9.

Tom Hanks collection

	Movie	Rent	Buy	Blue-ray	DVD release date	Wiki	
1	Forrest Gump	2.99	6.99	Available	Aug 01, 2001	Read	Edit Del
2	Cast Away	3.99	13.46	Not available	Feb 15, 2004	Read	Edit Del
3	Apollo 13	3.99	7.99	Available	Dec 23, 2002	Read	Edit Del

Figure 6-9. *Grid Panel with different column types*

The grid has the wikipedia field displayed as a hyperlink using TemplateColumn. The Blue-ray column is a boolean column and the dvd release date is formatted using the date column. The last column of the grid is an action column with two icons edit and delete added to it. The respective handlers will be called when you click on these icons.

You can incorporate more behavior into the the grid panel using plugins. Let's discuss the Grid plugins in detail.

Grid Plugins

Ext JS 4 provides a plugin concept that's used to attach additional functionalities to the UI components. The base class for any plugin is Ext.AbstractPlugin. The grid panel has behaviors like editing, grouping, drag and drop, etc., provided in the form of plugins. Table 6-3 shows the list of all plugins for a grid.

Table 6-3. List of Grid Plugins

Class	Description
Ext.grid.plugin.Editing	Used for editing the row and cells of the grid
Ext.grid.plugin.RowExpander	Used for creating expandable rows
Ext.grid.plugin.BufferedRenderer	Used to render large number of records in a grid
Ext.grid.plugin.DragDrop	Implements the drag and drop functionality in a grid
Ext.grid.feature.Feature	This plugin acts as a base class for a number of features like grouping, summary, etc.

These plugins can be added to the grid using the plugins array attribute. Each plugin has an alias name known as ptype similar to xtype. You can configure the plugin using its ptype or by using Ext.create() method. For example, if you want to add a RowExpander plugin to the grid, here's how you do that.

```
plugins : [
        Ext.create("Ext.grid.plugin.RowExpander",{})
]
```

You can use the ptype as shown below.

```
plugins : [
                {
                    ptype : "rowexpander"
                }
]
```

Ext.grid.plugin.Editing

This plugin provides the grid editing behavior. This plugin class has two subclasses, Ext.grid.plugin.CellEditing and Ext.grid.plugin.RowEditing, to either edit the cell or the row. The working of this plugin depends on a configuration attribute of the grid class called selType. The selType attribute denotes the selection model. You can select a cell or a row in a grid. The value of selType can either be cellModel or rowModel.

CellEditing

You can edit the cell of the grid using this plugin. The ptype or the alias name of this plugin class is cellediting. This plugin when added to the grid with the selType as cellModel, converts the cell to editable format when the cell is double-clicked.

The editable format is defined by the editor attribute of the column. The editor attribute is configured to be an UI control that has to be rendered when the cell is double-clicked.

Here's an example of the grid that has the cellediting plugin configured.

```
Ext.create("Ext.grid.Panel", {
            store: movieStore,
            height : 150,
            title : "Tom Hanks collection",
            selType : "cellmodel",
```

```
            plugins : [
                    {
                        ptype : "cellediting",
                        clicksToEdit : 2
                    }
            ],
            columns: [
                    {
                        text: 'Movie',
                        dataIndex: 'title',
                    },
                    {
                        text: 'Rent',
                        dataIndex: 'rent',
                    },
                    {
                        text: 'Buy',
                        dataIndex: 'buy',
                        editor : {
                            xtype : "numberfield",
                            step : 0.01
                        }
                    },
                    {
                        text: 'Blue-ray',
                        dataIndex: 'bluerayFormat',
                        xtype : 'booleancolumn',
                        trueText : "Available",
                        falseText : "Not available",
                        editor : {
                            xtype : "checkboxfield",
                        }
                    },
                    {
                        text: 'DVD release date',
                        dataIndex: 'dvdReleaseDate',
                        xtype : "datecolumn",
                        format : "M d, Y"
                    }
            ]
        });
```

The buy column is rendered as a numberfield in the editable format. The Blue-ray column is rendered as a checkboxfield in the editable format. Figure 6-10 shows the grid when you double click one of the buy cells.

Tom Hanks collection				
Movie	Rent	Buy	Blue-ray	DVD release date
Forrest Gump	2.99	6.99	Available	Aug 01, 2001
Cast Away	3.99	13.46	Not available	Feb 15, 2004
Apollo 13	3.99	7.99	Available	Dec 23, 2002

Figure 6-10. *CellEditing plugin with numberfield editor*

Figure 6-11 shows the grid when you double-click one of the Blue-ray cells.

Tom Hanks collection				
Movie	Rent	Buy	Blue-ray	DVD release date
Forrest Gump	2.99	6.99	☑	Aug 01, 2001
Cast Away	3.99	13.46	Not available	Feb 15, 2004
Apollo 13	3.99	7.99	Available	Dec 23, 2002

Figure 6-11. *CellEditing plugin with checkboxfield editor*

RowEditing

You can edit the row of the grid using this plugin. The ptype or the alias name of this plugin class is rowediting. This plugin, when added to the grid with the selType as rowModel, converts the row to the editable format when the row is double-clicked. It pops up update and cancel buttons that have to be clicked, indicating the completion of the editing.

The editable format is defined by the editor attribute of the column. The editor attribute is configured to be an UI control that has to be rendered when the row is double-clicked.

The code snippet that you wrote for the grid with the cellediting plugin has to be changed as shown below.

```
Ext.create("Ext.grid.Panel", {
            store: movieStore,
            height : 150,
            title : "Tom Hanks collection",
            selType : "rowmodel",
            plugins : [
              {
                 ptype : "rowediting",
                 clicksToEdit : 2
              }
            ],
            columns: [ ... ]
});
```

Figure 6-12 shows the grid when you double-click one of the rows.

Tom Hanks collection				
Movie	Rent	Buy	Blue-ray	DVD release date
Forrest Gump	2.99	6.99	Available	Aug 01, 2001
Cast Away	3.99	13.47 ⬍	☐	Feb 15, 2004
Apollo 13	3.99	Update Cancel		Dec 23, 2002

Figure 6-12. *RowEditing plugin*

The rowediting and cellediting plugins provide four events beforeedit, edit, canceledit, and validateedit. The validateedit event is called before updating the underlying record in the store.

These events can be registered with the grid to keep track of the editing. The event handlers for these events accept three parameters, the source plugin object, an object that holds the record and grid details, and the object that holds the optional data that's passed while registering the event.

Say you want to register the events while editing the buy column either using rowediting or cellediting plugin, you can use the following listeners block to keep track of what's going on.

```
listeners : {
            beforeedit : function(src,e){
              var record = e.record;
              console.log("beforeedit: " + record.get("buy"));
            },
            edit : function(src,e){
              var record = e.record;
              console.log("edit: " + record.get("buy"));
            },
            canceledit : function(src,e){
                var record = e.record;
                console.log("canceledit: " + record.get("buy"));
            },
            validateedit : function(src,e){
                var record = e.record;
                console.log("validateedit: " + record.get("buy"));
            }
}
```

Ext.grid.plugin.RowExpander

This plugin class provides the row in the grid to have contents that can be collapsed and expanded. It uses the RowBody feature we'll learn later in this chapter. You've to configure the rowBodyTpl attribute, with the template that'll be applied to the records.

Here's the grid that uses the RowExpander plugin. Let's modify the movie store with a field called description. The description of the movie will be shown while you expand the row.

```
var movieStore = Ext.create("Ext.data.Store", {
            fields: ["title", "rent", "buy","description"],
            data: [
                    { title: "Forrest Gump", rent: 2.99, buy:6.99, description:"Tom Hanks gives an
astonishing performance as Forrest, an everyman whose simple innocence comes to embody a generation."},
                    { title: "Cast Away", rent: 3.99, buy:13.46, description:"Academy Award-winning
filmmaker Robert Zemeckis and two-time Oscar winner Tom Hanks reunite to explore the blessings and
heartache of fate and the survival of the human spirit. Tom Hanks gives one of the towering screen
performances of all time as Chuck Noland, a FedEx systems engineer whose ruled-by-the-clock existence
abruptly ..."},
                    { title: "Apollo 13", rent: 3.99, buy:7.99, description:"A 'routine' space flight
becomes a desperate battle to survive in this breathtaking adventure of courage and faith starring Tom
Hanks, Kevin Bacon, Bill Paxton, Gary Sinise and Ed Harris."}
            ]
        });

Ext.create("Ext.grid.Panel", {
                store: movieStore,
                height : 300,
                title : "Tom Hanks collection",
                plugins: [
                    {
                      ptype: 'rowexpander',
                      rowBodyTpl : [
                        '<p>{description}</p>'
                      ]
                    }
                ],
                columns: [
                        {
                          text: 'Movie',
                          dataIndex: 'title',
                        },
                        {
                          text: 'Rent',
                          dataIndex: 'rent',
                        },
                        {
                          text: 'Buy',
                          dataIndex: 'buy',
                        }
                    ]
            });
```

The RowExpander plugin is configured using its ptype, rowexpander. The rowBodyTpl attribute has the description displayed in a paragraph element. Figure 6-13 shows the grid with row expander plugin.

Tom Hanks collection			
	Movie ▾	Rent	Buy
⊞	Forrest Gump	2.99	6.99
⊟	Cast Away	3.99	13.46
	Academy Award-winning filmmaker Robert Zemeckis and two-time Oscar winner Tom Hanks reunite to explore the blessings and heartache of fate and the survival of the human spirit. Tom Hanks gives one of the towering screen performances of all time as Chuck Noland, a FedEx systems engineer whose ruled-by-the-clock existence abruptly ...		
⊞	Apollo 13	3.99	7.99

Figure 6-13. *RowExpander plugin*

Ext.grid.plugin.BufferedRenderer

If you have a grid that displays a large number of records, scrolling the grid vertically may have a visual impact. When you try to scroll down a grid, the current viewable set of rows in the grid have to be replaced with a new set of data has to be shown in the grid. In the earlier versions of Ext JS 4, this feature was implemented by re-creating all the rows every time you scroll. In other words, the grid was being redrawn everytime. This may lead to a delayed response or a visual blur or sometimes the grid may even become unresponsive for a few seconds or more.

The latest version of Ext JS, 4.2 solves this problem by not replacing or re-rendering rows when you scroll. It just adds or removes the rows to the grid without re-rendering the entire grid panel. What they do is create a set of rows before and after the current viewable set of rows and store them in a buffer. When you scroll down the buffered set of rows is shown in the grid.

You can configure the grid with the BufferedRenderer plugin to configure the buffered rendering of the rows in the grid. The buffered rendering is also popularly known as *infinite scrolling*.

The Plugin has attributes like trailingBufferZone and leadingBufferZone to specify the number of rows that have to be buffered before and after the current viewable set of rows.

It also provides an attribute numFromEdge that indicates the number of rows from the edge of the table. Say the numFromEdge is 5, and if the viewable area is scrolled till you have 5 rows from the edge of the table, then the grid is appended with newer set of rows.

You can configure the plugin with the grid as shown below.

```
plugins : [
    {
        ptype :"bufferedrenderer",
        trailingBufferZone : 10,
        leadingBufferZone : 20,
        numFromEdge : 7
    }
]
```

One of the prominent grid plugins is the Feature plugin. Let's discuss the Feature plugin in detail.

Grid Features

Ext.grid.feature.Feature class is a grid plugin that provides functionalities like grouping, summary etc., Feature class is extended by several classes that provide the extra functionalities for the grid. The feature plugins can be wired up to the grid using the features attribute instead of the plugins attribute that you used earlier. Each feature class has an alias name or ftype, similarly to the xtype in components. Table 6-4 shows the list of feature classes that can be used with a grid panel.

Table 6-4. *Feature Classes*

Class	Description
Ext.grid.feature.RowBody	Used for adding additional contents to a grid row
Ext.grid.feature.Grouping	Used to create grouped records
Ext.grid.feature.Summary	Used for displaying summary data in a grid
Ext.grid.feature.GroupingSummary	Used to display summary data for each grouped set of records

Ext.grid.feature.RowBody

RowBody feature is used add additional contents to a grid row. In other words, it's used to implement a nested grid. It generates an additional <tr> element. The ftype of RowBody class is rowbody. The RowBody feature is pretty similar to the RowExpander plugin that we discussed earlier, the only difference being the lack of the expand/collapse functionality provided by RowExpander. You have to configure the getAdditionalData() method of the feature to return the contents of the additional row. Here's how you create a grid with rowbody feature.

```
Ext.create("Ext.grid.Panel", {
            store: movieStore,
            height : 350,
            title : "Tom Hanks collection",
            features: [
             {
               ftype: 'rowbody',
               getAdditionalData : function(data){
                return {
                        rowBody : "<p>" + data.description + "</p>",
                        rowBodyColspan : 3
                   };
               }
            }],
            columns: [
                    {
                      text: 'Movie',
                      dataIndex: 'title',
                    },
                    {
                      text: 'Rent',
                      dataIndex: 'rent',
                    },
```

```
                    {
                       text: 'Buy',
                       dataIndex: 'buy',
                    }
                  ]
});
```

The getAdditionalData() function returns a JSON object with rowBody and rowBodyColspan properties. Figure 6-14 shows the output of the code.

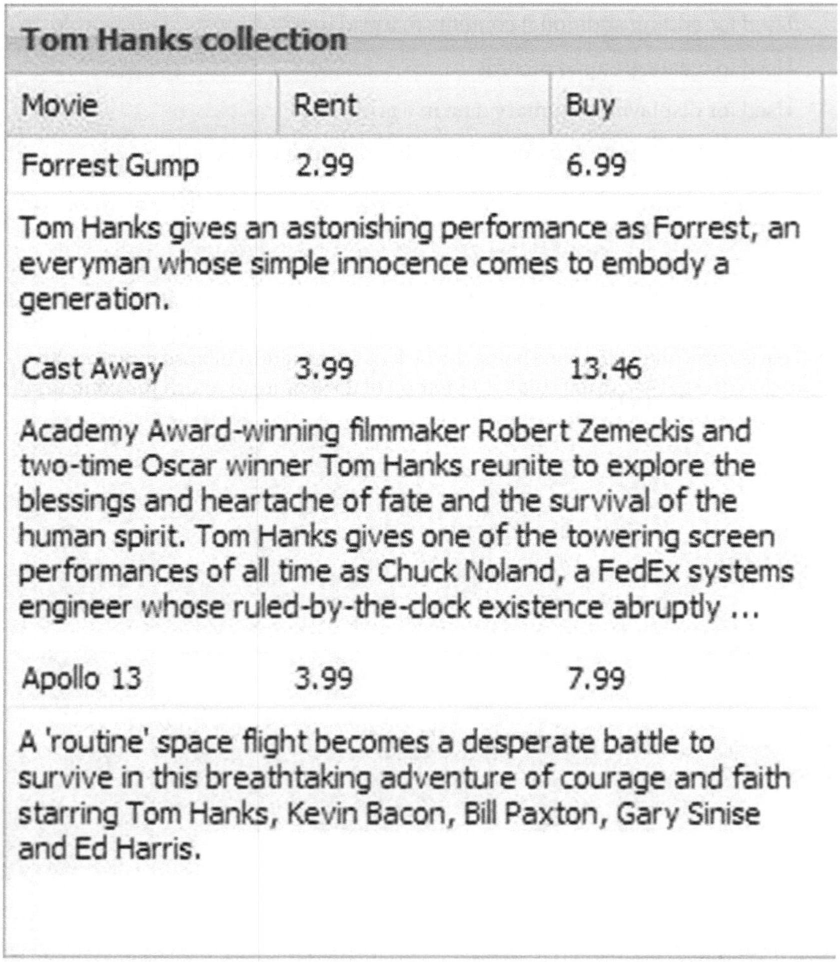

Tom Hanks collection		
Movie	Rent	Buy
Forrest Gump	2.99	6.99
Tom Hanks gives an astonishing performance as Forrest, an everyman whose simple innocence comes to embody a generation.		
Cast Away	3.99	13.46
Academy Award-winning filmmaker Robert Zemeckis and two-time Oscar winner Tom Hanks reunite to explore the blessings and heartache of fate and the survival of the human spirit. Tom Hanks gives one of the towering screen performances of all time as Chuck Noland, a FedEx systems engineer whose ruled-by-the-clock existence abruptly ...		
Apollo 13	3.99	7.99
A 'routine' space flight becomes a desperate battle to survive in this breathtaking adventure of courage and faith starring Tom Hanks, Kevin Bacon, Bill Paxton, Gary Sinise and Ed Harris.		

Figure 6-14. *RowBody feature*

Ext.grid.feature.Summary

The summary feature is a simple plugin used to display summary information of the records for each column. The summary for each column is specified using two properties, summaryType and summaryRenderer. The summaryType is a mathematical calculation attribute. You can set the summaryType to be one of the values in this list: *sum, count, average, max, min.* The summaryRenderer is a function that formats the display information. Figure 6-15 shows the grid with a summary feature.

Tom Hanks collection		
Movie	Rent	Buy
Forrest Gump	2.99	6.99
Cast Away	3.99	13.46
Apollo 13	3.99	7.99
Movie count: 3	**Average rent: $3.66**	**Total : $28.44**

Figure 6-15. *Summary feature*

Here's the code for the grid with the summary feature.

```
Ext.create("Ext.grid.Panel", {
            store: movieStore,
            height: 350,
            title: "Tom Hanks collection",
            features: [
            {
                ftype: 'summary'
            }],
            columns: [
                {
                    text: 'Movie',
                    dataIndex: 'title',
                    summaryType: "count",
                    summaryRenderer: function (value) {
                        return "<b>Movie count: " + value + "</b>";
                    }

                },
                {
                    text: 'Rent',
                    dataIndex: 'rent',
                    summaryType: "average",
                    summaryRenderer: function (value) {
                    return "<b>Average rent: $" + Ext.Number.toFixed(value, 2) + "</b>";
                    }
                },
```

```
                {
                    text: 'Buy',
                    dataIndex: 'buy',
                    summaryType: "sum",
                    summaryRenderer: function (value) {
                        return "<b>Total : $" + Ext.Number.toFixed(value, 2) + "</b>";
                    }
                }
            ]
        });
```

You can notice every column configured with summaryType and summaryRenderer attributes.

Ext.grid.feature.Grouping

Ext.grid.feature.Grouping plugin is used to group rows in a grid based on the group field that you configure in the data store. Let's modify our movie store to add a grouping field as shown below.

```
var movieStore = Ext.create("Ext.data.Store", {
        fields: ["title", "rent", "buy", "rating"],
        groupField : "rating",
        data: [
                { title: "Forrest Gump", rent: 2.99,buy:6.99,rating:"PG-13"},
                { title: "Cast Away", rent: 3.99,buy:13.46,rating:"PG-13"},
                { title: "Apollo 13", rent: 3.99, buy: 7.99, rating: "PG" },
                { title: "The Green Mile", rent: 1.99, buy: 9.99, rating: "R" },
                { title: "Sleepless in Seattle", rent: 1.99, buy: 11.97, rating: "PG" },
                { title: "Toy Story 3", rent: 1.99, buy: 14.99, rating: "G" },
        ]
    });
```

We've introduced a rating field that'll serve as the groupField. Let's display the grid where records are grouped based on their rating. Here's the grid where we've used the grouping feature.

```
Ext.create("Ext.grid.Panel", {
                store: movieStore,
                height: 350,
                title: "Tom Hanks collection",
                features: [
                    {
                        ftype: 'grouping',
                        groupHeaderTpl : "Rating: {name}",
                        collapsible : false,
                        showSummaryRow : true
                    }
                ],
                 columns: [
                        {
                            text: 'Movie',
                            dataIndex: 'title'
                        },
```

```
                        {
                            text: 'Rent',
                            dataIndex: 'rent'
                        },
                        {
                            text: 'Buy',
                            dataIndex: 'buy'
                        }
                    ],
                renderTo: Ext.getBody()
        });
```

We've used the grouping features along with few attributes. The groupHeaderTpl attribute represents the template for displaying the group header text. You'll get an output as shown in Figure 6-16.

Figure 6-16. *Grouping feature*

Ext.grid.feature.GroupingSummary

Ext.grid.feature.GroupingSummary plugin is used to add summary information for the group rows. It's a combination of the Grouping and Summary features. The code snippet for the grid panel with grouping summary feature is given below.

```
Ext.create("Ext.grid.Panel", {
               store: movieStore,
               height: 350,
               title: "Tom Hanks collection",
               features: [
               {
                   ftype: 'groupingsummary',
                   groupHeaderTpl: "Rating: {name}",
                   showSummaryRow : true
               }],
               columns: [
                       {
                           text: 'Movie',
                           dataIndex: 'title',
                           summaryType: "count",
                           summaryRenderer: function (value) {
                               return "<b>Movie count: " + value + "</b>";
                           }
                       },
                       {
                           text: 'Rent',
                           dataIndex: 'rent',
                           summaryType: "average",
                           summaryRenderer: function (value) {
                             return "<b>Average rent: $" + Ext.Number.toFixed(value, 2) + "</b>";
                           }
                       },
                       {
                           text: 'Buy',
                           dataIndex: 'buy',
                           summaryType: "sum",
                           summaryRenderer: function (value) {
                               return "<b>Total : $" + Ext.Number.toFixed(value, 2) + "</b>";
                           }
                       }
                   ],
           });
```

The grid is configured with groupingsummary feature and each column in the grid is configured with summaryType and summaryRenderer attributes. Figure 6-17 shows the output of the grid with the grouping summary.

Tom Hanks collection		
Movie	Rent	Buy
⊟ Rating: G		
Toy Story 3	1.99	14.99
Movie count: 1	**Average rent: $1.99**	**Total : $14.99**
⊟ Rating: PG		
Apollo 13	3.99	7.99
Sleepless in Seattle	1.99	11.97
Movie count: 2	**Average rent: $2.99**	**Total : $19.96**
⊞ Rating: PG-13		
Movie count: 2	**Average rent: $3.49**	**Total : $20.45**
⊟ Rating: R		
The Green Mile	1.99	9.99
Movie count: 1	**Average rent: $1.99**	**Total : $9.99**

Figure 6-17. *GroupingSummary feature*

Paginated Grid

The grid panel can be configured with a paging toolbar to enable pagination of the records. You can use the Ext.toolbar.Paging class for this purpose. The Paging toolbar object can be added as a docked item to the grid panel. Whenever you click the paging buttons like previous and next, the underlying store is populated with the next set of records through the proxy and displayed in the grid.

Let's create a paginated grid panel as shown in Figure 6-18.

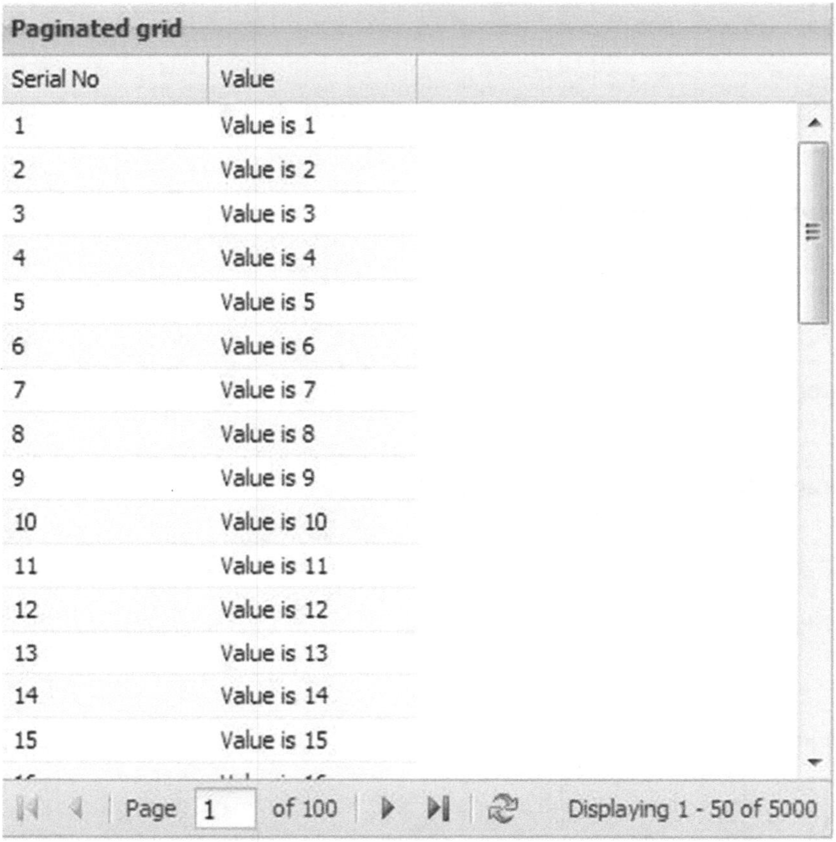

Paginated grid			
Serial No	Value		
1	Value is 1		▲
2	Value is 2		
3	Value is 3		≡
4	Value is 4		
5	Value is 5		
6	Value is 6		
7	Value is 7		
8	Value is 8		
9	Value is 9		
10	Value is 10		
11	Value is 11		
12	Value is 12		
13	Value is 13		
14	Value is 14		
15	Value is 15		
			▼

|◀ ◀ | Page `1` | of 100 | ▶ ▶| | ⟳ | Displaying 1 - 50 of 5000

Figure 6-18. *Paginated grid*

As shown in Figure 6-18, the paginated grid contains two columns and 5000 records. The page size is 50. The paging toolbar is docked to the bottom of the grid panel where you have the buttons to load the previous and subsequent pages. The paging toolbar contains a textbox to enter the page number.

Let's create a store with two fields namely sno and value as shown below. The store has the pageSize property configured as 50. It's registered with an Ajax proxy to load the records from the server.

```
var store = Ext.create("Ext.data.Store", {
        fields: ["sno", "value"],
        pageSize : 50,
        autoLoad : true,
        proxy : {
            type : "ajax",
            url : "server.ashx",
            reader : {
                type : "json",
                root : "output",
                totalProperty : "total"
            }
        }
    });
```

The proxy URL points to a server side implementation, `server.ashx` that I have used for this example. Server. ashx is a .NET implementation that has the following code snippet.

```
public void ProcessRequest (HttpContext context) {
        context.Response.ContentType = "application/json";
        HttpResponse Response = context.Response;
        int limit = int.Parse(context.Request["limit"]);
        int start = int.Parse(context.Request["start"]);
        //GENERATING JSON OUTPUT
        String output = "{total : 5000,output : [";
        for (int i = (start+1); i <= (start + limit); i++) {
            output += "{sno:" + i + ",value:'Value is " + i + "'}";
            if(i < (start + limit))
                output += ",";
        }
        output += "]}";
        Response.Write(output);
    }
```

In the code above we generate a JSON output based on two request parameters, start and limit. The limit will hold the value of the pageSize property configured in the store, which is configured as 50 in our example. The start parameter will have values in multiples of the pageSize. It will be 50 for page 1, 100 for page 2, 150 for page 3, and so on. The response will be a JSON formatted string that'll have the total property that represents the total size and an output property which is an array. The response for page 1 will look as shown below.

```
{total : 5000,output : [{sno:1,value:'Value is 1'},{sno:2,value:'Value is 2'},{sno:3,value:'Value
is 3'},{sno:4,value:'Value is 4'},{sno:5,value:'Value is 5'},{sno:6,value:'Value is 6'}... ]}
```

The grid panel that uses the paging toolbar is shown below.

```
Ext.create("Ext.grid.Panel", {
                store: store,
                title : "Paginated grid",
                height : 400,width:400,
                dockedItems: [{
                    xtype: 'pagingtoolbar',
                    store: store,
                    dock: 'bottom',
                    displayInfo: true
                }],
                columns: [
                        {
                          text: 'Serial No',
                          dataIndex: 'sno'
                        },
                        {
                          text: 'Value',
                          dataIndex: 'value',
                        }
                    ]
            });
        }
```

Whenever you click the next or previous button in the paging toolbar there'll be a request sent to server.ashx with page, start, and limit parameters in the querystring.

You can also configure the paging toolbar using the property bbar, which is a shortcut for bottom bar as shown below.

```
bbar : [
    {
       xtype:"pagingtoolbar",
       ...
    }
]
```

Tree

Ext.tree.Panel class represents a tree structured UI component. The tree panel is usually used to represent hierarchical data. The data for the tree panel is provided using an instance of Ext.data.TreeStore class.

The TreeStore like any other store can be configured with data from various sources and is collection of Model instances. Say we've the following data to be displayed in a tree format as shown in Figure 6-19.

```
{
   countries : [
{name:"USA",cities:[{name:"Houston"},{name:"Boston"},{name:"LA"}]}
{name:"UK",cities:[{name:"London"},{name:"Bristol"},{name:"Essex"}]}
{name:"India",cities:[{name:"Chennai"},{name:"Delhi"},{name:"Mumbai"}]}
   ]
}
```

Figure 6-19. *Tree Panel*

The records of the TreeStore have to be decorated with some extra properties for the tree panel to display the values as nodes. In other words, the records of the tree store have to be converted to nodes for proper display. The class Ext.data.NodeInterface is used for this purpose. The Model instances are automatically padded up with properties and methods of the NodeInterface class. Table 6-5 shows some of the config options of the NodeInterface class.

Table 6-5. *Config Options of NodeInterface Class*

Attribute	Description
Text	Represents the value to be displayed in the node
Leaf	Used to specify whether the node has children or not
Root	Used to specify whether the node is a root node or not
Children	Represents an array of child nodes
Checked	Used to display a checkbox for each node
Qtip	Used to specify the tooltip text for the node
Depth	Used to configure the depth of each starting from the root node. Root node has a depth of 0.
Expanded	Used to enable or disable expanding of the node
Icon	Represents an icon for the node

Table 6-6 shows some of the methods of the NodeInterface class.

Table 6-6. *Methods in NodeInterface Class*

Method	Description
appendChild	Used to append a node
Copy	Used for cloning the node
insertBefore	Used to insert a node before the given node
hasChildNodes	Specifies if the node has children or not
removeChild	Used to remove a given child node from its parent node
replaceChild	Used to replace a child node with the given node

The TreeStore instance with the data that's decorated using the NodeInterface attributes is given below.

```
var countryStore = Ext.create("Ext.data.TreeStore", {
        root: {
            text: "Countries",
            children: [

            { text: "USA", children: [{ text: "Houston", leaf: true }, { text: "Boston", leaf:
true }, { text: "LA", leaf: true}] },
            { text: "UK", children: [{ text: "London", leaf: true }, { text: "Bristol", leaf:
true }, { text: "Essex", leaf: true}] },
```

```
                 { text: "India", children: [{ text: "Chennai", leaf: true }, { text: "Delhi", leaf:
true }, { text: "Mumbai", leaf: true}] },
                 ]
              }
       });
```

You can notice the country and cities information has been converted to the format required by the tree panel. Each country record is decorated using the text, children, and leaf attributes. The code snippet for the tree panel that uses the countryStore is given below.

```
Ext.create('Ext.tree.Panel', {
                    title: 'Countries', height: 400,
                    store: countryStore,
              });
```

The tree panel instance will display the tree as shown in Figure 6-15.

Let's assume the data comes from the server in a JSON format and has to be decorated with NodeInterface attributes before displaying it in the tree. For example, we discussed the countries data where each record has a name of the country and a cities array. You can make use of the events provided by the NodeInterface class to decorate this data with the text and leaf attributes. NodeInterface class provides events like append, beforeappend, insert, remove, collapse, expand, and so on. We'll make use of the append event that'll be called after a node has been appended to the tree. The code snippet is shown below.

```
Ext.define("City", {
         extend: "Ext.data.Model",
         fields: ["name"]
      });
      Ext.define("Country", {
         extend: "Ext.data.Model",
         fields: ["name"],
         hasMany: [{ name: "cities", model: "City"}]
      });
      var countryStore = Ext.create("Ext.data.TreeStore", {
         model: "Country",
         autoLoad: true,
         proxy: {
             type: "ajax",
             url: "countries.txt",
             reader: {
                 type: "json",
                 root: "countries"
             }
         },
         listeners: {
             append: function (currentNode, newNode) {
                 if (!newNode.isRoot()) {
                     if (newNode.getDepth() == 1) {
                         newNode.set("text", newNode.get("name"));
                         for (var i = 0; i < newNode.cities().getCount(); i++) {
                             var city = newNode.cities().getAt(i).get("name");
                             var cityNode = newNode.copy();
```

```
                        cityNode.set("text", city);
                        cityNode.set("leaf", true);
                        newNode.appendChild(cityNode);
                    }
                }
            }
            else
                newNode.set("text", "Countries");
        }
    }
});
```

We've added an event handler for the append event. In the append handler function, we check for the depth of the node, and if it's one we add the country name. We iterate through the cities collection in the country and create a new node for every city and append it to the country node. You can notice the use of copy() and appendChild() functions that we've used to clone a node and add a node respectively.

Chart

Ext.chart.Chart class is used to create and render different types of charts. A chart renders the data from a Store object visually. The Chart class has to be configured with three attributes a store, axes that specify the boundary regions and the series that take care of the visual rendering of the data. Figure 6-20 shows the relationship between the Chart and these three attributes.

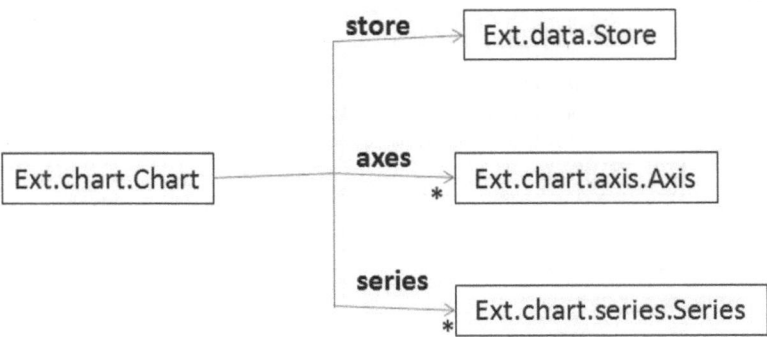

Figure 6-20. *Association of Chart class with Store, Axis and Series classes*

As shown in Figure 6-20, the Chart class has to be configured with a store attribute, an axes attribute that is an array of Ext.chart.axis.Axis objects and a series attribute that's an array of Ext.chart.series.Series objects.

Ext JS 4 provides different types of Axis classes and Series classes. Table 6-7 shows the list of Axis classes in Ext.chart.axis package.

Table 6-7. *Axis Classes*

Class	Description	Usage
Numeric	Used for setting numeric values.	```{ type:"Numeric", fields:[], position:"left" //"bottom", maximum: maximum value, minimum: minimum value }```
Time	Used for configuring the axes in time values	```{ type : "Time", fields : [], position : "left" //"bottom", dateFormat : "M d y", fromDate : "", toDate : "" }```
Category	Refers to the axes that have to be configured using non-quantitative values like names, etc.	```{ type:"Category" fields : [], position : "left"//"bottom", }```
Gauge	Refers to the Gauge axis and is used with Gauge series	```{ type : "Gauge", fields : [], position : "gauge", minimum: minimum value, maximum: maximum value }```

Table 6-8 shows the list of Series classes in Ext.chart.series package.

Table 6-8. *Series Classes*

Class	Description	Usage
Line	Used to create a line chart	```{ type:"line" xField : "", yField : "" }```
Pie	Used to create a pie chart	```{ type : "pie", angleField : "" }```

(*continued*)

Table 6-8. (*continued*)

Class	Description	Usage
Bar	Used to create a bar chart	```{ type : "bar", xField : "", yField : "" }```
Area	Used to create a stacked-up area chart. It can be used to display a stack of points for a category.	```{ type : "area", xField : "", yField : [] }```
Column	Used to create a column chart. It's a specialization of a bar chart.	```{ type : "column", xField : "", yField : "" }```
Gauge	Used to create a gauge chart. This chart is used to gauge the progression of an item.	```{ type : "gauge", field : "" }```
Radar	Popularly known as the spider chart or star chart, this class is used to analyze the behavior of data points in different categories.	```{ type : "radar" xField : "", yField : "" }```
Scatter	Used to display a scatter chart where values of different items are plotted in the chart	```{ type : "scatter", xField : "", yField : "" }```

There's neither time nor space to cover all of these Axis and Series classes. But a few of them are quite useful and worth a closer look.

Let's create a chart with some of these Axis and Series classes. We'll start with a store as shown below.

```
Ext.define('Employee', {
        extend: 'Ext.data.Model',
        fields: ['name', 'yearsOfExperience']
    });
var store = Ext.create('Ext.data.Store', {
        model: 'Employee',
        data: [
                { name: 'Sam', yearsOfExperience: 12 },
                { name: 'Ram', yearsOfExperience: 7 },
                { name: 'Kim', yearsOfExperience: 16 },
                { name: 'John', yearsOfExperience: 21 },
```

```
                        { name: 'Mary', yearsOfExperience: 13 }
            ]
    });
```

You have an employee store with the name and yearsOfExperience fields.
Let's create a bar chart and plot the store values as shown in Figure 6-21.

```
Ext.create('Ext.chart.Chart', {
                width: 500,
                height: 300,
                store: store,
                axes: [
        {
            title: 'Years of Experience',
            type: 'Numeric',
            position: 'bottom',
            fields: ['yearsOfExperience'],
            minimum: 0,
            maximum: 30
        },
        {
            title: 'Employee',
            type: 'Category',
            position: 'left',
            fields: ['name']
        }
    ],
        series: [
            {
                type : "bar",
                xField : "name",
                yField : "yearsOfExperience"
            }
        ]
    });
```

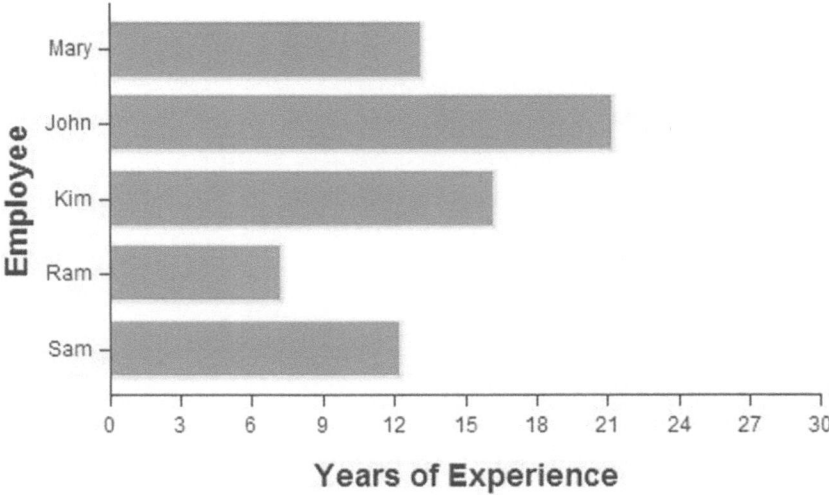

Figure 6-21. *Bar chart*

You can notice the use of Numeric and Category axes and bar series in the code snippet above. You can modify the axes and series as shown below to get a line chart as shown in Figure 6-22.

```
axes: [
        {
            title: 'Years of Experience',
            type: 'Numeric',
            position: 'left',
            fields: ['yearsOfExperience'],
            minimum: 0,
            maximum: 30
        },
        {
            title: 'Employee',
            type: 'Category',
            position: 'bottom',
            fields: ['name']
        }
    ],
series: [
            {
             type: 'line',
             xField: 'name',
             yField: 'yearsOfExperience'
             }
        ]
```

127

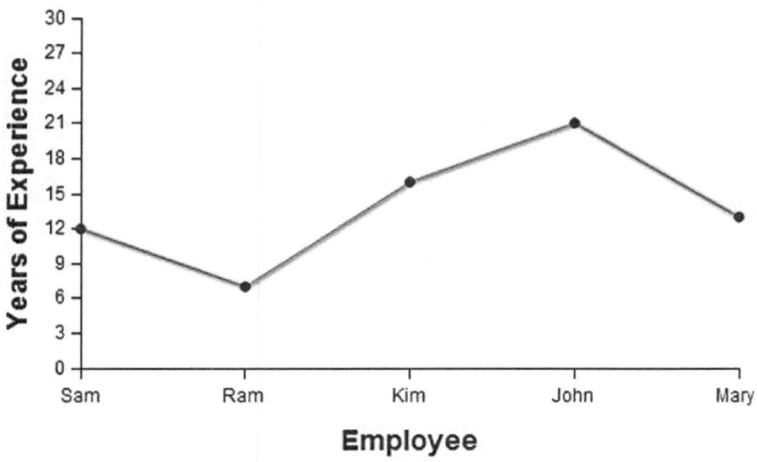

Figure 6-22. *Line chart*

You can display pie chart as shown in Figure 6-23 with the following series. Pie chart doesn't have the axes.

```
series: [
            {
                type: "pie",
                angleField: "yearsOfExperience",
                label: {
                    field : "name",
                    display: "middle",
                    contrast : true,
                    font : "20px"
                }
            }
]
```

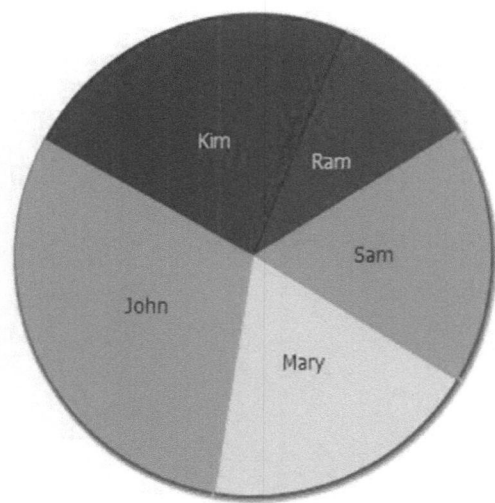

Figure 6-23. *Pie chart*

128

If you have to play with a Gauge chart, let's modify the store as given below.

```
var store = Ext.create('Ext.data.Store', {
        model: 'Employee',
        data: [
                { name: 'Sam', yearsOfExperience: 12 }
        ]
});
```

The store has one record that we want to show it in a gauge chart. The axes and series attributes for the gauge chart is shown below.

```
axes: [
            {
                type: 'gauge',
                position: 'gauge',
                minimum: 2,
                maximum: 30,
                steps: 15,
            }
],
series: [
            {
                type: 'gauge',
                field: 'yearsOfExperience'
            }
]
```

You have to configure the maximum, minimum, and the steps attributes for a gauge chart. You'll get a gauge chart as shown in Figure 6-24.

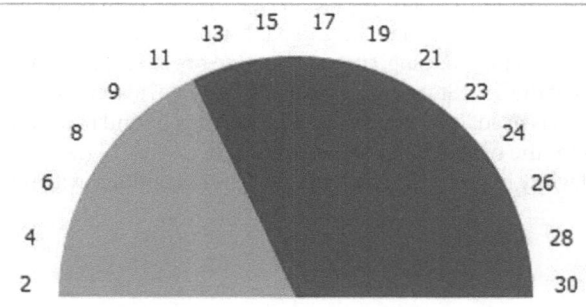

Figure 6-24. *Gauge chart*

The charts can be configured with a legend using the legend attribute. The legend attribute corresponds to the instance of Ext.chart.Legend class. You can set the legend attribute to true or configure it as an object by specifying the properties as shown below.

```
legend : {
 position : "right",
 labelColor : "#00F"
 ...
}
```

The line chart with the legend attribute will look as shown in Figure 6-25.

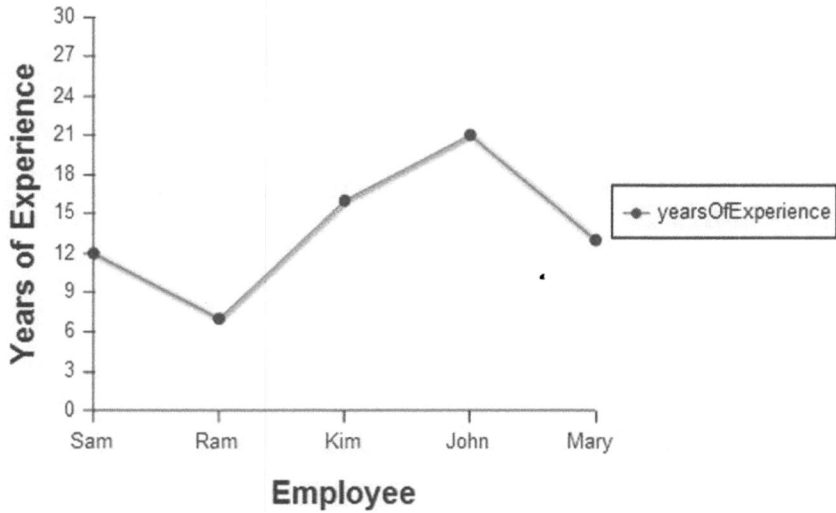

Figure 6-25. *Line chart with a legend*

Summary

In this chapter you learned various data controls like combobox, grid, tree, and chart. All these controls are bound to the data store and render the data automatically. XTemplate class provides an HTML-based template that can be applied to the data to produce custom HTML output. XTemplate has its own syntax to access the data. Ext.form.field.ComboBox class represents a dropdownlist. Ext.grid.Panel represents a data grid. Grid panel is configured with columns array. You can use different types of columns in a grid. The grid panel functionalities can be enhanced by using plugins. You have various plugins and features for grouping, summary and so on. Ext.tree.Panel represents a tree that's bound to a TreeStore. The records of the TreeStore are decorated with NodeInterface attributes to convert them to a node. Ext.chart.Chart class is used to create charts. Each chart is bound to a store for data, Axis classes for the boundary and the Series classes for the type of chart like Pie, Bar, etc.

In the next chapter you will learn the drag and drop facility in Ext JS 4. I'll discuss the various options available to perform drag and drop of UI components.

CHAPTER 7

Drag and Drop

Drag and Drop (DnD) is a prominent feature in modern web applications. Various UI controls in a web page can be dragged, moved around, and dropped in different spots effortlessly, thus saving a number of mouse click operations. A number of JavaScript libraries provide their own APIs for implementing the drag and drop behavior. DnD is now a part of the standard HTML 5 specification as well.

Ext JS 4 provides a well-structured API for implementing DnD behavior. You can use the Ext JS 4 API to incorporate a DnD facility in your applications easily. You can make any UI control draggable and able to be dropped to any type of container.

In this chapter you'll learn how to implement DnD in Ext JS 4.

Drag and Drop behavior

The drag and drop behavior involves dragging a component and dropping it into another component.

The drag behavior of a component X can be split into various steps.

- Configure the component X to be draggable, so that it can be dragged around.

- Place the mouse on X, click on it and holding the mouse button down, move the mouse.

- Reach a spot or the component and release the mouse button.

- Perform the necessary action so the dragged component X appears in that particular spot or component.

- If something goes wrong while dragging and dropping X perform the necessary repair.

The drop behavior of a component X can be split into various steps.

- Configure the component X to be drop area, so that you can drop other components in it.

- Drag other components to X while holding the mouse button down and release the mouse button once you reach X.

- Perform the necessary action so the dragged component appears in X.

- If something goes wrong while dropping components into X, perform the necessary repair.

In a nutshell, the components that can be dragged or dropped should be configured to have those facilities using the API.

You can drag and drop any type of UI component in Ext JS 4. You can drag and drop a panel or a button or a text field or grid items or tree nodes and so on. You can provide the DnD behavior to the components by overriding some of the methods or configuring some properties.

The simple way of configuring the components to be draggable is by using the draggable attribute available in the Component class.

131

The draggable property

The Ext.Component class that serves as the base class for all the components has a configuration attribute *"draggable".* This attribute can be configured to be true to make any component draggable. If you want to make a panel draggable, here's how you do that.

```
Ext.create("Ext.panel.Panel", {
  title: "Drag",
  id : "mypanel",
  draggable: true,
  padding: 20, height: 100, width: 100,
});
```

You can set the panel's draggable attribute to true. You can place the mouse over the panel's titlebar and notice that the cursor changes, indicating that it can be dragged now. You can drag the panel and drop it wherever you want in the page. Figure 7-1 shows the browser window when the panel is being dragged. Figure 7-2 shows the browser window after the panel is dropped onto a spot.

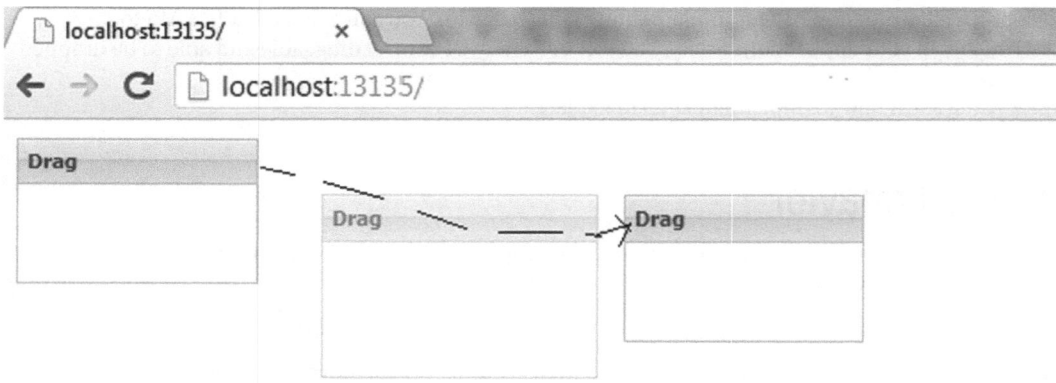

Figure 7-1. *Panel that is being dragged*

Figure 7-2. *Panel after dragging is over*

In Figure 7-1 the arrow mark indicates the dragged path. When the panel is dragged you will notice a ghost panel created that will be seen during the dragging process. The source panel gets hidden during this time. The ghost panel holds the top and left position coordinates as it is being dragged. Once the mouse button is released the ghost disappears and the source panel is rendered to the region using the top and left position coordinates of the ghost panel. Figure 7-3 shows the HTML code snippet while dragging the panel and after completing the drag operation.

```
▶<div id="mypanel" class="x-panel x-panel-default" style="padding: 10px; width: 150px; height: 100px; display: none;">..</div>
▶<div id="panel-1009" class="x-panel x-panel-ghost x-layer x-panel-default" style="height: 100px; left: 132px; top: 40px; z-index: 19000; width: 150px;" aria-
labelledby="panel-1009_header_hd" tabindex="-1">..</div>
▶<div id="mypanel-drag-status-proxy" class="x-component x-dd-drag-proxy x-dd-drop-nodrop x-layer x-component-default" style="visibility: hidden;">..</div>
```

```
▶<div id="mypanel" class="x-panel x-panel-default" style="padding: 10px; width: 150px; height: 100px; left: 132px; top: 40px" tabindex="-1">..</div>
▶<div id="panel-1009" class="x-panel x-panel-ghost x-layer x-panel-default" style="height: 100px; left: 132px; top: 40px; z-index: 19000; width: 150px; display:
none;" aria-labelledby="panel-1009_header_hd" tabindex="-1">..</div>
▶<div id="mypanel-drag-status-proxy" class="x-component x-dd-drag-proxy x-dd-drop-nodrop x-layer x-component-default" style="visibility: hidden;">..</div>
```

Figure 7-3. *HTML code snippet generated during drag and drop*

In Figure 7-3, the first part shows the HTML code when you are dragging the panel. The mypanel element is hidden as you can infer from the display:none style. The ghost panel element with the id panel-1009 has the style attribute where the left and top positions hold the value of the current position of the panel.

The second part of the figure shows the HTML code after completing the drag operation. The mypanel element has the left and top positions modified with the ghost panel's values and it is shown. The ghost panel is hidden now.

You will also notice a <div> element with the id attribute as mypanel-drag-status-proxy. We'll discuss this later in the chapter.

We have discussed a very simple DnD example using the draggable property. If you want to customize the drag and drop operation and scale it up to suit your needs we need to take a look at the Ext.dd package.

Ext.dd package

The Ext.dd package provides the classes for performing DnD operations. The classes are related either to the drag operations or to the drop operations. These classes speed up the development by providing the basic DnD behavior to the components.

Ext.dd.DragDrop serves as the parent class for all the DnD operations related classes.

Ext.dd.DragDrop class

Ext.dd.DragDrop is the base class for all the classes that implement the DnD behavior. You can encapsulate any HTML element in a DragDrop instance and the HTML element becomes draggable and a drop area. The DragDrop instance has an isTarget property that can be configured with a boolean value to make the underlying component a drop target. The DragDrop class provides the following event handler methods that can be overridden.

- startDrag
    - Called when the draggable item is clicked and ready to be moved.
- onDragEnter
    - Called when the draggable item is dragged and enters another DragDrop instance whose isTarget attribute is configured as true.
- onDrag
    - Called when the item is being dragged.

- onDragOver

  - Called when the draggable item is dragged over another DragDrop instance whose isTarget attribute is configured as true.

- onDragOut

  - Called when the draggable item is dragged out of the DragDrop instance whose isTarget attribute is configured as true.

- onDragDrop

  - Called when the draggable item is dropped on a DragDrop instance whose isTarget attribute is configured as true.

- onInvalidDrop

  - Called when the draggable item is dropped on a DragDrop instance usually on an item whose isTarget attribute is configured as false.

- endDrag

  - Called when drag operation is over and the mouse button is released.

You can also configure items to be part of a logical group. Draggable items in a particular group can be dropped only into other items that are configured as drop areas of that group. For example, if Item1 and Item2 belong to group A, they can only be dragged into drop areas that belong to group A. You can add an item to a group by using the groups property or the addToGroup method.

Let's create two HTML elements and configure them as DragDrop instance. One of the elements will be a draggable item and the other will be a drop target. We'll implement the event handler methods as well. Figure 7-4 shows the page that we'll create.

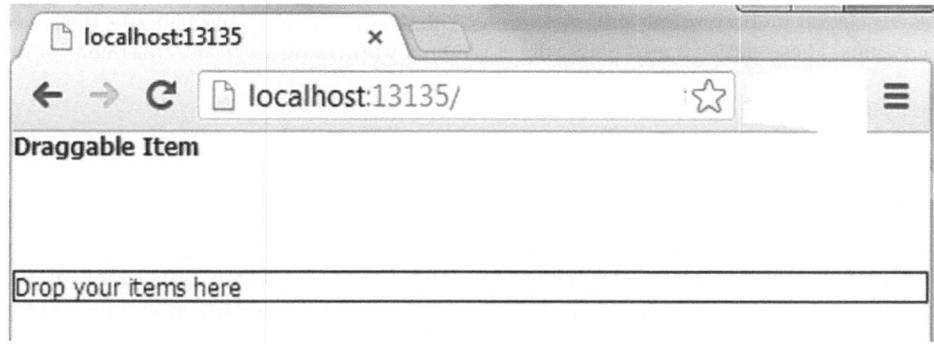

Figure 7-4. *Page that uses DragDrop*

Listing 7-1 shows the code for the example.

Listing 7-1. DragDrop

```
<script>
    Ext.onReady(function () {
        var ddItem1 = Ext.create("Ext.dd.DragDrop", "item1", "A", { isTarget: false });
        ddItem1.startDrag = function () {
            console.log("startDrag");
        }
```

```
            ddItem1.onDrag = function () {
                console.log("onDrag");
            }
            ddItem1.onDragEnter = function () {
                console.log("onDragEnter");
            }
            ddItem1.onDragOut = function () {
                console.log("onDragOut");
            }
            ddItem1.onDragOver = function () {
                console.log("onDragOver");
            }
            ddItem1.onDragDrop = function () {
                console.log("onDragDrop");
            }
            ddItem1.endDrag = function () {
                console.log("endDrag");
            }
            ddItem1.onInvalidDrop = function () {
                console.log("onInvalidDrop");
            }
            var ddItem2 = Ext.create("Ext.dd.DragDrop", "item2", "A", {isTarget:true});
        });
    </script>
</head>
<body>
    <h5 id="item1">
        Draggable Item
    </h5>
     <br /><br /><br /><br />
    <div id="item2" style="border-width:.1em;border-style:double; height:130;width:30;">
        Drop your items here
    </div>
</body>
```

As shown in Listing 7-1, we have <h5> and <div> elements that configured as DragDrop instances. The <h5> element with **item1** as the id is configured as a draggable item and <div> element with **item2** as the id is configured as a drop target. Both the elements belong to the group **A**. The dragdrop instance ddItem1 is configured with all the event handlers.

You can click on the <h5> element and drag it and drop it on the <div> element. You'll not find any effect in the UI when you perform a drag and drop as the DragDrop class is the basic class without any such UI changes. However, when you drag the <h5> element and drop it on the <div> element, the event handlers will get called. The console window provides the following output.

startDrag

35onDrag

onDragEnter

onDrag

onDragOver

onDrag

onDragOver

onDrag

onDragOver

onDragDrop

endDrag

As you can see in the output, the startDrag event handler is called in the beginning and onDrag is called several times when you drag to the <div> element. According to the results the onDrag was called 35 times when I executed this example. The onDragEnter method is called when you enter the <div> element and onDragOver is called when you move inside the <div> element. After you release the mouse button the onDragDrop method is called followed by the endDrag method.

Say, you drag the <h5> element and move beyond the <div> element and drop it outside the <div> element, here's the output you get in the console.

startDrag

11onDrag

onDragEnter

onDrag

onDragOver

onDrag

onDragOut

10onDrag

onInvalidDrop

endDrag

As you can notice in the output, when you drag on the <div> element, onDragEnter is called, and when you move out of the <div> element, onDragOut is called. When the item is dropped outside the <div> element, onInvalidDrop is called.

As mentioned earlier, all the classes related to DnD operations inherit the DragDrop class. Figure 7-5 shows the core classes related to Drag operations.

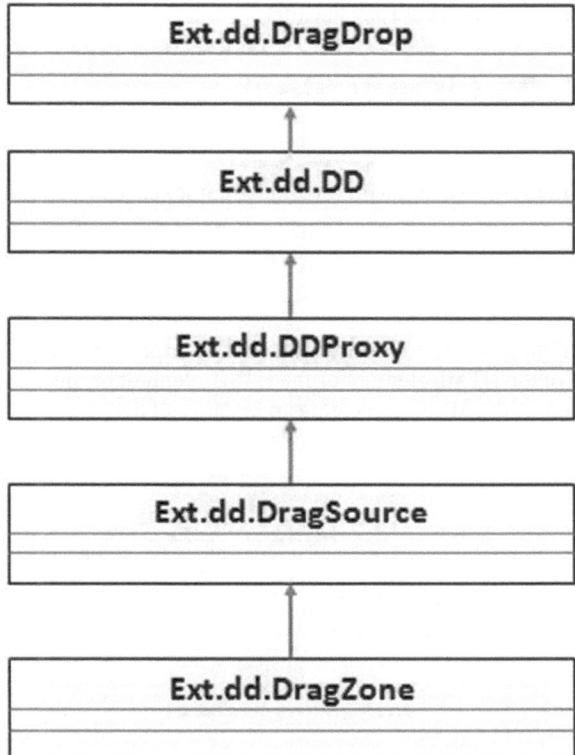

Figure 7-5. *Drag classes*

Let's discuss these classes in detail.

Ext.dd.DD class

The Ext.dd.DD class extends the DragDrop class. This class provides the drag facility where you can find the dragged element moving along with the mouse cursor.

You can modify the code in Listing 7-1 to create an instance of Ext.dd.DD like this.

```
Ext.onReady(function () {
    var ddItem1 = Ext.create("Ext.dd.DD", "item1", "A", { isTarget: false });
        ...
});
```

When you run the code you can see the dragged item move along with the mouse cursor as it is being dragged.

Ext.dd.DDProxy class

The Ext.dd.DDProxy class inherits the Ext.dd.DD class. This class provides the drag behavior where you can find a <div> element with a border being rendered when you drag an item.

You can modify the code in Listing 7-1 to create an instance of Ext.dd.DDProxy like this.

```
Ext.onReady(function () {
    var ddItem1 = Ext.create("Ext.dd.DDProxy", "item1", "A", { isTarget: false });
    ...
});
```

When you run the code you can see a bordered `<div>` element move along with the mouse cursor as it is being dragged.

Ext.dd.DragSource class

The Ext.dd.DragSource class that inherits the Ext.dd.DDProxy class is the commonly used class to implement drag behavior. You can create a DragSource object by passing the id of the HTML element or the HTML element or the Ext.Element object itself. If you have a `<div>` element with item1 as the id you can create an instance of the DragSource like this.

```
Ext.create("Ext.dd.DragSource","item1",{
  ddGroup : "A"
});
```

The DragSource object is configured to be in group A using the ddGroup attribute.

If you have a UI component like a Panel or Button and configure it as a drag source you can do it as shown in Listing 7-2.

Listing 7-2. DragSource

```
{
    xtype : "button",
    text : "Draggable button",
    listeners : {
      render : function(src){
        Ext.create("Ext.dd.DragSource",src.getEl(),{
                          ddGroup : "A"
                      });
      }
    }
}
```

You can create a DragSource instance only after the component is loaded, and the best place to do this is in the render event handler. The getEl() method is called on the Button object and passed into the DragSource constructor.

DragSource class provides a wide range of methods, most of them serving as the event handler methods. Table 7-1 shows some of the event handler methods in DragSource class.

Table 7-1. *Event Handler Methods in DragSource Class*

Method	Description
onBeforeDrag	Called before the drag operation begins
onStartDrag	Called when the drag operation begins
onDrag	Called when the item is being dragged
beforeDragEnter	Called before the dragged item enters the drop area

(*continued*)

Table 7-1. (*continued*)

Method	Description
afterDragEnter	Called after the dragged item enters the drop area
beforeDragOver	Called before the item is dragged over the drop area
afterDragOver	Called after the item is dragged over the drop area
beforeDragOut	Called before the item is dragged out of the drop area
afterDragOut	Called after the item is dragged out of the drop area
beforeDragDrop	Called before the dragged item is dropped and mouse button is released
afterDragDrop	Called after the dragged item is dropped and the mouse button is released
beforeInvalidDrop	Called before the dragged item is dropped in an invalid drop area
afterInvalidDrop	Called after the dragged item is dropped in an invalid drop area
afterValidDrop	Called after the dragged item is dropped in a valid drop area

Let's create two panels and drag the button from one panel and drop it to the other as shown in Figures 7-6 and 7-7.

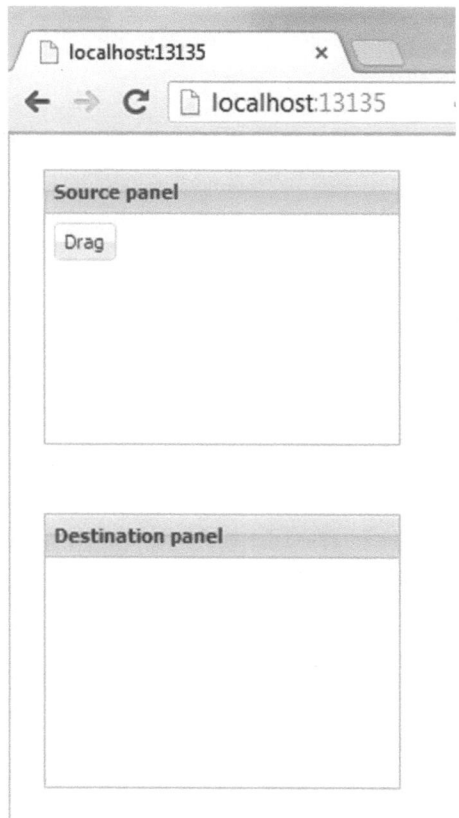

Figure 7-6. *Before drag and drop*

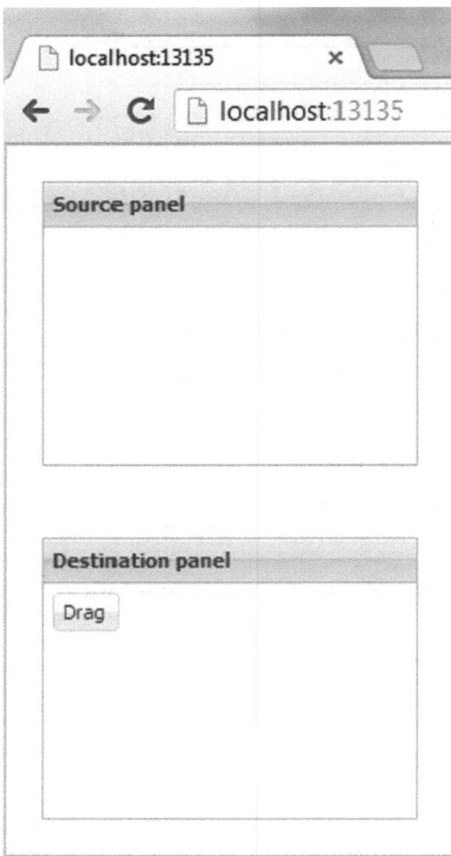

Figure 7-7. *After drag and drop*

Listing 7-3 shows the code snippet for creating these two panels and a button. The button is configured as a DragSource. The destination panel is configured to be a drop area.

Listing 7-3. Drag and Drop Button

```
Ext.onReady(function () {
  Ext.create("Ext.panel.Panel", {
    title: "Source panel",
    height: 200, width: 250, padding: 20,
    renderTo : Ext.getBody(),
    items: [
            {
              xtype : "button",
              text : "Drag",margin:5,
              listeners : {
                render : function(src){
                  Ext.create("Ext.dd.DragSource",src.getEl(),{
                    ddGroup : "A",
                    afterValidDrop : function(dropSrc){
                     var target = Ext.getCmp(dropSrc.id);
```

```
                    target.add(src);
                  },
                });
              }
            }
          }
        ]
  });
  Ext.create("Ext.panel.Panel", {
    title: "Destination panel",
    height: 200, width: 250, padding: 20,
    renderTo : Ext.getBody(),
    listeners: {
      render: function (src) {
        Ext.create("Ext.dd.DDTarget",src.getEl(),"A");
      }
    },
  });
});
```

In Listing 7-3 we've created the two panel objects. The Source panel has a Button object that is configured to be a drag source. The DragSource object implements the afterValidDrop event handler. In the event handler we get the drop target object, which is the destination panel, and add the button into it. The destination panel has been configured to be a DDTarget. You'll learn DDTarget in detail later in the chapter.

Ext.dd.DragZone class

The Ext.dd.DragZone class is used when you have to configure a number of elements as draggable. If you have a container where all the elements can be dragged, it's difficult to configure every individual element as a drag source. Instead, you can configure the container as a drag zone and all the elements in the container become draggable automatically. Typically components like grid and trees use the DragZone class.

Say you have a <div> element with a list of paragraph elements like this. These paragraph elements should be dragged and dropped in the <div> element with item2 as the id.

```
<div id="item1">
 <p>Item1</p>
 <p>Item2</p>
 <p>Item3</p>
</div>
<div id="item2">
Drop here...
</div>
```

Each paragraph element can be made draggable by configuring the <div> element as a DragZone as shown here.

```
Ext.create("Ext.dd.DragZone", "item1", {});
```

The DragZone does not move the child items from their positions when they are dragged. When you click on every item and drag it a proxy element is created and rendered to the screen. This proxy element appears along side the mouse cursor when you drag the item. You have to specify the proxy element by overriding the getDragData() method of DragZone class. The getDragData() method needs to return an object that has a mandatory property called ddel. The ddel property refers to the HTML element that will act as a proxy. It's this element that will appear near the mouse cursor when you drag the item. The object that getDragData() method returns is also used to pass extra information to the drop area. You can consume this information from the drop area. Listing 7-4 shows the code snippet that contains the DragZone object with getDragData() method.

Listing 7-4. getDragData( ) Method

```
Ext.create("Ext.dd.DragZone", "item1", {
     getDragData: function (e) {
         var elem = document.createElement("span");
         elem.innerHTML = "Draggable item";
         return {
           ddel : elem
         };
     }
});
```

As shown in Listing 7-4, the getDragData() method returns an object that contains a ddel property. We have created a <span> element that contains a text *Draggable item*. Figure 7-8 shows the proxy element that is created when you click on one of the items and drag it.

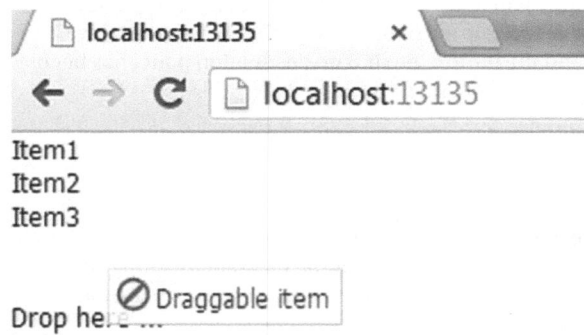

Figure 7-8. *Dragging an item in a DragZone*

Let's modify the getDragData() method in Listing 7-3 to show the text of the item that is being dragged. Let's pass some additional information along with ddel as shown here.

```
getDragData: function (e) {
   var sourceElem = e.getTarget();
   var clonedSourceElem = sourceElem.cloneNode(true);
   clonedSourceElem.innerHTML = "Dragging " + clonedSourceElem.innerHTML;
   return {
     ddel: clonedSourceElem,
     source: sourceElem,
     text : sourceElem.innerHTML
   };
}
```

We have modified the getDragData() method above where the ddel property refers to a clone of the original elemen that's being dragged. We modify the inner HTML of the cloned element. The object that's returned contains ddel, and source and text properties additionally. Figure 7-9 shows what happens when you drag item2 for instance.

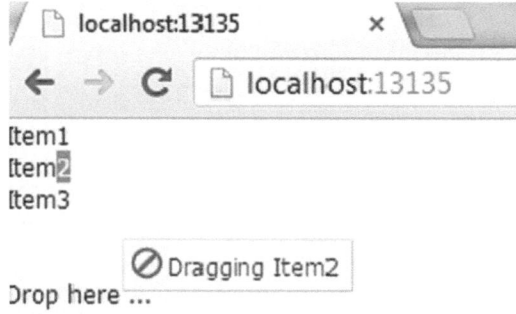

Figure 7-9. *DragZone with modified getDragData( ) method*

We've been discussing drag operation related classes so far. Let's dicuss the classes related to the drop operations. The drop operation related classes inherit the DragDrop class as shown in Figure 7-10.

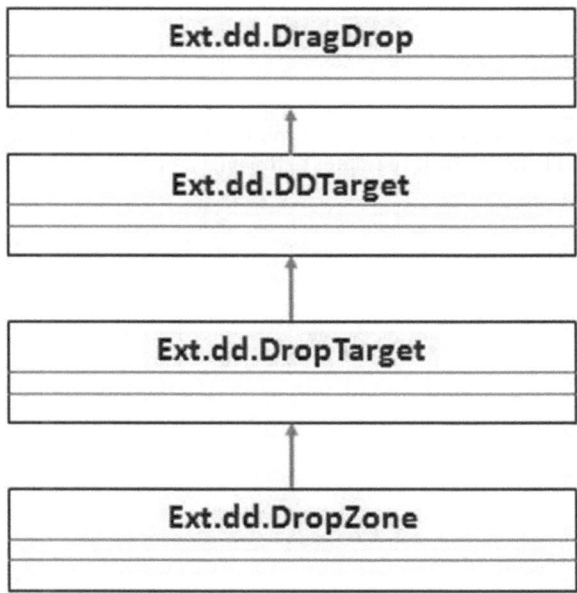

Figure 7-10. *Drop classes*

Ext.dd.DDTarget class

The Ext.dd.DDTarget class is a simple implementation of the Ext.dd.DragDrop class, which configures the element as a drop area where you can drag and drop your items. It doesn't provide any drop event handlers. If you have a <div> element with div1 as the id, you can configure it to be a DDTarget like this.

```
Ext.create("Ext.dd.DDTarget","div1","GroupName");
```

If you have a panel that needs to be configured as a DDTarget, you can do so after the panel is rendered like this.

```
Ext.create("Ext.panel.Panel",{
  ...
 listeners : {
   render : function(src){
     Ext.create("Ext.dd.DDTarget",src.getEl(),"GroupName");
   }
 }
});
```

Ext.dd.DropTarget Class

The Ext.dd.DropTarget class is a specialization of DDTarget class with drop event handlers. You can create an instance of DropTarget similar to creating an object of DDTarget class. The main difference between the two classes is DropTarget object should provide an implementation of an event handler method called notifyDrop(). The notifyDrop() method is called with the reference to the dragged object and the data that is passed while dragging. The general format of using DropTarget is given below.

```
Ext.create("Ext.dd.DropTarget","element or the id",{
 notifyDrop : function(dragSource,e,data){
 }
});
```

Let's create an empty fieldset element that can be dragged and dropped into a panel. We'll configure the fieldset to be a DragSource and the panel to be a DropTarget. Figure 7-11 shows the three states of the page, the initial, dragging and dropped state.

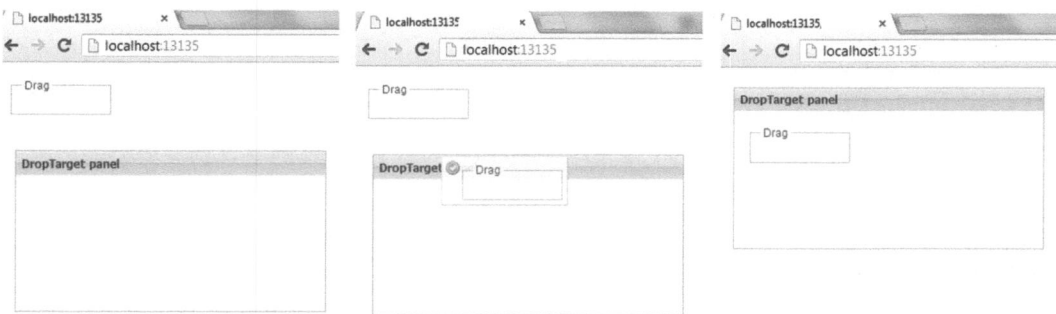

Figure 7-11. *The initial, dragging and dropped state*

Listing 7-5 shows the code snippet for implementing the example.

Listing 7-5. DropTarget

```
Ext.create("Ext.form.FieldSet",{
  renderTo : Ext.getBody(),
  width : 100,margin:15,
  title : "Drag",
  listeners : {
    render : function(src){
      Ext.create("Ext.dd.DragSource",src.getEl(),{
```

```
      ddGroup : "A"
    });
  }
 }
}
});

Ext.create("Ext.panel.Panel", {
  title: "DropTarget panel",
  height: 200, width: 350, padding: 20,
  renderTo : Ext.getBody(),
  listeners: {
    render: function (src) {
      Ext.create("Ext.dd.DropTarget",src.getEl(),{
        ddGroup : "A",
        notifyDrop : function(dragSource,e,data){
         var elem = Ext.getCmp(dragSource.id);
         src.add(elem);
        }
      });
    }
  },
});
```

As shown in Listing 7-5, the Panel is configured as a DropTarget with an implementation of notifyDrop() method. The notifyDrop() method gets the fieldset element and adds it to the panel. In this example we don't pass any data from the drag source.

Ext.dd.DropZone class

The Ext.dd.DropZone class similar to the DragZone class is used to configure a collection of elements as drop targets. Configuring the container as a drop zone makes the items in the container become drop targets. For example, you can use the DropZone in a Panel where you want to rearrange its items. The DropZone class provides a number of methods that you can choose to override. Some of the methods are listed below.

- getTargetFromEvent
  - This method returns the target object on which you are going to drop your item. This returned object is passed as the first parameter to the onNodeXXX methods.
- onNodeEnter
  - This method is called when the dragged item enters the drop zone.
- onNodeOut
  - This method is called when the dragged item moves out of the drop zone without getting dropped.
- onNodeOver
  - This method is called when the dragged item moves over the drop zone.
- onNodeDrop
  - This method is called when the item is dropped in the drop zone.

145

The onNodeXXX methods accept four arguments. The first one is the nodeData object that is returned from the getTargetEvent() method. The second argument is the DragSource instance, the third argument is the event object and the last argument is the data object returned by the DragSource.

Let's create a list of items that can be dragged into a container that is configured as a DropZone object. Figure 7-12 shows the screen shots of the page that we'll develop. You have to read the figure from left to right.

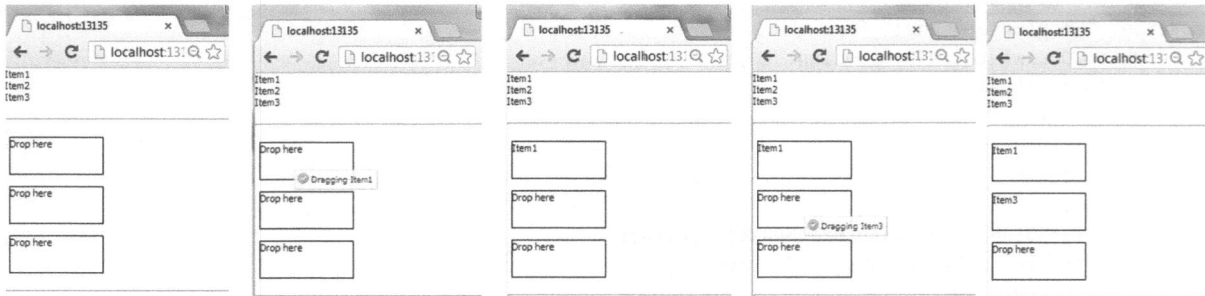

Figure 7-12. *DropZone example*

Listing 7-6 shows the HTML code snippet for the UI elements.

Listing 7-6. HTML Code Snippet for DropZone Example

```
<html>
<head>
<style>
.dnd{
        border-width:.1em;
        border-style:double;
        margin-left:5px;
        height:4em;
        width:10em;
    }
</style>
</head>
<body>
<div id="zone1">
   <p>Item1</p>
   <p>Item2</p>
   <p>Item3</p>
   </div>
  <br /><hr /><br />
  <div id="zone2" >
    <p class="dnd">Drop here</p><br />
    <p class="dnd">Drop here</p><br />
    <p class="dnd">Drop here</p><br />
 </div>
 <hr />
</body>
</html>
```

As shown in Listing 7-5, the `<div>` element with zone1 as the id will be configured as a DragZone object and `<div>` element with zone2 as the id will be configured as DropZone. Listing 7-7 shows the code to do that.

Listing 7-7. DragZone and DropZone

```
Ext.create("Ext.dd.DragZone", "zone1", {
  getDragData: function (e) {
    var sourceElem = e.getTarget();
    var clonedSourceElem = sourceElem.cloneNode(true);
    clonedSourceElem.innerHTML = "Dragging " + clonedSourceElem.innerHTML;
    return {
          ddel: clonedSourceElem,
          source: sourceElem,
          text : sourceElem.innerHTML
        };
  },
});

Ext.create("Ext.dd.DropZone", "zone2", {
  getTargetFromEvent: function (e) {
    if(e.getTarget().id != "zone2")
      return e.getTarget();
    return null;
  },
  onNodeDrop: function (target, dd, e, data) {
    target.innerHTML = data.text;
    return true;
  }
});
```

As shown in Listing 7-7, the zone2 is configured as a DropZone instance. We've overridden the getTargetFromEvent() method that returns the target object. As we want the items to be dropped into one of the three containers and not on the main container itself, we check for the id. If the id of the target is zone2 null is returned. In other words, returning a null is equivalent to canceling the drop operation. The onNodeDrop() method adds the text of the dragged item in the drop area.

Let's discuss the DnD operations related to data controls like grid and tree.

Drag and Drop in Grid Panel

Drag and Drop behavior in grid panels is available in the form of a plugin. You have a plugin class `Ext.grid.plugin.DragDrop` that can be configured with the grid for enabling drag and drop support. The DragDrop plugin with an alias name gridviewdragdrop needs to be configured in the viewConfig property of the grid as shown here.

```
Ext.create("Ext.grid.Panel",{
 viewConfig : {
  plugins : {
    ptype : "gridviewdragdrop"
  }
 }
});
```

This plugin automatically configures the grid to be DragZone and DropZone objects. You can rearrange rows of a grid easily by configuring this plugin. Figure 7-13 shows a grid panel whose rows can be rearranged using DnD operation.

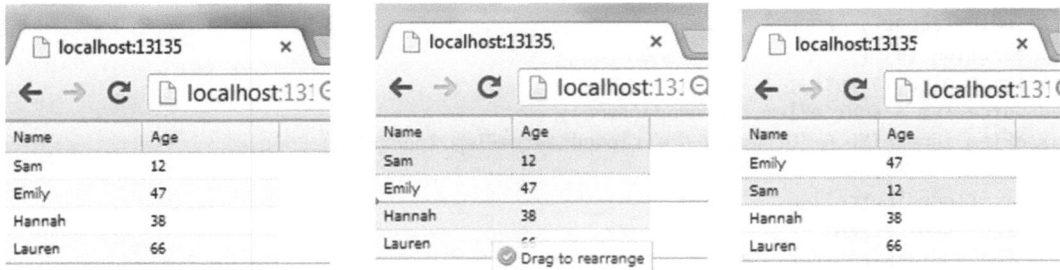

Figure 7-13. *Drag and Drop in a grid*

Figure 7-13 shows the grid where the first row is dragged and dropped to the second position. Listing 7-8 shows the code snippet for doing this.

Listing 7-8. Drag and Drop With Grid

```
var store = Ext.create("Ext.data.Store", {
    fields: ["name", "age"],
    data: [
      { name: "Sam", age: 12 },
      { name: "Emily", age: 47 },
      { name: "Hannah", age: 38 },
      { name: "Lauren", age: 66 },
    ]
});
Ext.create("Ext.grid.Panel", {
  store: store,
  viewConfig: {
    plugins: {
      ptype: 'gridviewdragdrop',
      dragText: 'Drag to rearrange',
    }
  },
  columns: [
      { text: "Name", dataIndex: "name" },
      { text: "Age", dataIndex: "age"}
  ]
});
```

We've used the dragText property of the plugin to configure the text that appears in the proxy element when you drag a row.

The plugin provides **dragGroup** and **dropGroup** properties that can be used to configure the group names. These properties are used when you want to drag and drop items to and from other components.

Say you want to drag and drop rows between two grid panels. You can configure the dragGroup property of Grid 1 and dropGroup property of Grid 2 to be the same. Figure 7-14 shows two grids whose rows can be moved between them. You have to read the diagrams from left to right. The rows from the members grid are dragged and dropped to the favorites grid.

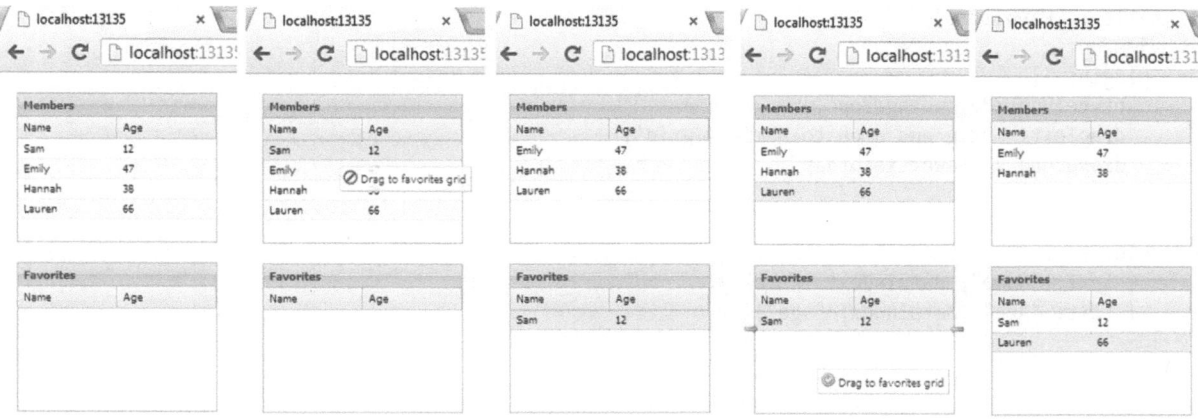

Figure 7-14. *Drag and Drop behavior between two grid panels*

Listing 7-9 shows the code snippet that contains two grids with drag and drop plugin configured along with their group names.

Listing 7-9. Drag and Drop Between Two Grids

```
var store1 = Ext.create("Ext.data.Store", {
  fields: ["name", "age"],
  data: [
    { name: "Sam", age: 12 },
    { name: "Emily", age: 47 },
    { name: "Hannah", age: 38 },
    { name: "Lauren", age: 66 },
  ]
});
var store2 = Ext.create("Ext.data.Store", {
    fields: ["name", "age"],
});
Ext.create("Ext.grid.Panel", {
  store: store1,
  title : "Members",
  viewConfig: {
    plugins: {
      ptype: 'gridviewdragdrop',
      dragText: 'Drag to favorites grid',
      dragGroup : "FavoritesGroup"
    }
  },

  columns: [
    { text: "Name", dataIndex: "name" },
    { text: "Age", dataIndex: "age"}
  ]
});
Ext.create("Ext.grid.Panel", {
  store: store2,
```

```
    title : "Favorites",
    viewConfig: {
     plugins: {
       ptype: 'gridviewdragdrop',
       dragText: 'Drag and drop to Members grid',
       dropGroup : "FavoritesGroup",
     }
    },
    columns: [
      { text: "Name", dataIndex: "name" },
      { text: "Age", dataIndex: "age"}
    ]
});
```

The plugin has two event handler methods: beforedrop and drop. Say you want to move only persons with age greater than 30 years to the favorites grid. You can add a beforedrop event handler to the code snippet in Listing 7-9.

```
Ext.create("Ext.grid.Panel", {
    store: store2,
    title : "Favorites",
    viewConfig: {
     plugins: {
       ptype: 'gridviewdragdrop',
       dragText: 'Drag and drop to Members grid',
       dropGroup : "FavoritesGroup",
     },
     listeners : {
        beforedrop : function(node,data){
          //Assuming only one row is dragged
          var records = data.records;
          var person = records[0];
          if(person.get("age") < 30)
            return false;
        }
     }
    },
    ...
});
```

The beforedrop() method checks the person's age. Returning false in the beforedrop method cancels the drop operation. You can also use the beforedrop() method if you want to perform an asynchronous operation by talking to the server.

Drag and Drop in Tree Panel

Drag and Drop behavior in tree panels is available in the form of a plugin similar to the grid panel. You have a plugin class Ext.tree.plugin.TreeViewDragDrop that can be configured with the tree for enabling drag and drop of nodes. The TreeViewDragDrop plugin with an alias name treeviewdragdrop, needs to be configured in the viewConfig property of the tree panel as shown here.

```
Ext.create("Ext.tree.Panel",{
 viewConfig : {
  plugins : {
    ptype : "treeviewdragdrop"
  }
 }
});
```

The plugin has properties like dragText, dragGroup, and dropGroup and event handler methods like beforedrop and drop similar to the grid DragDrop plugin.

Let's create a tree where the leaf nodes can be dragged and dropped to other child nodes. You cannot drop a leaf node to the root node and non-leaf nodes into other non-leaf nodes. Figure 7-15 shows a draggable tree panel.

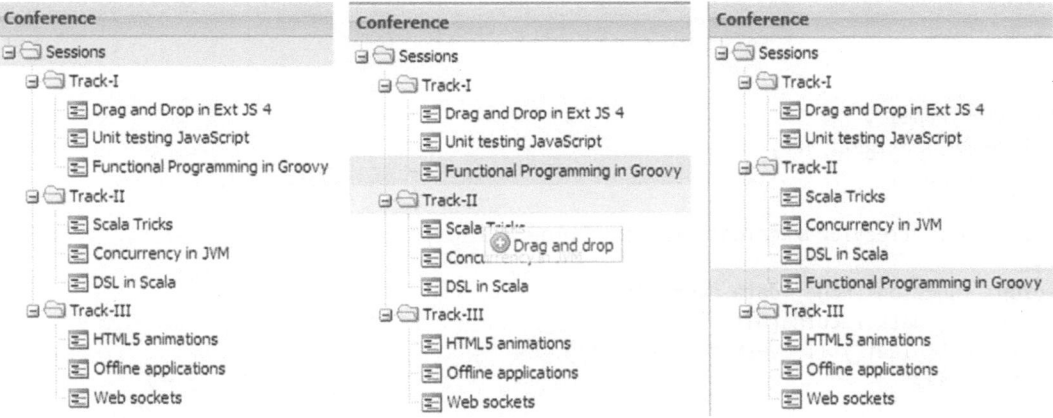

Figure 7-15. *Draggable tree panel*

As shown in Figure 7-15, the *Functional Programming in Groovy* node in Track-I is dragged and dropped to Track-II.

Listing 7-10 shows the code snippet for the drag and drop behavior in tree panels.

Listing 7-10. Drag and Drop in Tree Panels

```
var conferenceStore = Ext.create("Ext.data.TreeStore", {
  root: {
        text: "Sessions",
        children: [
          { text: "Track-I", children:
            [
              { text: "Drag and Drop in Ext JS 4", leaf: true },
              { text: "Unit testing JavaScript", leaf: true },
              { text: "Functional Programming in Groovy", leaf: true }
            ]
          },
```

```
            { text: "Track-II", children:
              [
               { text: "Scala Tricks", leaf: true },
               { text: "Concurrency in JVM", leaf: true },
               { text: "DSL in Scala", leaf: true}
              ]
            },
            { text: "Track-III", children:
              [
                { text: "HTML5 animations", leaf: true },
                { text: "Offline applications", leaf: true },
                { text: "Web sockets", leaf: true}
              ]
            },
         ]
        }
});

Ext.create('Ext.tree.Panel', {
    title: 'Conference', height: 400,
    store: conferenceStore,
    viewConfig: {
      plugins: { ptype: 'treeviewdragdrop',dragText:"Drag and drop" },
      listeners: {
        beforedrop: function (node, data,overModel) {
          var session = data.records[0];
          (!session.get("leaf") || overModel.isRoot())
            return false;
        }
      }
    },
    rootVisible: true
});
```

As shown in Listing 7-10, the beforedrop() method checks if the dragged node is a leaf node and the drop target is not the root element.

Summary

In this chapter I discussed the Drag and Drop API in Ext JS 4. Ext.dd package provides the classes that are used to implement DnD operations. Ext.dd.DragDrop class serves as the base class for all the DnD-related classes. This class provides a number of event handler methods to keep track of the drag operation. You can configure an element to be draggable by creating an instance of Ext.dd.DragSource. A group of elements can be configured as draggable by using the DragZone class. Ext.dd.DropTarget can be used to configure an item as a drop area. Group of elements can be configured as drop targets by using the DropZone class. The grid and tree panels provide gridviewdragdrop and treeviewdragdrop plugins, respectively, for DnD operations.

In the next chapter you will learn about themes in Ext JS 4. I'll discuss the various options used for styling the UI components and creating custom themes.

CHAPTER 8

■ ■ ■

Theming and Styling

You will have noticed by now that the UI components in Ext JS 4 have a common look and feel. The UI components appear with a tinge of light blue in color, by default. The buttons, panels, toolbars, grids, and so on have a uniform appearance. In our applications we may have to customize the appearance of these components. In a traditional UI-based application, this involves modifying the stylesheets of the components. You identify the CSS classes and id(s) of the UI components and start making changes to them.

Customizing the look and feel of the components by modifying their CSS properties, one by one, is an uphill task for a rich UI library like Ext JS 4. Identifying the CSS properties of each and every component that we use in our application and modifying them is very time consuming. In the process of doing this you may end up changing some of the fundamental properties of the UI components like borders, fonts, etc.

While Ext JS 4 provides placeholders for modifying the styles of components programmatically, it offers a much more sophisticated approach than merely changing the CSS properties. Ext JS 4 provides a rich set of extensible and customizable themes. The light blue-colored components belong to the classic theme. You can simply fork a theme and modify the common properties and change the complete look and feel of the components. Now, what's unique about this is that you will not modify the CSS files but work with a bunch of SASS files. You will learn about SASS in a short while.

Ext JS 4 provides a whole new set of tools to customize the look and feel of the application. In this chapter you will learn how to create custom themes for your application. I'll also discuss the basic set of CSS properties of the UI components that can be used to customize them.

Styling

The UI components in Ext JS 4 provide a common set of attributes that can be used to style the components. Table 8-1 shows a list of some CSS attributes that are used while creating the UI components.

Table 8-1. *Styling Attributes*

Attribute	Description
Style	Custom style object provided to the UI elements.
Cls	Used to specify additional CSS class to the component.
baseCls	The fundamental CSS class for the UI components. For example, the base CSS class for panel is x-panel and the base CSS class for button is x-btn. You have to be careful overriding this attribute.
componentCls	Very similar to the cls attribute in purpose. The cls attribute is used while creating instances of UI components, while componentCls is used to specify the CSS classes while defining custom UI classes.
bodyCls	This attribute is available for the container controls like Panel to specify the CSS class for the body region.

Let's write some code using the attributes listed in Table 8-1.

Listing 8-1 shows a simple component that uses the style attribute. The style attribute has some common CSS properties like background color, border width, etc.

Listing 8-1. Using the Style Attribute

```
Ext.create("Ext.Component", {
html: "Sample component",
style : {
  backgroundColor : "yellow",
  width : "100px",
  height : "40px",
  color: 'red',
  padding : "5px",
  borderWidth: "2px",
  borderStyle : "solid",
  borderColor : "black"
 },
});
```

The code fragment in Listing 8-1 shows an instance of a raw component class created using the style attribute. The code emits the following HTML snippet during runtime.

```
<div id="component-1009" class="x-component x-component-default" style="background-
color:yellow;width:100px;height:40px;color:red;padding:5px;border-width:2px;border-
style:solid;border-color:black;">Sample component</div>
```

Let's create an `Ext.panel.Panel` object with the CSS class `mypanel` as shown below.

```
<style>
  .mypanel
  {
    border-width:thick;
    border-style:double;
    font-size:larger;
  }
</style>
```

Listing 8-2 shows the `Panel` instance configured using the CSS class `mypanel`. You can configure the `Panel` using `cls` or `bodyCls` or `baseCls`.

Listing 8-2. A Panel With cls Attribute

```
Ext.create("Ext.panel.Panel", {
   title: "Custom panel",
   html: "Stylized",
   id : "pnl1",
   cls: "mypanel", //or baseCls : "mypanel"  or bodyCls: "mypanel"
});
```

Table 8-2 shows the generated HTML code based on the attributes used in Listing 8-2.

Table 8-2. *Generated HTML Code for the Style Attributes*

Code	Generated HTML
cls : "mypanel"	`<div id="pnl1" class="x-panel `**`mypanel`**` x-panel-default">` ...`</div>`

bodyCls : "mypanel"	`<div id="pnl1" class="x-panel x-panel-default">`
	`<div id="pnl1_header">`...`</div>`
	`<div id="pnl1_body" class="x-panel-body mypanel x-panel-body-default">`...`</div>`
	`</div>`

baseCls : "mypanel"	`<div id="pnl1" class="`**`mypanel`**`">`
	`<div id="pnl1_header" class="`**`mypanel-header`**`">`...`</div>`
	`<div id="pnl1_body" class="mypanel-body">`...`</div>`
	`</div>`

As shown in Table 8-2, configuring the CSS class mypanel in different ways generates different HTML code. Configuring the cls attribute adds mypanel to the existing class attribute of the generated HTML code. The bodyCls attribute just modifies the `<div>` element that represents the body of the panel. The interesting aspect is when you configure baseCls attribute. This attribute replaces the default look and feel of a panel and you may have to be careful in doing so.

As mentioned earlier, modifying the CSS properties of every control that we use in our application is a tedious task. You can customize the themes of the application and provide a uniform look and feel.

Let's discuss the theming concepts in Ext JS 4 and find out how we can customize and build our own themes for the application.

Theming

Ext JS 4 applications use the classic blue theme by default. This theme contains a set of images and a CSS file decorated with the properties for the UI components. The theme can be found in the resources folder of the Ext JS 4 directory as shown in Figure 8-1. It contains a number of CSS files, but what we need is the *ext-theme-classic-all.css* file.

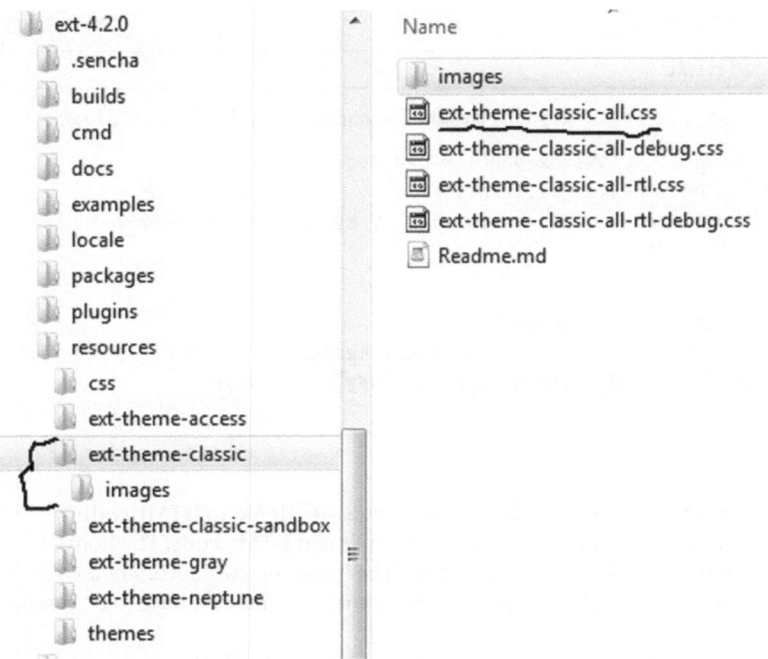

Figure 8-1. *Classic blue theme folder*

The ext-theme-classic-all.css file contains a complex set of CSS rules for the components. It's really difficult to manually edit the properties if we have to customize it. Moreover this CSS file is programmatically generated and not handwritten.

The Ext JS 4 directory contains a folder called packages that contains the *ext-theme-classic* folder as shown in Figure 8-2. This folder is composed of SCSS files.

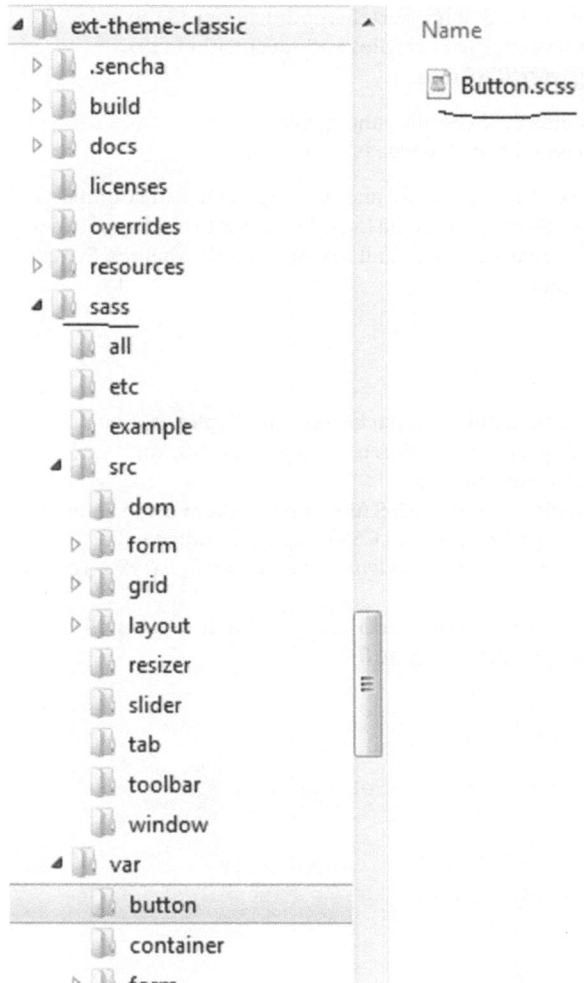

Figure 8-2. ext-theme-classic folder containing SCSS files

The ext-theme-classic folder contains a SASS folder that contains SCSS files. The SCSS files are executed by a Ruby program that produces the CSS files that you use in your Ext JS 4 application. *Therefore, customizing the themes involves playing with the SCSS files.*

Let's briefly introduce Ruby, SASS, SCSS, and Compass before we proceed with creating custom themes.

- **Ruby** is an interpreted, dynamic, and agile programming language. The official site is http://www.ruby-lang.org/en/. You'll need to install a Ruby interpreter v1.9 or above, in your machine to work with the themes.

- **SASS** stands for Syntactically Awesome StyleSheets. The official site is http://sass-lang.com/. It's a style sheet language written in Ruby. You can create stylesheets using SASS syntax and generate CSS3 files by executing them. The SASS syntax provides support for declaring variables, mixins, inheritance, nested rules and so on.

157

- **SCSS** stands for Sassy StyleSheets. It's an extension of SASS. It has certain modifications to the SASS syntax that make the code resemble CSS. You can create SCSS files and execute them to generate CSS3 files. In Ext JS 4 you will be working with SCSS files.

- **Compass** is an open source Ruby library that executes the SCSS files and generates well-formatted CSS files. The official site of Compass is http://compass-style.org/.

Working with themes in Ext JS 4 involves working with the SCSS files provided and running them using Compass. Compass will execute the SCSS files and generate a compressed CSS file that can be included in our Ext JS 4 application.

If you are already wondering about the number of tools you may have to install to work with the themes, Sencha comes to your rescue with a command line tool called Sencha Cmd.

Sencha Cmd

Sencha Cmd is a command line tool provided by Sencha for creating, building, packaging, and deploying Sencha projects. You can create an Ext JS 4 project, package it, and deploy it to production using Sencha Cmd. You can download Sencha Cmd from http://www.sencha.com/products/sencha-cmd.

Sencha Cmd is also used to build custom themes. You can play with the SCSS files and run them using Sencha Cmd. Sencha Cmd internally uses the SASS and Compass libraries and generates CSS files. It is bundled with Compass and SASS libraries also known as gems in the Ruby world. *Therefore, to work with themes in Ext JS 4, you just need to install Ruby and Sencha Cmd in your machine.*

At the time of writing the latest version of Sencha Cmd is 3.1. You can download the executable and install it. After installation, open the command prompt and type sencha as shown in Figure 8-3.

```
C:\>sencha
Sencha Cmd v3.1.0.256
Sencha Cmd provides several categories of commands and some global switches. In
most cases, the first step is to generate an application based on a Sencha SDK
such as Ext JS or Sencha Touch:

    sencha -sdk /path/to/sdk generate app MyApp /path/to/myapp

Sencha Cmd supports Ext JS 4.1.1a and higher and Sencha Touch 2.1 and higher.

To get help on commands use the help command:

    sencha help generate app

For more information on using Sencha Cmd, consult the guides found here:

http://docs.sencha.com/ext-js/4-1/#!/guide/command
http://docs.sencha.com/ext-js/4-2/#!/guide/command
http://docs.sencha.com/touch/2-1/#!/guide/command

Options
  * --cwd, -cw - Sets the directory from which commands should execute
  * --debug, -d - Sets log level to higher verbosity
  * --nologo, -n - Suppress the initial Sencha Cmd version display
  * --plain, -pl - enables plain logging output (no highlighting)
  * --quiet, -q - Sets log level to warnings and errors only
  * --sdk-path, -s - The location of the SDK to use for non-app commands
  * --time, -ti - Display the execution time after executing all commands

Categories
  * app - Perform various application build processes
  * compass - Wraps execution of compass for sass compilation
```

Figure 8-3. Sencha Cmd from Command prompt

I'll explain how to use the commands in Sencha Cmd to generate themes and compile them to CSS files later in this chapter.

You will learn more about Sencha Cmd in Chapter 10, when we discuss packaging and optimizing Ext JS 4 applications.

Basics of SASS

Before we start customizing the Ext JS 4 themes by modifying the SCSS files you need to understand some of the basics of SASS syntax like declaring variables, defining mixins and including mixins. The complete language reference can be found at http://sass-lang.com/docs/yardoc/file.SASS_REFERENCE.html.

Variables

You can declare variables in SCSS with a dollar ($) prefix. Variables help us reuse the style properties. Say you want to generate the CSS content shown in Listing 8-3.

Listing 8-3. Sample CSS Style

```
.mypanel1 {
  color: yellow;
  background-color: red;
  height: 3px;
  width: 3px; }

.mypanel2 {
  color: red;
  background-color: yellow;
  height: 5px;
  width: 2px; }
```

You can generate the CSS data shown in Listing 8-3 by using the SCSS code shown in Listing 8-4.

Listing 8-4. SCSS With Variables

```
$color-yellow : yellow;
$color-red : red;
$width1 : 2px;
$width2 : 3px;
$height1 : 3px;
$heightt2 : 5px;

.mypanel1{
    color : $color-yellow;
    background-color:$color-red;
    height : $height1;
    width : $width2;
}
.mypanel2{
    color : $color-red;
    background-color:$color-yellow;
    height : $height2;
    width : $width1;
}
```

In Listing 8-4 we have declared variables $color-yellow, $color-red, $width1, $width2, $height1, and $height2. These variables are used in the classes mypanel1 and mypanel2. When the SCSS file is executed it generates the CSS files with each variable replaced by its values as shown in Listing 8-3.

Say you have stored the code in Listing 8-4 in panel.scss file. You want to use the override *panel.scss* and create a new SCSS file *custom-panel.scss*. In custom-panel.scss, you want to override the values of the $color-yellow and $color-red variables to a light yellow and light red color. You can create custom-panel.scss like this.

```
$color-yellow : #ffffcc;
$color-red : #ff0a0a;
@import "panel"
```

When the code in custom-panel.scss is executed, $color-yellow and $color-red are assigned the new values. As the panel.scss is imported, the $color-yellow and $color-red variables get reassigned to the original yellow and red values as defined in the panel.scss file. In order to make the variables use the overridden values, you have to modify the variables declaration in Listing 8-4 like this.

```
$color-yellow : yellow !default;
$color-red : red !default;
```

The !default flag added to the variables indicate that the variables will be initialized only if they haven't been yet. In our example, as these variables get initialized in custom-panel.scss they are not re-initialized later. Running the *custom-panel.scss* will give you the CSS code shown in Listing 8-3 with the modifications to the color properties as shown here.

```
.mypanel1 {
  color: #ffffcc;
  background-color: #ff0a0a;
  height: 3px;
  width: 3px; }

.mypanel2 {
  color: #ff0a0a;
  background-color: #ffffcc;
  height: 5px;
  width: 2px; }
```

Mixins

Mixins in SCSS are similar to the #define directives that are used in C programming language. They let you define and re-use a chunk of CSS code. You can define a mixin with a name and arguments using the following syntax.

```
@mixin nameOfTheMixin(comma separated arguments){
}
```

You can include the mixin using @include like this.

```
@include nameOfTheMixin(argument values);
```

Listing 8-5 shows the SCSS code for generating the CSS content shown in Listing 8-3.

Listing 8-5. SCSS Using Mixins

```
$color-yellow : yellow;
$color-red : red;
$width1 : 2px;
$width2 : 3px;
$height1 : 3px;
$heightt2 : 5px;

@mixin panel($classname,$color,$bgcolor,$height,$width){
  .#{$classname}{
     color : $color;
     background-color:$bgcolor;
     height : $height;
     width : $width;
  }
}

@include panel('mypanel1',$color-yellow,$color-red,$height1,$width2);
@include panel('mypanel2',$color-red,$color-yellow,$height2,$width1);
```

In the code snippet in Listing 8-5, we have a mixin called panel defined. We invoke the panel mixin using @include by passing the class name and the arguments. The variable $classname is accessed using #{}, which is called the interpolation syntax.

In Listing 8-5 you can modify the @include syntax to improve readability by specifying the name of the arguments while passing the values like this.

```
@include panel($classname:'mypanel1',
          $color:$color-yellow,
          $bgcolor:$color-red,
          $height:$height1,
          $width:$width2);

@include panel($classname:'mypanel2',
             $color:$color-red,
             $bgcolor:$color-yellow,
             $height:$height2,
             $width:$width1);
```

That concludes this brief explanation of the basics of the SASS language. If you have installed Ruby and Sencha Cmd, let's start creating custom themes for our Ext JS 4 application.

Creating Custom Themes

As I said earlier, we are going to modify the SCSS files of the UI components and run them using Sencha Cmd, which will generate a CSS file. Modifying the SCSS files involves modifying the variables and including the mixins provided for the components. For instance if I have to modify the values for the SCSS variables for the Ext.button.Button class, you can create a *Button.scss* file in the *button* folder and provide values for the variables. You can get the variables list from the API documentation. Figure 8-4 shows the API documentation for the Button class, which has the CSS vars and mixins.

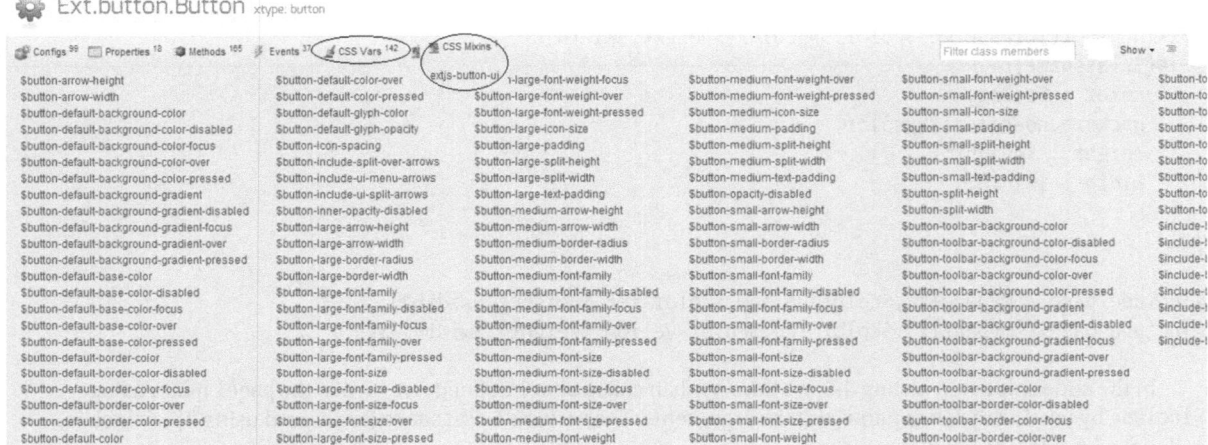

Figure 8-4. *CSS vars and mixins for the Button class*

Figure 8-4 shows the list of CSS vars and mixins of the Button class. All these variables have some default values that you can modify in the Button.scss file.

We know that all the UI components inherit from the Ext.Component class. Component.scss provides a global list of variables and mixins. The values of these variables can be changed, which will result in the change in the appearance of all the UI components. Figure 8-5 shows the list of CSS vars and mixins in the Component class. They are available in the documentation as Global_CSS.

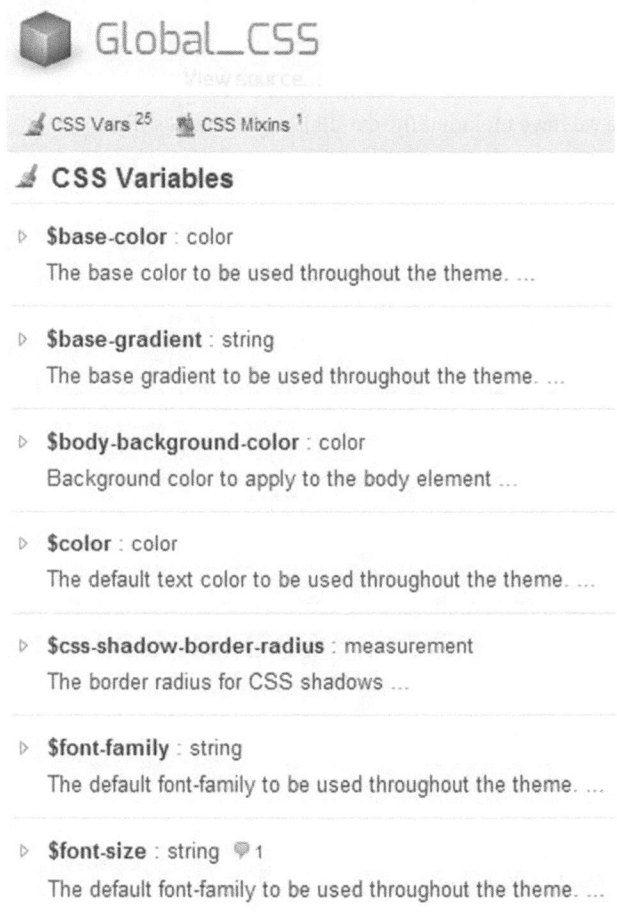

Figure 8-5. *Global_CSS*

Let's create an Ext JS 4 application called *ThemingAndStyling* that uses the default classic theme. We will create a page that uses a `Panel` with a `Textfield` and `Button`. We'll create a custom theme and use it in this application. Figure 8-6 shows the project structure.

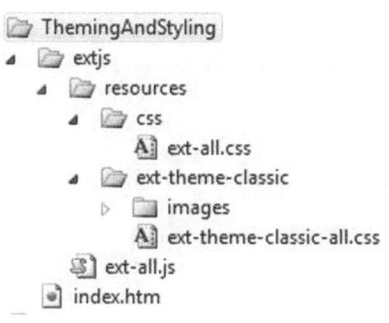

Figure 8-6. *ThemingAndStyling application*

The *ext-all.css* file just imports the *ext-theme-classic-all.css* file like this.

```
@import '../ext-theme-classic/ext-theme-classic-all.css';
```

Listing 8-6 shows the code in index.htm file. In this file we have included the ext-all.js and ext-all.css files.

Listing 8-6. index.htm

```
<!DOCTYPE html>
<html>
<head>
<link href="extjs/resources/css/ext-all.css" rel="stylesheet" type="text/css" />
<script src="extjs/ext-all.js"></script>
<script>
  Ext.onReady(function () {
    Ext.create("Ext.panel.Panel", {
      title: "Theme panel",
      items: [
              { xtype:"textfield",fieldLabel:"First name" },
              { xtype : "button",text:"Submit"}
      ],
      renderTo: Ext.getBody()
    });
 });
</script>
</head>
<body>
</body>
</html>
```

The code snippet in Listing 8-6 provides the output shown in Figure 8-7.

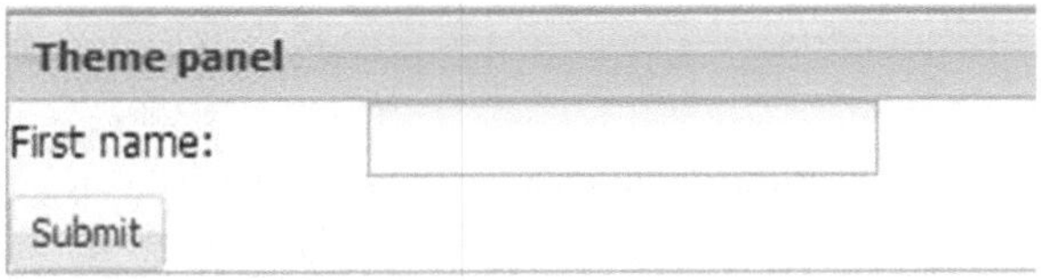

Figure 8-7. *Output of index.htm that Uses Classic Theme*

Let's create a custom theme and play with the options available. We'll use the Sencha Cmd to generate a custom theme. Sencha Cmd provides commands for creating a workspace, project, themes, etc. You can create a workspace, then a project, and then generate a theme for the project. To keep things simple, we'll focus on creating a custom theme and apply it to the *ThemingAndStyling* application that we have created.

Let's generate a theme called **my-theme1**. Let's open the command prompt and go to the Ext JS 4 directory and run the following command to generate the theme.

```
sencha generate theme my-theme1
```

Figure 8-8 shows the command run in the command prompt window.

```
C:\ext-4.2.0>sencha generate theme my-theme1
Sencha Cmd v3.1.0.256
[INF]
[INF]  init-plugin:
[INF]
[INF]  init-plugin:
[INF]  Invoking plugin (C:\ext-4.2.0\.sencha\workspace\plugin.xml) - suppor
rgets: -before-generate-theme
[INF]
[INF]  -before-generate-theme:
[INF]  Invoking plugin (C:\ext-4.2.0\.sencha\workspace\plugin.xml) - suppor
rgets: generate-theme
[INF]
[INF]  cmd-root-plugin.init-properties:
[INF]
[INF]  init-properties:
[INF]
[INF]  init-sencha-command:
[INF]
[INF]  init:
[INF]
[INF]  -before-generate-theme:
[INF]
[INF]  generate-theme-impl:
[INF]
[INF]  init-plugin:
[INF]
[INF]  init-plugin:
[INF]  Invoking plugin (C:\ext-4.2.0\.sencha\workspace\plugin.xml) - suppor
rgets: -before-generate-package
```

Figure 8-8. *Generating my-theme1 from command prompt*

In the Ext JS 4 directory, under the packages folder you will notice a folder called my-theme1 generated. The contents of the *my-theme1* folder are shown in Figure 8-9.

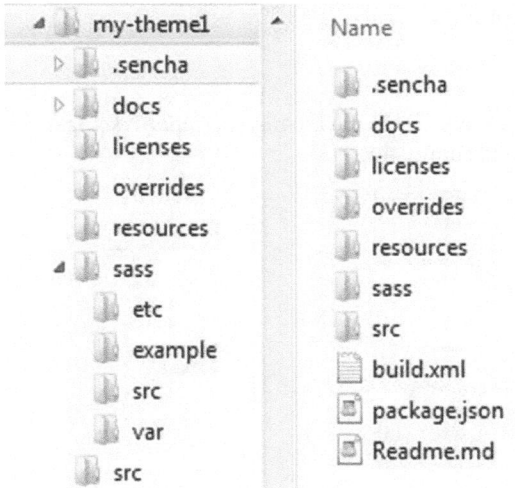

Figure 8-9. *Contents of my-theme1 folder*

As shown in Figure 8-9, what's interesting and important is the *sass* folder. The sass folder contains various other folders where we'll create the SCSS files.

- *var* folder will contain the definitions of the variables of the UI components

- *src* folder will contain the @include calls to the mixins and SASS rules.

- *etc* folder will contain additional SASS mixins and other utility functions.

The *resources* folder will contain the images that you want to use for the components.

165

The *package.json* file in my-theme1 folder serves as the manifest for the theme. It contains information like the name, version, base theme, etc. The contents of the package.json file are shown below.

```
{
    "name": "my-theme1",
    "type": "theme",
    "creator": "anonymous",
    "version": "1.0.0",
    "compatVersion": "1.0.0",
    "local": true,
    "requires": [],
    "extend": "ext-theme-classic"
}
```

As you will notice, the *ext-theme-classic* serves as the base theme for our *my-theme1* theme.

Let's start defining our SCSS files. Say we want to change the font size and font family of all the components. Let's create a *Component.scss* file *my-theme1/sass/var folder*. We'll use the CSS variables $font-size and $font-family as shown in Listing 8-7.

Listing 8-7. Component.scss File

```
$font-size:18px !default;
$font-family:Courier New !default;
```

Let's build our theme now that'll generate a modified CSS file using the SCSS file we've created. You can run the following command from the *my-theme1* directory in the command prompt.

```
sencha package build
```

The build command will invoke the compass library and generate CSS files in the *my-theme1/build/resources* folder. Figure 8-10 shows the command prompt where we run the build command.

```
C:\ext-4.2.0\packages\my-theme1>sencha package build
Sencha Cmd v3.1.0.256
[INF]
[INF] init-plugin:
[INF]
[INF] init-plugin:
[INF] Invoking plugin (C:\ext-4.2.0\packages\my-theme1\.sencha\package\plu
1) - supported targets: -before-pkg-build
[INF]
[INF] -before-pkg-build:
[INF] Invoking plugin (C:\ext-4.2.0\packages\my-theme1\.sencha\package\plu
1) - supported targets: pkg-build
[INF]
[INF] cmd-root-plugin.init-properties:
[INF]
[INF] init-properties:
[INF]
[INF] init-sencha-command:
[INF]
[INF] init:
[INF]
[INF] -before-pkg-build:
[INF]
[INF] pkg-build-impl:
[INF]
[INF] init-local:
[INF]
[INF] -before-init-local:
[INF]
[INF] -after-init-local:
[INF]
[INF] find-cmd:
[INF]
```

Figure 8-10. *Building my-theme1*

166

The CSS files and images are generated in the *build/resources* folder. The contents of *my-theme1/build/resources* are shown in Figure 8-11.

Figure 8-11. *Contents of my-theme1/build/resources folder*

As shown in Figure 8-11, we need to add the *my-theme1-all.css* file and the *images* folder in our *ThemingAndStyling* application. Let's modify the ThemingAndStyling application to include my-theme1 as shown in Figure 8-12.

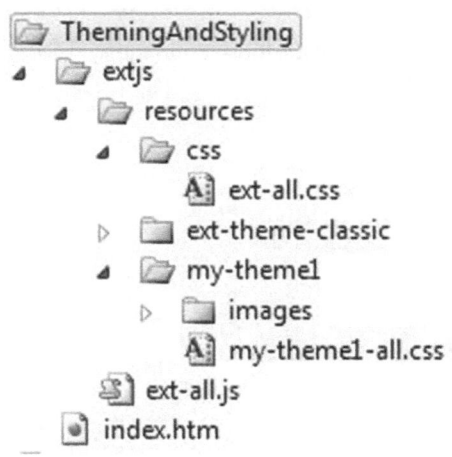

Figure 8-12. *ThemingAndStyling application with my-theme1*

We've created a *my-theme1* folder in *ThemingAndStyling/resources* folder and included the *my-theme1-all.css* file and images folder. Let's modify the ext-all.css to import the *my-theme1-all.css* file like this.

```
@import '../my-theme1/my-theme1-all.css';
```

Running index.htm will show you the output with modified font size and font family as shown in Figure 8-13.

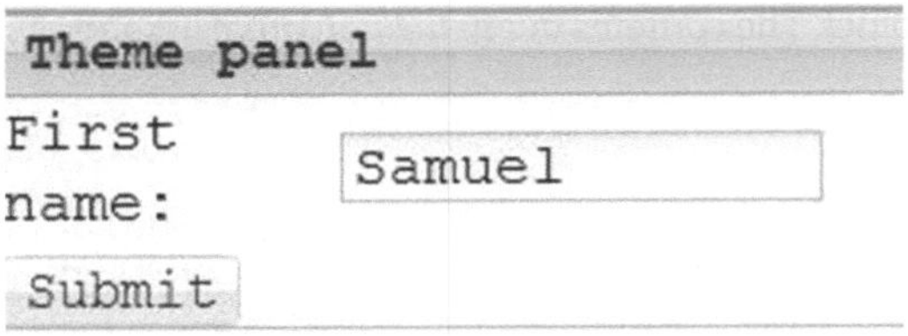

Figure 8-13. *Output of index.htm that uses my-theme1*

Let's modify the style of the textfield. You can find out the CSS vars from the documentation for the
`Ext.form.field.Text` class. In the *my-theme1/sass/var* folder let's create a *form/field* folder and *Text.scss* in inside it.
We'll modify some CSS variables of the Text class as shown in Listing 8-8.

Listing 8-8. Text.scss

```
$form-field-border-style:groove !default;
$form-field-color:red !default;
$form-field-font-weight: italic !default;
$form-field-font-size: 12px !default;
$form-field-height: 16px !default;
```

We have modified the border style, color, textbox height, and the weight and size of the fonts. Build the `my-theme1`
package to produce a modified *my-theme1-all.css* file. You will get the output shown in Figure 8-14.

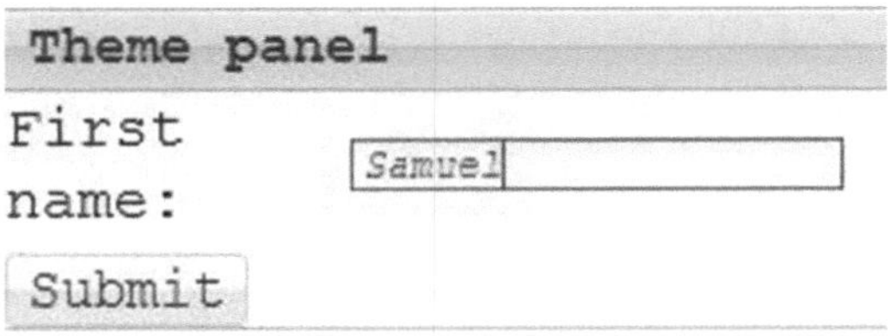

Figure 8-14. *Output of index.htm with modified textfield theme*

I've discussed modifying the *Component* class and *Text* class variables. Let's include a mixin with custom values
now. We'll include the mixin for the `Ext.panel.Panel` class. The Panel class documentation shows that it has a CSS
mixin `extjs-panel-ui`. Let's include this mixin with default values. We'll create a new panel `ui` style called 'cool'. Let's
create a Panel.scss file in *sass/src/panel* folder. The contents of Panel.scss are shown in Listing 8-9.

Listing 8-9. Panel.scss

```
@include extjs-panel-ui(
    $ui-label: 'cool',
    $ui-border-color: black,
    $ui-border-width: 3px,
    $ui-border-radius: 3px,

    $ui-header-font-family: Times New Roman,
    $ui-header-font-size: 16px,
    $ui-header-font-weight: bold,
```

```
    $ui-header-color: white,
    $ui-header-background-color: black,

    $ui-header-border-color: black,
    $ui-header-border-width: 3px,
    $ui-header-padding: 2px,

    $ui-body-border-width: 5px,
    $ui-body-border-color: black,
    $ui-body-background-color: yellow
);
```

As shown in Listing 8-9, we include the extjs-panel-ui mixin by passing various arguments. We create a ui label called cool, as mentioned earlier. We have modified the background color and color of the header and body of the panel.

After running the sencha build command again and updating the *my-theme1-all.css* in our application, let's make a change to the panel instance in index.htm. We will add a ui attribute to the code in Listing 8-6 like this.

```
Ext.create("Ext.panel.Panel", {
    title: "Theme panel",
    ui : "cool",
    items: [ ... ]
    ...
});
```

Executing the index.htm will produce an output with a modified look and feel of the panel as shown in Figure 8-15.

Figure 8-15. *Output of index.htm with modified Panel panel theme*

Summary

In this chapter, I explained the basic styling attributes of the UI components. You have configuration attributes like cls, bodyCls, baseCls, style, etc. to manipulate the style of the components. Ext JS 4 applications use ready-made themes, such as a classic theme which is the default. Working with themes in Ext JS 4 involves working with the SASS language. You can customize the themes by modifying the SCSS files and running them using the Sencha Cmd tool. Sencha Cmd executes the SCSS files and generates the CSS files. Modifying the SCSS files involves modifying the variables and including the mixins.

In the next chapter you will learn about MVC architecture in Ext JS 4. I'll show you how to develop Ext JS 4 applications by applying the MVC architecture.

■ ■ ■

CHAPTER 9

MVC with Ext JS 4

Working with JavaScript libraries poses an important challenge to developers in the form of lack of modularity. JavaScript does not provide any facility to modularize the code, unlike languages like Java that provide concepts like packages to organize our code. Creating and developing applications in JavaScript usually leads to code that is very hard to maintain and reuse. One of the significant advantages of Ext JS 4 is the ability to create maintainable code by providing a template to implement the Model-View-Controller (MVC) architecture.

Ext JS 4 helps you to develop applications that implement the MVC architecture. You can segregate your code into Models, Views, and Controllers and build an application that can be maintained easily. This approach also paves way for extensibility and reusability, usually rare in JavaScript applications.

In this chapter you'll learn to develop Ext JS 4 applications that implement the MVC architecture. We'll discuss the API support for implementing MVC architecture and build an application using MVC.

A Short Introduction to MVC

Most Java, C#, Rails, or Grails developers who have built Web applications will be aware of the MVC architecture. It's a widely adapted software pattern in Web applications. If you know the basics of MVC, you can safely skip this section.

MVC is a simple mechanism by which you organize your code into three categories: the models, views and controllers.

The View entity represents the UI or the display. It's the UI component (such as a form) that the user interacts with. The user interacts with the View and provides input. A View accepts input from the user and displays output to the user.

The Model entity represents the data models. It contains the data and business logic. The View populates the Model with user input and pulls out the data from the Models and displays it to the users.

The Controller entity controls the flow in the application. It takes in the input from the Views, gives it to the Models and creates the output View and gives it to the users. You can read more about MVC at http://en.wikipedia.org/wiki/Model-view-controller.

MVC API in Ext JS 4

As mentioned earlier Ext JS 4 application is organized into models, views and controllers. Table 9-1 shows the classes that make up the models, views and controllers.

Table 9-1. *The Models, Views and Controller Classes*

Entity	Class	Description
Model	Ext.data.Model	The Model classes that are used in data handling. Custom Ext JS 4 classes with business logic also fall under this category.
View	Ext.Component	All the Ext.Component classes fall under the View category.
Controller	Ext.app.Controller	This class serves as the controllers where you write the event handling and navigation logic.

Ext.app.Controller Class

All the controller classes that we create will extend the Ext.app.Controller class. We will manage the views and models in the controller classes. There are no hard and fast rules on the number of controllers that you can create. Practically you will have a controller for a group of related operations or a use case. For instance, you can have a Controller class for user authentication related operations like login, logout, forgotten password, etc. The Controller class provides a number of useful attributes and methods. Here's a list of attributes in the Controller class.

- The models attribute represents an array of Model names that will be loaded before instantiating the Controller.

- The stores attribute represents an array of Store names that will be loaded before instantiating the Controller

- The views attribute represents an array of View component names that will be loaded before instantiating the Controller.

- The refs attribute represents an array of references to UI components. Each reference has a reference variable name and an expression to resolve the UI component. The expression is resolved by the Ext.ComponentQuery class. The variable names will have a getter method generated automatically. For example, in the statement refs: [{ref:"username",selector:"#usernametext field"}], the *username* ref refers to the UI component with an id usernametextfield. You'll have a getUsername() method generated automatically to access the component

Table 9-2 shows the list of methods in the Controller class.

Table 9-2. *Methods in Controller Class*

Method	Description
Init	Acts like a constructor of the Controller class. It's called even before the Ext.Viewport is created.

Control	This method is used to add event handlers for the UI components. The general format of this method is
	
	`"component selector expression" : {`
	`eventName : this.eventHandlerFunction`
	`}`
	
	The component selector expression is resolved by Ext.ComponentQuery class.

getApplication	Used to access the Ext.app.Application instance. I'll discuss the Application class in detail later.
getStore	This method is used to access the Store instance. If the store instance is not available, a new instance is created and returned.

Listing 9-1 shows a skeleton of Controller class definition.

Listing 9-1. Custom Controller Class

```
Ext.define("MyController",{
  extend : "Ext.app.Controller",
  refs : [
      {ref:"referenceVariable1", selector:"component selector expression"},
      {ref:"referenceVariable2", selector:"component selector expression"},
  ],
  models : [],
  stores : [],
  views : [],
  init : function(){
    this.control({
        "component selector expression1" : {
          eventName : this.eventHandlerFunction1
        },
        "component selector expression2" : {
          eventName : this.eventHandlerFunction2
        }
      },
    });
  },
  eventHandlerFunction1 : function(){},
  eventHandlerFunction2 : function(){}
});
```

As shown in Listing 9-1, the MyController class extends Ext.app.Controller and overrides the init() method. We've registered the events with event handler functions using control() method. The MyController class has the views, models, stores, and refs attributes. I'll discuss a practical example where you can create controller classes later in this chapter.

Ext.app.Application Class

The Models, Views, Stores and Controllers in an Ext JS 4 application are brought together by Ext.app.Application class. This class represents the complete application. The Application instance binds all the entities of an Ext JS 4 application.

You can create an instance of the Application class by using Ext.application() method. Listing 9-2 shows the code for instantiating an Application object.

Listing 9-2. Creating an Application

```
Ext.application({
  name : "NameOfTheApplication",
  appFolder : "",
  controllers : [],
  launch : function(){

  }
});
```

In the code snippet shown in Listing 9-2, an Application object is created when we call `Ext.application()` method.

- The `Ext.application()` method is configured with a `name` attribute that represents the name of the application. This name also serves as the root namespace for all the classes in our application.

- The `appFolder` attribute is supplied with the folder that contains all the MVC classes. The `appFolder` has a value called "*app*" by default.

- The `controllers` array is supplied with the list of `Controller` names that are loaded and instantiated before the `Application` object is created.

- The `launch()` method is the last piece of code to be executed. You can create the root view instance usually a `Viewport`, in this method.

At any point of time in your application, you can access the instance of the `Application` class by calling the `getApplication()` method on the root namespace. For example, if you have written `Ext.application({name:"MVC"})`, you can get the instance of `Application` by calling **MVC.getApplication()** method.

You can access the models, stores, views, and controllers using the `getModel()`, `getStore()`, `getView()`, and `getController()` methods, respectively, on the `Application` instance.

We discussed that the models, views, stores, and controllers are configured in arrays and are loaded before the Application instance is created. So, where are these entities loaded from? As mentioned earlier, the appFolder contains all these entities. If your appFolder attribute is configured as *Chapter09,* the application structure will look as shown in Figure 9-1.

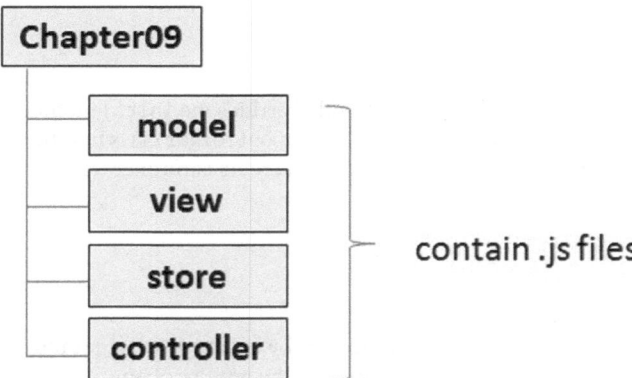

Figure 9-1. *Structure of an MVC application*

Let's build an application using MVC architecture. For brevity's sake we will keep it simple and focus on the important concepts. Figure 9-2 shows the screen shots of the application we will develop. It has a login page and a home page. On clicking the login button in the login page, the home page is displayed. The home page displays has a placeholder for displaying a menu at the top of the page. The body of the home page displays a data grid and the details of each row in the grid.

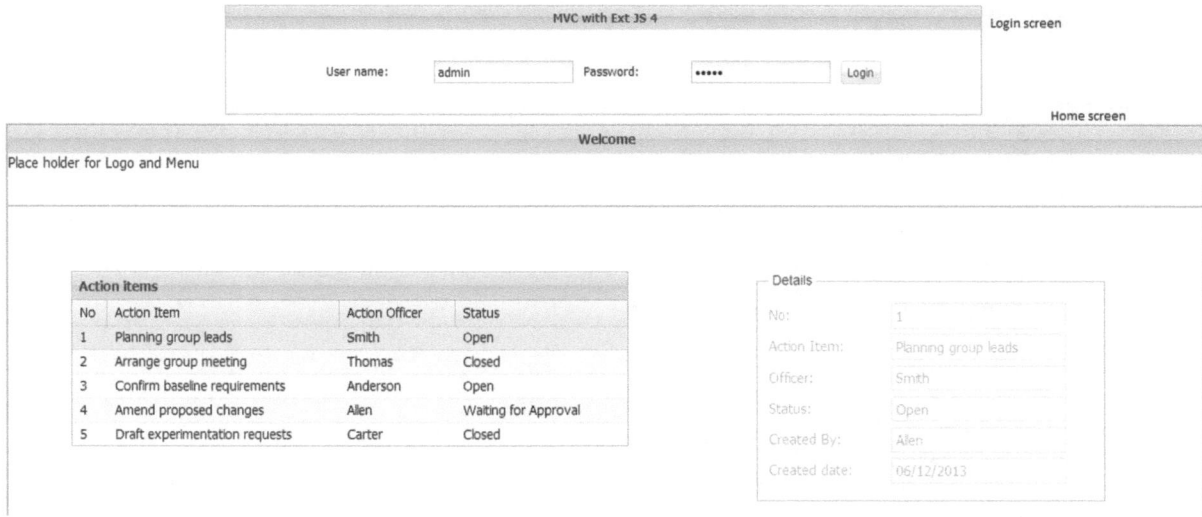

Figure 9-2. Sample MVC application

Let's split the application into views, models, stores, and controllers as shown in the list below.

- We have two main view entities login screen and home screen.

- The login screen has the basic login form. We will define this view in a class say **LoginScreen**.

- The home screen is composed of a grid Panel and a panel where we display the details. The grid panel displays the project action items. The details panel displays the detail of every action item. Let's define the view for the home in a class **HomeScreen**. We'll define the grid and details panel in separate classes **ProjectActionItemGrid** and **ProjectActionItemDetailsPanel**.

- We can create a controller for login screen where we have the event handling logic for the login button and navigation logic to navigate to the home screen. Let's define a controller called **LoginController** for this purpose.

- We'll create a controller for handling the logic like populating the grid and displaying the details of an action item in the panel, whenever a row in the grid is selected. Let's define a controller called **HomeController** for this purpose.

- Let's define a model class **ProjectActionItem** and a store **ProjectActionItemStore** to load the list of all action items. We'll have the sample data for the action items in a file **actionitems.txt**.

Now that we have a basic idea of the list of classes that we may need for implementing this application, let's create an application with the folder structure for storing all these classes in individual files. Let's create an Ext JS 4 application called **MVCWithExtJS4** with all the entities stored in a folder called app. Figure 9-3 shows the structure of the application MVCWithExtJS4 with all the files created.

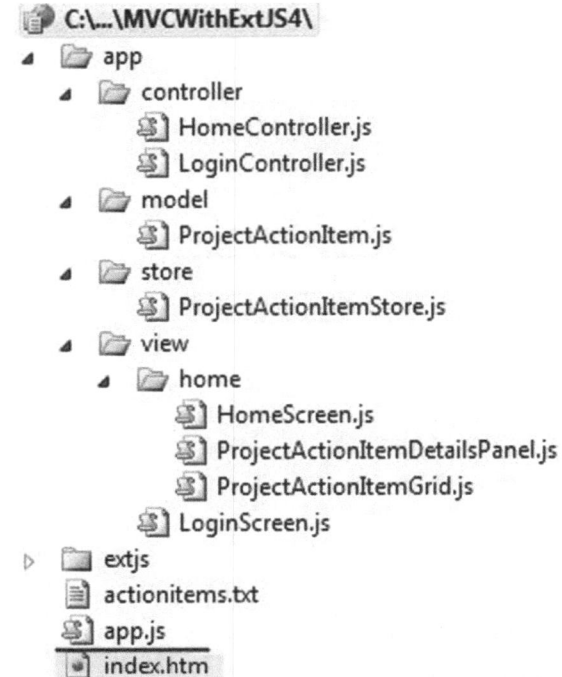

Figure 9-3. *Structure of MVCWithExtJS4 application*

You can generate the application using Sencha Cmd, which will create the basic folder structure along with the index.htm and app.js files. We can build our components using the structure created. You will learn about generating a sample application using Sencha Cmd in Chapter 10. In this chapter you can create the application and the folder structure manually.

There are different ways to implement this application using MVC architecture. As our focus is to learn the nuances of MVC architecture in Ext JS 4, we'll keep it simple so that it's easier to understand the concepts.

Let's start coding with the index.htm file as shown in Listing 9-3.

Listing 9-3. index.htm

```
<!DOCTYPE html>
<html>
<head>
    <link href="extjs/resources/css/ext-all.css" rel="stylesheet" type="text/css" />
    <script src="extjs/ext-all.js"></script>
    <script src="app.js"></script>
</head>
<body>
</body>
</html>
```

In the code above we have added the reference to the ext-all.css, ext-all.js, and app.js files. When you use Sencha Cmd to create the project, the index.htm is automatically created with the reference to these files added. As mentioned earlier, you'll learn about Sencha Cmd in Chapter 10.

The next step is to create the app.js file and configure the `Ext.app.Application` object. Listing 9-4 shows the code snippet for app.js file.

Listing 9-4. app.js

```
Ext.Loader.setConfig({ enabled: true });

Ext.application({
  name: "Chapter09",
  appFolder: "app",
  controllers: ["LoginController","HomeController"],
  launch: function () {
    this.viewport = Ext.create("Ext.container.Viewport", {
      renderTo: Ext.getBody(),
      layout: "card",
      items: [
        //We'll add the view later
      ]
  });
    }
});
```

Here's a description of the contents of the app.js file.

- The first line of app.js has the `Ext.Loader` configured to load the dependent JavaScript files. This line enables loading of the controller, model, view, and store files.

- The name of the application is configured to be *Chapter09*. The root namespace of all the classes that we create in this application henceforth will be Chapter09.

- We have configured the LoginController and HomeController files in the controllers array.

- In the `launch()` function, we have created an instance of `Ext.container.Viewport` class with a `card` layout and rendered it to the body of the page. The items array of the Viewport is empty right now. We'll add the items once we complete the creation of the views.

- The `Viewport` instance is assigned to a variable called `viewport` in the `Application` instance. The code `this.viewport = Ext.create("Ext.container.Viewport",{...})` creates an instance of Viewport class and assigns to a viewport variable. You can now access the Viewport instance from anywhere in the application by writing `this.application.viewport`

Let's build the application by developing the data components first.

Developing the data components

Our application involves loading JSON data from the server and displaying it in a grid panel. The data provides the list of action items in a project. Each action item has a serial number, description of the item, creation date, status, and the names of the officer and the person who created it. We'll define this JSON data in *actionitems.txt* file as shown in Listing 9-5.

Listing 9-5. actionitems.txt

```
{
    "actionitems" : [
        {"sno":1,"item":"Planning group leads","officer":"Smith","status":"Open","createdby":"Allen","
createddate":"06/12/2013"},
        {"sno":2,"item":"Arrange group meeting ","officer":"Thomas","status":"Closed","createdby":
"Thomas","createddate":"05/28/2013"},
        {"sno":3,"item":"Confirm baseline requirements","officer":"Anderson","status":"Open","createdby
":"Carter","createddate":"06/14/2013"},
        {"sno":4,"item":"Amend proposed changes","officer":"Allen","status":"Waiting for Approval",
"createdby":"Yong","createddate":"06/27/2013"},
        {"sno":5,"item":"Draft experimentation requests","officer":"Carter","status":"Closed",
"createdby":"Turner","createddate":"06/01/2013"}
    ]
}
```

Let's define the Model class for the project action item. Listing 9-6 shows the ProjectActionItem model class defined with the fields.

Listing 9-6. ProjectActionItem.js

```
Ext.define("Chapter09.model.ProjectActionItem", {
    extend : "Ext.data.Model",
    fields : ["sno","item","officer","status","createdby","createddate"]
});
```

Let's define the Store class for loading the data from actionitems.txt file. Listing 9-7 shows the ProjectActionItemStore class. The Store class is defined using an Ajax proxy and a JSON reader. We will configure the autoLoad attribute to be false for the store. Later in our Controller class we'll populate the store dynamically.

Listing 9-7. ProjectActionItemStore.js

```
Ext.define("Chapter09.store.ProjectActionItemStore", {
    extend: "Ext.data.Store",
    model: "Chapter09.model.ProjectActionItem",
    proxy: {
        type: "ajax",
        url: "actionitems.txt",
        reader: {
            type : "json",
            root : "actionitems"
        }
    }
});
```

Let's build the view classes now.

Developing the View Components

Let's create the login screen with the username and password text fields and a login button. We'll not handle any event in this view class. Listing 9-8 shows the code snippet for login screen.

Listing 9-8. LoginScreen.js

```
Ext.define("Chapter09.view.LoginScreen", {
    extend: "Ext.form.Panel",
    xtype: "login",
    layout: {
        type : "hbox",
        pack : "center",
        align : "middle"
    },
    defaults : {margin:5},
    title: "MVC with Ext JS 4",
    titleAlign: "center",
    padding : 250,
    items: [
        {
            xtype: "textfield",
            id: "usernametext",
            fieldLabel: "User name"
        },
        {
            xtype: "textfield",
            id: "passwordtext",
            fieldLabel: "Password",
            inputType: "password"
        },
        {
            xtype: "button",
            id: "loginbutton",
            text: "Login"
        }
    ]
});
```

In Listing 9-8 we have a defined a class LoginScreen with login as the xtype. The LoginScreen class inherits the Ext.panel.Panel class and is configured to have a horizontal box layout.

In our application we have a login screen and a home screen. The home screen contains the grid panel and the detail panel. We'll define the grid panel in a separate class. Listing 9-9 shows the ProjectActionItemGrid class that extends the Ext.grid.Panel class.

Listing 9-9. ProjectActionItemGrid.js

```
Ext.define("Chapter09.view.home.ProjectActionItemGrid", {
    extend: "Ext.grid.Panel",
    xtype: "projectactionitemgrid",
    title: "Action items",
    store: null,
    columns: [
```

```
                   { header: "No", dataIndex: "sno", width: 30 },
                   { header: "Action Item", dataIndex: "item", width: 200 },
                   { header: "Action Officer", dataIndex: "officer" },
                   { header: "Status", dataIndex: "status", width: 150 }
              ]
});
```

As shown in Listing 9-9, the code contains the ProjectActionItemGrid class. The xtype of the class is configured to be projectactionitemgrid. The class contains the columns configured. We have configured the store to be null. You can wire up the ProjectActionItemStore with the store attribute, but it's better to remove the coupling and wire up the store dynamically using the reconfigure() method of the grid panel class.

Listing 9-10 shows the ProjectActionItemDetailsPanel class, which is the detailed panel where you will display the details of the project action item.

Listing 9-10. ProjectActionItemDetailsPanel.js

```
Ext.define("Chapter09.view.home.ProjectActionItemDetailsPanel", {
    extend : "Ext.form.Panel",
    xtype: "projectactionitemdetails",
    border: false,
    items: [
        {
          xtype: "fieldset", title: "Details",
          defaults: { xtype: "textfield", disabled: true },
          items: [
                { name: "sno", fieldLabel: "No" },
                { name: "item", fieldLabel: "Action Item" },
                { name: "officer", fieldLabel: "Officer" },
                { name: "status", fieldLabel: "Status" },
                { name: "createdby", fieldLabel: "Created By" },
                { name: "createddate", fieldLabel: "Created date" },
          ]
        }
    ]
});
```

As shown in Listing 9-10, the code contains the ProjectActionItemDetailsPanel class. The xtype of the class is configured to be projectactionitemdetails. This class extends Ext.form.Panel class and has a fieldset and textfields where we'll display the details of the project action item. The textfield components in this class have the name attribute configured to be the field name in the ProjectActionItem model class.

Let's create a HomeScreen class that's composed of the ProjectActionItemGrid and ProjectActionItemDetailsPanel instances as shown in Listing 9-11.

Listing 9-11. HomeScreen.js

```
Ext.define("Chapter09.view.home.HomeScreen", {
    extend: "Ext.panel.Panel",
    xtype: "home",
    layout: "border",
    padding: 30,
    items: [
```

```
        { region: "north", height: 70,
          title:"Welcome",titleAlign:"center",
          html: "Place holder for Logo and Menu"
        },
        {
          region: "center",
          items: [
            {
              xtype: "panel", layout: "hbox",
              defaults: { margin: 5, padding: 50 },
              border: false,
              items: [
                { xtype: "projectactionitemgrid", width: 580 },
                { xtype: "projectactionitemdetails", width: 400, height: 400 }
              ]
            }
          ]
        }
      ]
    },
  ]
});
```

As shown in Listing 9-11, the code contains the HomeScreen class. The xtype of the class is configured to be home. This class extends Ext.panel.Panel class and is configured with a border layout with the north and center regions. The north region can be configured with a menu, logo, etc. We have left this region intentionally blank for brevity's sake.

The center region of the HomeScreen contains a panel that has the projectactionitemgrid and the projectionactionitemdetails instances.

We have created the *ProjectActionItemGrid.js*, *ProjectActionItemDetailsPanel.js* and *HomeScreen.js* in the *view/home* folder. You'll notice that the namespace of these classes are Chapter09.view.home.

Let's bind the model, store and the view classes together by creating the controller classes.

Developing the Controller Components

Listing 9-12 shows the LoginController class, which has the authenticate() function that'll be called when login button is clicked. This method will just check if the credentials are equal to **admin**. If the authentication is successful, you will display the home screen. You'll display an error dialog otherwise.

Listing 9-12. LoginController.js

```
Ext.define("Chapter09.controller.LoginController", {
    extend: "Ext.app.Controller",
    refs: [
        { ref: "userName", selector: "login textfield[id=usernametext]" },
        { ref: "password", selector: "#passwordtext" }
    ],
    views: ["LoginScreen"],
    init: function () {
        this.control({
            "#loginbutton": {
                click: this.authenticate
            }
        });
    },
```

```
        authenticate: function () {
            if (this.getUserName().getValue() == "admin" &&
                this.getPassword().getValue() == "admin") {
                this.application.viewport.add({ xtype: "home", id: "homescreen"});
                this.application.viewport.getLayout().setActiveItem(1);
            }
            else
                Ext.Msg.alert("Invalid credentials");
        }
});
```

Here's a list of things to notice in the LoginController class defined in Listing 9-12.

- The LoginController class has two reference variables—namely, userName and password defined. The username variable refers to the selector expression **"login textfield[id=usernametext]"**. This expression searches for a textfield with usernametext as the id inside the **login** xtype—i.e., the LoginScreen object. The password variable is mapped to the expression **"#passwordtext"**. The different selector expressions have been used differently to only highlight various options.

- The actual loading of the LoginScreen.js file happens only when LoginController class is instantiated. The views array has the LoginScreen configured.

- The authenticate() function validates the credentials. On successful validation the HomeScreen instance is created and added to the Viewport.

Let's define the HomeController class as shown in Listing 9-13.

Listing 9-13. HomeController.js

```
Ext.define("Chapter09.controller.HomeController", {
    extend: "Ext.app.Controller",
    id: "HomeController",
    refs: [
        { ref: "actionItemsGrid", selector: "home grid" },
        { ref: "actionItemDetailsPanel", selector: "home form" }
    ],
    models: ["ProjectActionItem"],
    stores: ["ProjectActionItemStore"],
    views: ["home.ProjectActionItemDetailsPanel", "home.ProjectActionItemGrid", "home.HomeScreen"],
    init: function () {
        this.control({
            "home": {
                beforerender: this.loadProjectActionItems
            },
            "home grid": {
                itemclick: this.displayProjectActionItemDetails
            }
        });
    },
    displayProjectActionItemDetails: function (src, record) {
        this.getActionItemDetailsPanel().loadRecord(record);
    },
```

```
    loadProjectActionItems: function () {
        var store = Ext.getStore("ProjectActionItemStore");
        store.load();
        this.getActionItemsGrid().reconfigure(store);
    }
});
```

Here's a list of things that we've written in the HomeController class defined in Listing 9-13.

- The class has the ProjectActionItem and ProjectActionItemStore files configured in the models and stores attributes, respectively.

- The views attribute has home.ProjectActionItemGrid, home.ProjectActionItemDetailsPanel, and home.HomeScreen files configured. The *home.* prefix is due to the home folder where these files are stored.

- We've handled the beforerender event of the home xtype. We load the ProjectActionItemStore only before the home screen is rendered to the page.

- The Ext.getStore() method is used to access the ProjectActionItemStore instance. If the instance is available, it returns a reference to the same. If the instance is not available, a new one is created and returned. All the store instances are essentially available as global variables that you can access from anywhere in your application using the Ext.getStore() method. It's usually a good practice to access Store instances from the Controller classes only as it's easier to maintain.

- The ProjectActionItemStore instance is wired up to the grid using the reconfigure() method.

- The displayProjectActionItemDetails() method is used to display the details of the selected row in the grid. The update() method on the ProjectActionItemDetailsPanel instance is invoked by passing the selected record.

As we've completed creating all the entities, let's modify the app.js code shown in Listing 9-4. We'll create an instance of the LoginScreen and add it to the Viewport as shown here.

```
this.viewport = Ext.create("Ext.container.Viewport", {
  renderTo: Ext.getBody(),
  layout: "card",
  items: [
    {
      xtype: "login"
    }
  ]
});
```

You can execute index.htm file and get the output as shown in Figure 9-2.

Summary

In this chapter I discussed developing Ext JS 4 applications following the MVC architecture. The complete Ext JS 4 code is organized into separate folders for storing the models, views, stores, and controllers. The Ext.app.Application is the class that holds references to the Controller, Model, Store, and View objects. Ext.application() method is used to create an instance of Application class and configure the application. The controller classes extend Ext.app.Controller. The controller classes have the event handling and navigation logic of the application.

In the next chapter you will learn about customizing the Ext JS 4 API. You will also learn packaging and deploying Ext JS 4 applications. We'll discuss unit testing Ext JS 4 applications using the *Jasmine* unit-testing library.

■ ■ ■

CHAPTER 10

Extending, Unit Testing, and Packaging

In the first nine chapters of this book we have analyzed various features of Ext JS 4. You learned how to use the UI controls, work with data components, create custom themes, and build applications that follow the MVC architecture. In this chapter you'll find out about some miscellaneous features in Ext JS 4. For example, you'll see how to extend the UI controls by creating custom components. I'll discuss various options involved in creating custom components and plugins. You'll also learn how to write unit tests in JavaScript to test our Ext JS 4 application. Finally you'll learn how to create an Ext JS 4 application from scratch, package it, and deploy it to the web server.

Extending the UI

In Chapter 9 when I discussed the MVC architecture, we created classes that extended some built-in classes such as `Ext.panel.Panel`, `Ext.grid.Panel`. These derived classes just modified the attributes of the built-in classes without really making a drastic change to their look and feel or behavior. In this section let's take a look at how to create custom UI components, custom plugins, etc., from scratch.

Custom Components

Let's start with a HelloWorld component that we will use, like this.

```
{xtype:"helloworld"}
```

Let's implement the helloworld component in such a way that it emits the following HTML code.

```
<span>Hello World</span>
```

We can implement this component by extending the `Ext.Component` class. The `autoEl` attribute of the Component class can be configured to provide the tag name and inner HTML of the element that you want to create.

Listing 10-1 shows the code for the HelloWorld component.

Listing 10-1. HelloWorld Component

```
Ext.define("HelloWorld",{
  xtype : "helloworld",
  extend : "Ext.Component",
  autoEl : {
   tag : "span",
   html : "Hello World"
  }
});
```

When you use an instance of the HelloWorld component in an application you will get the Hello World text displayed on the screen with the following generated HTML code snippet.

```
<span id="helloworld-1010" class="x-component x-component-default">Hello World</span>
```

As shown in Listing 10-1 we have specified the HTML data using the autoEl attribute. The autoEl attribute corresponds to the Ext.DomHelper object. The autoEl attribute can have properties like tag, html, cls, and children for decorating the HTML code that will be generated. Any property other than these four items is treated as the attribute of the generated HTML tag.

Let's create a hyperlink component that will be used like this.

```
{
  xtype:"link",
  url:"http://www.apress.com",
  text:"Apress Inc"
}
```

Listing 10-2 shows the code snippet for the link component built using autoEl attribute.

Listing 10-2. Link Component

```
Ext.define("Link",{
  extend : "Ext.Component",
  xtype : "link",
  autoEl : {
   tag : "a",
   html : "Click",
   href : "#"
  },
  initComponent : function(){
    if(this.text)
      this.autoEl.html = this.text;
    if(this.url)
      this.autoEl.href = this.url;
    this.callParent(arguments);
  }
});
```

As shown in Listing 10-2, we have used the autoEl property of the Component class to create an anchor element. We've overridden the `initComponent()` method where we initialize the autoEl attribute using the values passed while creating the instance of this component. The `initComponent()` method can be treated as the constructor for custom components. You can write your initialization logic in it. You need to have a call default `initComponent()` method in the Component class using `this.callParent()` method.

When you use the Link component in an application you will get a hyperlink on the screen with the following generated HTML code snippet.

```
<a id="link-1010" class="x-component x-component-default"
href="http://www.apress.com">Apress Inc</a>
```

Figure 10-1 shows the output of the link component.

Figure 10-1. *Link component*

The autoEl attribute of the Component class can become tedious if you want to build a complex component where the HTML snippet that you're generating is a lot more verbose—such as a `<table>` element, for instance. Here's where you can use Ext.XTemplate. The Ext.Component class has two attributes: *tpl* for configuring XTemplate, and data for providing values to the template.

Let's build our link component using XTemplate. Listing 10-3 shows the code for the link component using XTemplate.

Listing 10-3. Link Component Using XTemplate

```
Ext.define("Link",{
  xtype : "link",
  extend : "Ext.Component",
  tpl : '<a href="{url}">{text}</a>',
  initComponent : function(){
    this.data = {
      text : this.text,
      url : this.url
    };
    this.callParent(arguments);
  }
});
```

As shown in Listing 10-3, the Link class has the tpl attribute configured. In the `initComponent()` method, we initialize the data attribute with the values for the url and text properties.

Let's throw in some validation for the url that's passed to the link component. You can write a validation function in the XTemplate instance and invoke it. In Listing 10-3, the tpl attribute can be modified to include the function like this:

```
Ext.define("Link",{
  ...
  tpl : Ext.create("Ext.XTemplate",
                 '<a href="{[this.validateUrl(values.href)]}">{text}</a>',
                 {
                      validateUrl: function (url) {
                          var valid = url.match(/^(ht|f)tps?:\/\/[a-z0-9-\.]+\.[a-
z]{2,4}\/?([^\s<>\#%"\,\{\}\\|\\\^\[\]`]+)?$/);
                          return valid?url:"#";
                      }
                 }
                 ),
  ...
});
```

As you notice in the tpl attribute, we've created an instance of XTemplate using Ext.create() method and have a validateUrl() function that validates the url using a regular expression. If the url is valid, the function returns the url. Otherwise it returns a hash (#). We've invoked this function using the expression {[this.validateUrl(values.url)]} where values refers to the data attribute of the XTemplate class.

Let's add a custom event to this component. When you click the anchor element, let's alert a message. Handling the click event for an anchor element is really easy in the traditional approach where you use the onclick handler, but it's not the same in this case. We may have to wire up the click event programmatically with the generated anchor element. Let's override the onRender() method in our Link class where we programmatically wire up the click event on the anchor element. In Listing 10-3 we modify the Link class to add the onRender() method.

```
Ext.define("Link",{
  ..
  onRender: function () {
   this.callParent(arguments);
   this.mon(this.el,
           "click",
           function () {
              alert("Clicked");
           },
           this);
  }
});
```

We have overridden the onRender() method, where the click event is registered with a handler function using the mon() method. The mon() method is used for adding listeners to events. The arguments for the mon() method are the HTML element, event name, event handler function, and the scope in which the handler function is executed.

Let's create our own event—say, "**go**"—which will be called when you click the link component. Also, you want to add a listener using the listeners property as shown below.

```
{
  xtype:"link",
  url:"http://www.apress.com",
  text:"Apress Inc",
  listeners : {
    go : function(){
          alert("You clicked the link");
    }
  }
}
```

Ext.Component class provides a addEvents() method that can be used to add custom events. You can raise the event using the fireEvent() method. Listing 10-4 shows the link component with a custom event called go. The go event is fired when you click the anchor element.

Listing 10-4. Link Component With go Event

```
Ext.define("Link", {
  xtype: "link",
  extend: "Ext.Component",
  tpl: '<a href="{url}">{text}</a>',
  initComponent: function () {
    this.data = {
          text: this.text,
          url: this.href
    };
    this.addEvents("go");
    this.callParent(arguments);
  },
  onRender: function () {
    this.callParent(arguments);
    this.mon(this.el,
            "click",
            function () {
              this.fireEvent("go}
            },
            this);
  }
});
```

As shown in Listing 10-4, in the initComponent() method we have the go event added using addEvents() method. In the onRender() method, we have the go event fired using the fireEvent() method. The fireEvent() method is called from the event handler of the traditional click event.

I explained the use of plugins in components like grid in Chapter 6. Let's develop a custom plugin now.

Custom Plugin

Plugins in Ext JS 4 (which you saw in Chapter 6 on data controls) are used to inject custom functionality to the UI components.

Let's create a plugin for the Ext.panel.Panel class. We'll develop a timer plugin and apply it to the panel. The timer plugin will display a timer for 10 seconds. After 10 seconds, the timer is stopped and the panel is disabled. Figure 10-2 shows the screenshot of the Panel with a timer plugin.

```
Time left : 9 seconds
This is a panel with timer plugin
```

After 10 seconds panel is disabled

```
Time left : 0 seconds
This is a panel with timer plugin
```

Figure 10-2. *Panel with a timer plugin*

You can create a custom plugin by extending the Ext.AbstractPlugin class. The AbstractPlugin class has an init(component) method where the component argument corresponds to the underlying UI component where the plugin is used. In our case the component refers to the Panel object. Inside this init() method we'll start a timer that runs for 10 seconds. Listing 10-5 shows the timer plugin.

Listing 10-5. Timer Plugin

```
Ext.define("TimerPlugin", {
  extend: "Ext.AbstractPlugin",
  alias: "plugin.timerplugin",
  limit: 10,
  count: 0,
  intervalId: null,
  init: function (component) {
    var me = this;
    this.intervalId = window.setInterval(function () {
                         me.timer(component);
                         }, 1000);
  },
  timer: function (component) {
   if (this.count != this.limit) {
    this.count += 1;
    component.setTitle("Time left : " + (this.limit - this.count) + " seconds");
   }
   if(this.count == this.limit) {
     component.disable();
     window.clearInterval(this.intervalId);
   }
 }
});
```

In Listing 10-5 we've created a TimerPlugin class that extends AbstractPlugin. The init() method users the window.setInterval() method, which runs every 1000 milliseconds and calls a timer() method.

In the timer() method we have the logic to compute the end time and update the panel's title. When the count variable reaches the limit, the panel is disabled.

Listing 10-6 shows the Panel object that uses the timer plugin.

Listing 10-6. Panel that Uses the Timer Plugin

```
Ext.create("Ext.panel.Panel", {
    title: "Timer",
    html: "This is a panel with timer plugin",
    plugins : [{ptype:"timerplugin"}]
});
```

Unit Testing Ext JS 4

Code written in any language needs to be tested. That is a well-accepted fact in the programming world, and JavaScript code is no exception. Since JavaScript is used on the client side and a lot of developers mix it with HTML, it can be difficult to test the JavaScript code alone. It's important to keep the JavaScript code decoupled from the UI until you can test it.

We don't have to worry about writing modularized and decoupled JavaScript code in Ext JS 4 due to the MVC architecture we follow. So it's pretty easy to test the Ext JS 4 code. There are a number of tools and libraries like Ext Spec, Siesta, Jasmine, etc., available for testing Ext JS 4 code. We'll use the Jasmine toolkit for testing Ext JS 4 code.

Jasmine is a JavaScript unit testing library. In fact, it's more than a mere testing library. Jasmine is a Behavior-Driven Development (BDD) library. BDD is a development methodology based on Test-Driven Development and Domain-Driven Design. We'll not delve into BDD, however; instead, we'll focus on the unit testing abilities of Jasmine. Jasmine has a simple syntax to unit-test JavaScript code. Jasmine API does not come with the burden of DOM on its shoulders.

While this section is about using Jasmine to test Ext JS 4 code, let's start with an example of using Jasmine for testing plain JavaScript code, where you'll learn the basics of Jasmine. After that, we'll discuss how to use Jasmine to test an Ext JS 4 application.

You can visit https://github.com/pivotal/jasmine/downloads and download the latest stable version of Jasmine. At the time of writing, the latest version is 1.3.1. When you download the standalone zip file and extract it, you get the files shown in Figure 10-3.

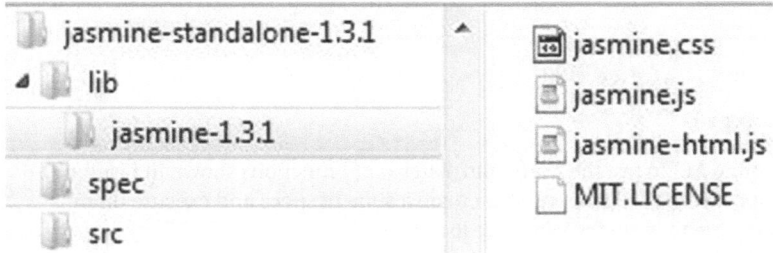

Figure 10-3. *Jasmine extract*

As shown in Figure 10-3, you need the contents of the lib folder in your application. In our case you need the jasmine-1.3.1 folder. The three files jasmine.css, jasmine.js, and jasmine-html.js need to be referenced in our web page that runs all the tests. Let's create a HTML page—say, sample-tests.html—and set up a Jasmine environment. Listing 10-7 shows the code snippet for the sample-tests.html file.

Listing 10-7. sample-tests.html

```html
<!DOCTYPE html>
<html>
<head>
  <link rel="stylesheet" type="text/css" href="jasmine-1.3.1/jasmine.css">
  <script type="text/javascript" src="jasmine-1.3.1/jasmine.js"></script>
  <script type="text/javascript" src="jasmine-1.3.1/jasmine-html.js"></script>
  <script>
   function init() {
     jasmine.getEnv().addReporter(new jasmine.HtmlReporter());
     jasmine.getEnv().execute();
   }
   window.onload = init;
</script>
</head>
<body>
</body>
</html>
```

As shown in Listing 10-7, we've added the Jasmine stylesheet and scripts. In the init() function we add an HtmlReporter provided by the Jasmine API to the Jasmine environment that will generate an HTML report for the tests we execute. You can run *sample-tests.html* file just to make sure there are no errors reported by the browser.

Let's write some simple JavaScript code and test it using Jasmine. As our intention is to get accustomed to Jasmine basics, let us write simple add() and subtract() functions. We'll create a file calc.js and implement the add() and subtract() functions over there. Listing 10-8 shows calc.js with add() and subtract() functions.

Listing 10-8. calc.js

```javascript
function add(num1, num2) {
  return num1 + num2;
}

function subtract(num1, num2) {
  return num1 - num2;
}
```

Let's start writing the tests, using the Jasmine API to test the add() and subtract() functions shown in Listing 10-8. In Jasmine terminology the tests are called specifications, or specs. You create a suite of specs and execute them.

The basic functions you would use in Jasmine to write the specs are listed below.

- describe()

  - You create a test suite using the describe function. The describe() function is composed of specs. The general format of the describe() function is

    ```
    describe("name of the test suite", function(){
    //collection of specs
    })
    ```

- it()

  - Each spec or the test is specified by the it() function. The format of the it() function is

    ```
    it("name of the spec",function(){
      //the actual test code
    })
    ```

- expect()

  - The expect() function specifies the expectations and is used for performing the actual check or the test. For the Java or C# developers, expect() is equivalent to the assert() function. The expect() function is chained with Matcher functions to perform the test. The expect() function takes in a value that is matched with the expected value. Here are some examples of using the expect() function:

    ```
    expect(123).toEqual(123)
    expect(someVar).toBeDefined()
    expect(true).toBe(true)
    ```

There are some more functions in Jasmine, such as the describe(), it(), and expect(), that we can use. We'll not get into those as it's beyond the scope of this chapter. If you want to read more about the Jasmine API, you can read its documentation at http://pivotal.github.io/jasmine/.

Let's develop our specs for the add() and subtract() methods as shown in Listing 10-9. We'll write our code in a file called 'calcspecs.js'.

Listing 10-9. calcspecs.js

```
describe("Addition", function () {
    it("test add() is defined", function () {
        expect(add).toBeDefined();
    });
    it("test add 2 simple numbers", function () {
        expect(add(1,2)).toEqual(3);
    });
});

describe("Subtraction", function () {
    it("test  subtract() is defined", function () {
        expect(subtract).toBeDefined();
    });
    it("test subtract 2 simple numbers", function () {
        expect(subtract(11, 2)).toEqual(9);
    });
});

describe("Multiplication", function () {
    it("test  multiply() is defined", function () {
        expect(multiply).toBeDefined();
    });
});
```

We've created three suites—namely, Addition, Subtraction, and Multiplication. The Addition and Subtraction suites have two specs each. The Multiplication suite has a spec that checks whether multiply function is defined. This spec will throw an error obviously.

You have to modify the sample-tests.html file to include calc.js and calcspecs.js files. Figure 10-4 shows the output when you run the sample-tests.html file.

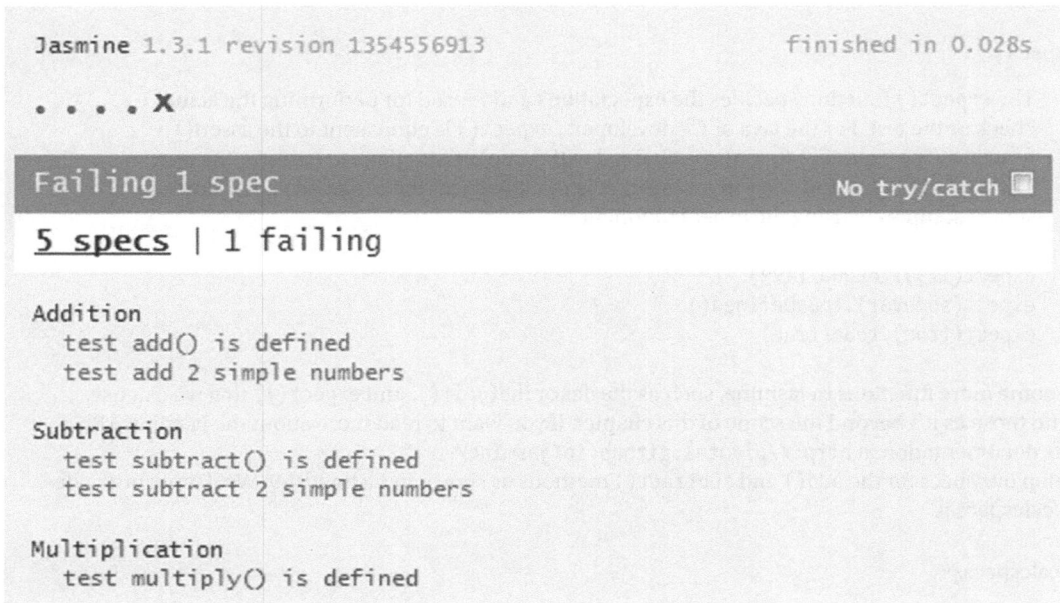

Figure 10-4. *Output of sample-tests.html*

Now that you've learned the basics of Jasmine, let's test our Ext JS 4 application using Jasmine.

To begin with, let's create a simple MVC application where we display a grid and the details of each item in the grid in a window as shown in Figure 10-5.

Name ▼	Capital
India	New Delhi
USA	Washington, D.C
France	Paris
Brazil	Brasilia

USA ✕
Washington, D.C
North America

Figure 10-5. *MVC application to be tested using Jasmine*

As shown in Figure 10-4, the grid shows a list of countries and when you click on any item you see the details of the country shown in a pop-up window. Let's implement this application using the MVC architecture. As we have discussed MVC in detail in Chapter 9, we'll take a fast-track approach to get to the testing part. Figure 10-6 shows the app folder that contains the code for the application.

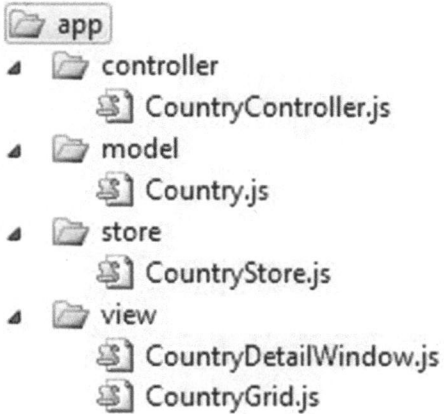

Figure 10-6. File structure for the MVC application to be tested using Jasmine

Listing 10-10 shows the code for the Country and CountryStore classes.

Listing 10-10. Country and CountryStore

```
Ext.define("Chapter10.model.Country",{
    extend : "Ext.data.Model",
    fields : ["name","capital","continent"]
});
Ext.define("Chapter10.store.CountryStore",{
    extend : "Ext.data.Store",
    autoLoad : false,
    model : "Chapter10.model.Country",
    proxy : {
      url : "countries.txt",
      type : "ajax",
      reader : {
          type : "json",
          root : "countries"
      }
    }
});
```

Listing 10-11 shows the code for the view classes CountryGrid and CountryDetailWindow.

Listing 10-11. CountryGrid and CountryDetailWindow Classes

```
Ext.define("Chapter10.view.CountryGrid", {
  extend: "Ext.grid.Panel",
  xtype: "countrygrid",
  store: "CountryStore",
  columns: [
  { header: "Name", dataIndex: "name" },
  { header: "Capital", dataIndex: "capital" }
  ]
});
Ext.define("Chapter10.view.CountryDetailWindow", {
  extend: "Ext.window.Window",
  xtype: "countrydetail",
  title: "Detail", height: 75, width: 200, padding: 2,
  layout : "vbox",
  items: [
  { xtype: "label", id: "capitallabel" },
  { xtype: "label", id: "continentlabel" }
  ]
});
```

Listing 10-12 shows the code for the CountryController class.

Listing 10-12. CountryController Class

```
Ext.define("Chapter10.controller.CountryController", {
  extend: "Ext.app.Controller",
  models: ["Country"],
  stores: ["CountryStore"],
  views: ["CountryGrid", "CountryDetailWindow"],
  refs: [
    { ref: "countryGrid", selector: "countrygrid" },
    { ref: "countryDetail", selector: "countrydetail" },
    { ref: "continent", selector: "countrydetail label[id=continentlabel]" },
    { ref: "capital", selector: "countrydetail label[id=capitallabel]" },
  ],
  init: function () {
   Ext.getStore("CountryStore").load();
   this.control({
     "countrygrid": {
       itemclick: this.onCountryClicked
     }
   });
  },
  onCountryClicked: function (src, record) {
    if (!this.getCountryDetail())
      Ext.create("Chapter10.view.CountryDetailWindow");
    this.getCountryDetail().setTitle(record.get("name"));
    this.getCapital().setText(record.get("capital"));
```

```
        this.getContinent().setText(record.get("continent"));
        this.getCountryDetail().show();
    }
});
```

The root namespace name of the application is Chapter10, as you can notice from the code snippets above. We'll ignore the app.js file as it's not of much importance in this example.

Let's set up the Jasmine environment and create the specs. We'll create two specs—one each for testing the CountryStore and CountryController classes. Let's create a folder called app-test and store the jasmine library and the specs in it. We'll configure the test application in a file called app-test.js and the main HTML file that will be executed will be tests.html file. Figure 10-7 shows the file structure of the project after adding the above mentioned files.

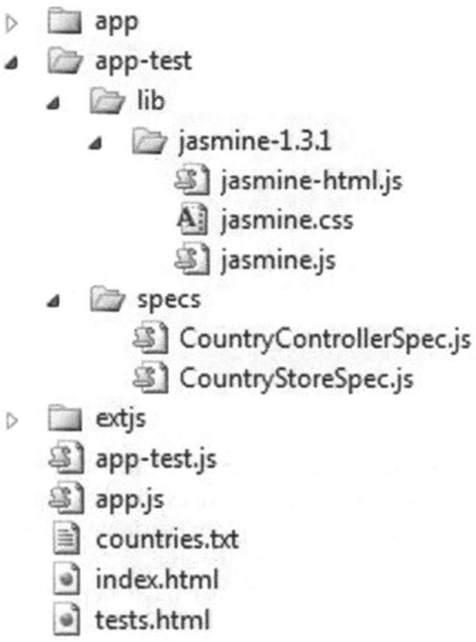

```
▷  📁 app
◢  📂 app-test
   ◢  📂 lib
      ◢  📂 jasmine-1.3.1
              📄 jasmine-html.js
              📄 jasmine.css
              📄 jasmine.js
   ◢  📂 specs
              📄 CountryControllerSpec.js
              📄 CountryStoreSpec.js
▷  📁 extjs
   📄 app-test.js
   📄 app.js
   📄 countries.txt
   📄 index.html
   📄 tests.html
```

Figure 10-7. *File Structure of the MVC application with Jasmine library*

As you notice in Figure 10-7, I have used Jasmine version 1.3.1.

Listing 10-13 shows the code snippet for tests.html file that will be executed in the browser.

Listing 10-13. tests.html

```html
<!DOCTYPE html>
<html>
<head>
 <link rel="stylesheet" type="text/css" href="app-test/lib/jasmine-1.3.1/jasmine.css">
 <script src="extjs/ext-all.js"></script>
 <script type="text/javascript" src="app-test/lib/jasmine-1.3.1/jasmine.js"></script>
 <script type="text/javascript" src="app-test/lib/jasmine-1.3.1/jasmine-html.js"></script>
 <script src="app-test.js"></script>
```

```html
<script src="app-test/specs/CountryStoreSpec.js"></script>
<script src="app-test/specs/CountryControllerSpec.js"></script>
</head>
<body>
</body>
</html>
```

We've added the Jasmine related files, app-test.js and the two specs in tests.html.

Listing 10-14 shows the code snippet for app-tests.js file where the test environment is set up.

Listing 10-14. app-test.js

```javascript
Ext.Loader.setConfig({enabled : true});

var Application = null;

Ext.onReady(function() {
 Application = Ext.create('Ext.app.Application', {
    name: 'Chapter10',
    controllers: ["CountryController"],
    launch: function() {
     jasmine.getEnv().addReporter(new jasmine.HtmlReporter());
     jasmine.getEnv().execute();
    }
 });
});
```

The interesting difference between what we wrote in app.js and what we've written in app-test.js is the way we create the instance of Ext.app.Application class. As shown in the code snippet in Listing 10-14, we explicitly create an instance of the Application class and assign it to a global variable called Application. This global variable will be used in the specs we'll implement later. The launch() function has the Jasmine environment configured.

Let's create the specs now. You can create any number of specs. You have to add them to the test page. Let's create a spec to test the CountryStore. You can give any name for the spec file. The CountryStore spec will load the store data and test if the data is properly loaded. Listing 10-15 shows the code snippet for CountryStoreSpec.js.

Listing 10-15. CountryStoreSpec.js

```javascript
describe("Country Store", function () {
var store = null;

beforeEach(function () {
 store = Application.getStore("CountryStore");
 store.load();
 waitsFor(function () {
   return !store.isLoading(); },
   "Unable to load countries.txt",
   5000);
});

 it("test store data", function () {
  expect(store.getCount()).toEqual(4);
  var country = store.getAt(0);
```

```
    expect(country.get("name")).toEqual("India");
    expect(country.get("capital")).toEqual("New Delhi");
    expect(country.get("continent")).toEqual("Asia");
  });
});
```

In Listing 10-15 we have written a spec to test the store data, where we test for the record count and also check the first records' details. The beforeEach() function in Jasmine is a set up method that is called before running each spec. It's not of prime importance here as there's only one spec in this suite.

In the beforeEach() function we access the store instance and call the load() method. Since the store loads records asynchronously, we give it 5000 milliseconds and check if the store has completed loading the records. The whole asynchronous loading process is achieved using the waitsFor() function provided in Jasmine.

You can add more specs to test the CountryStore instance based on your needs.

Let's create the CountryControllerSpec.js, which has the specs to test the CountryController class. We'll test the references in the CountryController and check if the details of the country are displayed in a window when the row in the grid is clicked. Listing 10-16 shows the code for CountryControllerSpec.js.

Listing 10-16. CountryControllerSpec.js

```
describe("CountryController", function () {
 var countryController = null;
 var countryGrid = null;
 var countryStore = null;

   beforeEach(function () {
      countryController = Application.getController("CountryController");
      countryGrid = Ext.create("Chapter10.view.CountryGrid");
      countryStore = Application.getStore("CountryStore");
      countryStore.load();
      waitsFor(function () {
       return !countryStore.isLoading();
      }, "Unable to load countries.txt", 5000);
   });

   it("test Country Grid", function () {
      var grid = countryController.getCountryGrid();
      expect(grid).toBeDefined();
      expect(grid.columns.length).toEqual(2);
   });

   it("test country grid item click", function () {
      var grid = countryController.getCountryGrid();
      grid.fireEvent("itemclick", grid.getView(), countryStore.getAt(0));
      expect(countryController.getCountryDetail()).toBeDefined();
   });
});
```

In the code snippet in Listing 10-16 we've a beforeEach() function where we initialize the countryStore, countryController and create an instance of the CountryGrid.

In the *'test country grid'* spec we access the country grid using the getCountryGrid() method generated for the reference variable countryGrid in the CountryController.

The *'test country grid item click'* spec is interesting. We programmatically fire the itemclick event using the fireEvent() method by passing the first record in the store as one of the arguments. According to the code in Listing 10-12, clicking the item in the grid will invoke the onCountryClicked() method and create an instance of the CountryDetailWindow. We check if the CountryDetailWindow object is created or not.

Running tests.html page will give you the output shown in Figure 10-8.

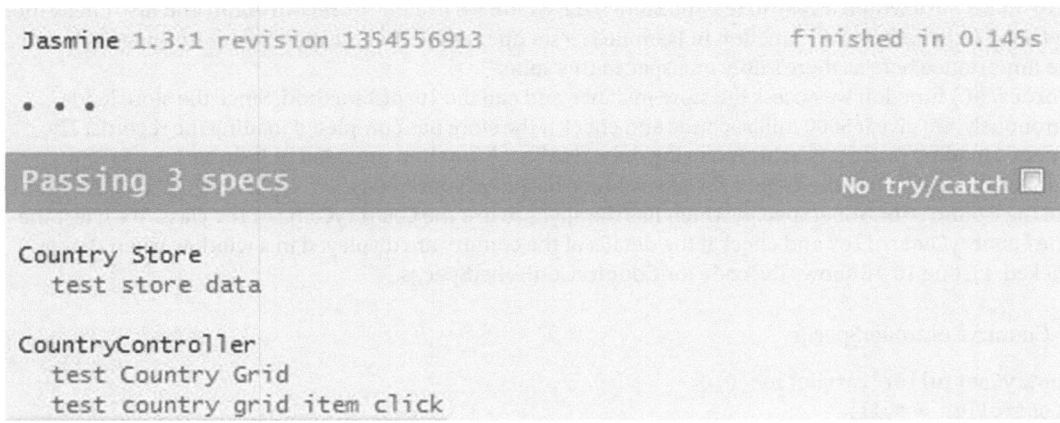

Figure 10-8. *The output of the tests.html page*

We've explored the basics of testing an Ext JS 4 application using Jasmine. Apart from the options discussed here, there are various parts of an Ext JS 4 application that you can effectively test using Jasmine to make your application foolproof. You also need to be careful while unit testing Ajax calls to the server resources as it will take a long time to do that. You can do it by creating mock data and unit testing it. It's also important to be a little cautious while unit testing complex UI interactions like drag and drop behavior, grid, and tree interactions as you may have to tweak your code a bit to make it suitable for testing.

Let's try creating and deploying an Ext JS 4 application using the Sencha Cmd tool.

Packaging

We have been creating an Ext JS 4 application manually from scratch, adding all the source files, CSS files, themes folder, and the MVC folder structure so far. Though it's a one-time job in a project, it's a tedious one.

You can use the Sencha Cmd tool that you met in Chapter 8, while learning about Theming and Styling, to generate an Ext JS 4 application that creates a complete template for generating the application. In technical circles this is commonly referred to as *Scaffolding*.

Let's generate an Ext JS 4 application using the generate command shown below.

```
sencha –sdk PathToSDK generate app NameOfTheApp PathToTheApp
```

Figure 10-9 shows the screenshot of the generate command run from the command prompt.

```
C:\>sencha -sdk c:\ext-4.2.0 generate app Chapter10 C:\Chapter10
Sencha Cmd v3.1.0.256
[INF]
[INF]   init-plugin:
[INF]
[INF]   init-plugin:
[INF]   Invoking plugin (C:\ext-4.2.0\.sencha\workspace\plugin.xml) - suppor
rgets: -before-generate-workspace
[INF]
[INF]   -before-generate-workspace:
[INF]   Invoking plugin (C:\ext-4.2.0\.sencha\workspace\plugin.xml) - suppor
rgets: generate-workspace
[INF]
[INF]   cmd-root-plugin.init-properties:
[INF]
[INF]   init-properties:
[INF]
[INF]   init-sencha-command:
[INF]
[INF]   init:
[INF]
[INF]   -before-generate-workspace:
[INF]
```

Figure 10-9. *sencha generate command*

As shown in Figure 10-9 we've generated the *Chapter10* application. Figure 10-10 shows the contents of the Chapter10 application.

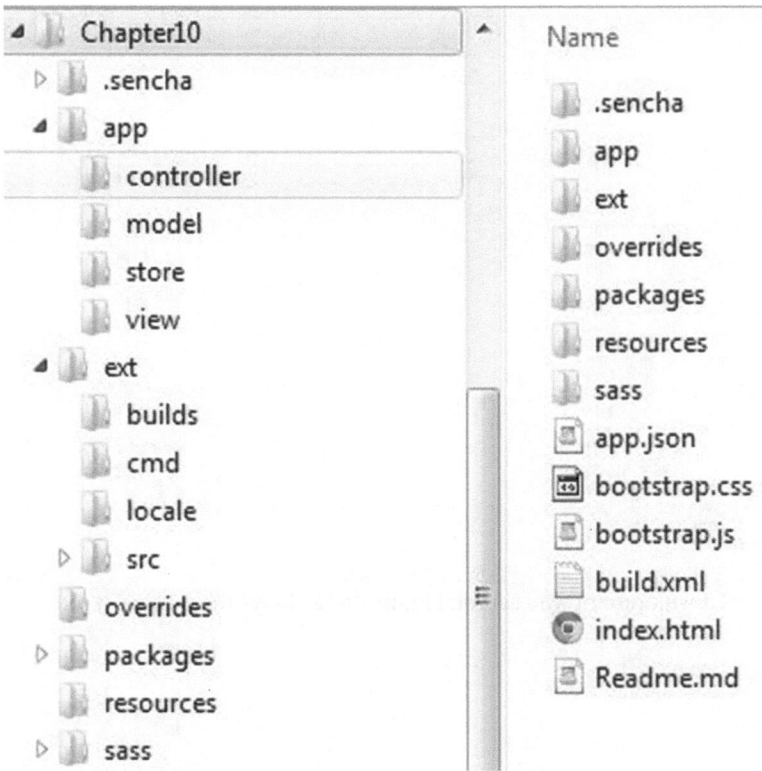

Figure 10-10. *Contents of Chapter10 application*

As shown in Figure 10-10, the Chapter10 seems to be loaded with all the basic folders and files.

- **.sencha** folder contains the project-related configuration files.
- **app** folder has the MVC folder structure. This folder contains the **app.js** file also.
- **ext** folder contains the source files.
- **packages** folder contains the custom packages that you may want to use in your application, like the themes.
- **resources** folder contains the images that you want to use in your application.
- **index.html** file is the executable web page where all the appropriate files have been referenced.

As a developer all you need to do now is load this generated application folder in the IDE of your choice and start building the models, views, controllers, and stores. You can also play with themes and other resources. I loaded this application in Visual Studio, one of my favorite IDEs, as a web application like that shown in Figure 10-11.

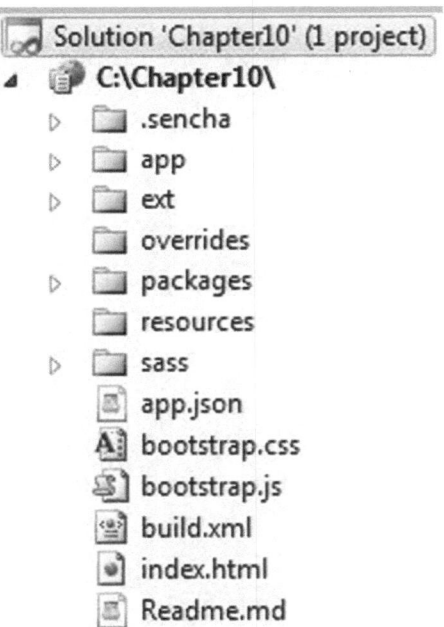

Figure 10-11. *Chapter10 application loaded in IDE*

I launched the index.html page in a local development web server. Figure 10-12 shows the output of the index.html page.

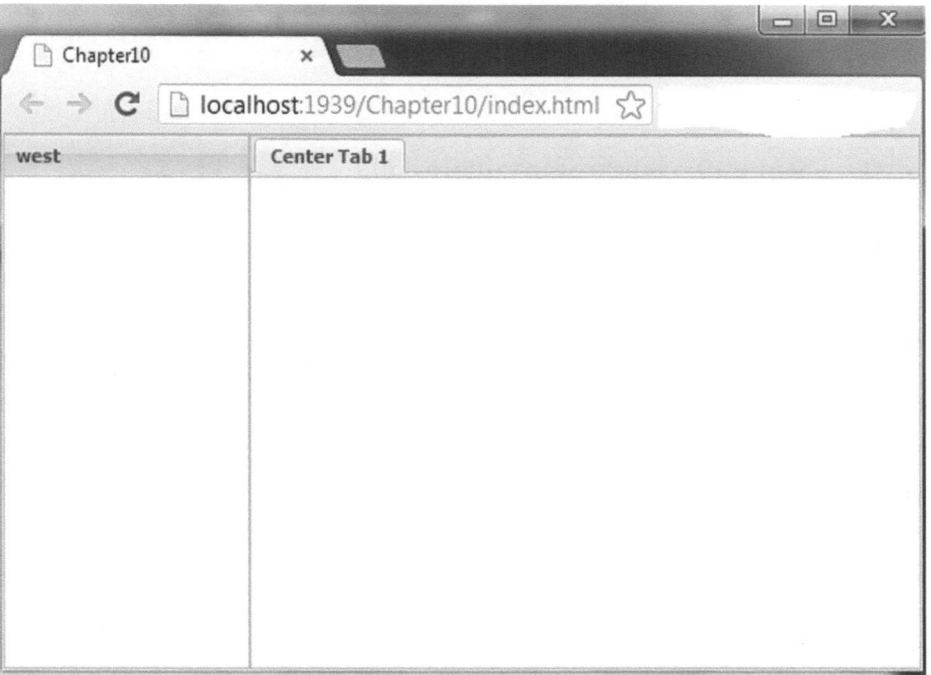

Figure 10-12. *Output of index.html page*

As shown in Figure 10-12, the default view is the Ext.container.Viewport instance with border layout. The center region of the Viewport is a tab panel.

You can now modify the code and start building your application. After completing development we need to build it so that it can be deployed to the production web server. Building the application involves tasks like minifying the JavaScript files, generating CSS from SCSS files, finding and including only the source code of those components used in the application, etc. All these tasks can be implemented using the simple build command shown here.

```
sencha build app production
```

You can build the application for a production or a testing environment.
Figure 10-13 shows the build command run from the command prompt.

```
C:\Chapter10>sencha app build production
Sencha Cmd v3.1.0.256
[INF] Including theme package ext-theme-classic for app.theme=ext-theme-cl
build
[INF]
[INF] init-plugin:
[INF]
[INF] init-plugin:
[INF] Invoking plugin (C:\Chapter10\.sencha\app\plugin.xml) - supported ta
-before-app-build
[INF]
[INF] -before-app-build:
[INF] Invoking plugin (C:\Chapter10\.sencha\app\plugin.xml) - supported ta
  app-build
[INF]
[INF] cmd-root-plugin.init-properties:
[INF]
[INF] init-properties:
[INF]
[INF] init-sencha-command:
[INF]
[INF] init:
[INF]
[INF] -before-app-build:
[INF]
[INF] app-build-impl:
[INF]
[INF] production:
[INF]
[INF] -before-init-local:
[INF]
```

Figure 10-13. *sencha build command*

The build command generates a build folder in your application. The build folder contains the production code that can be copied to the production web server. Figure 10-14 shows the generated build folder.

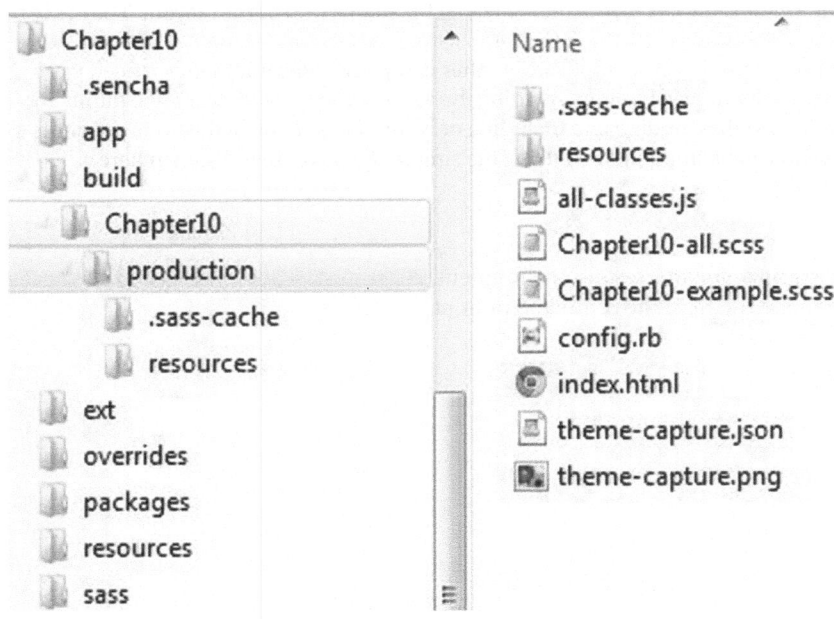

Figure 10-14. *build folder*

As shown in Figure 10-14, the build folder contains *Chapter10/production* folder, which has the files that you can deploy to the application. Ideally you just need to copy the *resources folder, index.html,* and *all-classes.js* files to the production server. The all-classes.js file contains all the JavaScript code used in the application. This includes the API code that our application needs and the code that we've written. The all-classes.js has the JavaScript code in a compressed format, thereby reducing the size. Sencha Cmd uses the YUI (Yahoo User Interface) JavaScript compressor to compress the JavaScript code.

Summary

In this chapter you learned how to extend the Ext JS 4 API by creating custom components and plugins. You can create a custom component by using the autoEl attribute to specify the HTML element. If you want to build a complex component, you can use the XTemplate using the tpl attribute and a data attribute for supplying data to the template. Plugins can be developed by inheriting the Ext.AbstractPlugin class and overriding the init() method.

You can test Ext JS 4 applications using the Jasmine toolkit. You can create specs and specify the expectations on the Ext JS4 application. Ext JS 4 applications can be created from scratch using Sencha cmd tool. You can use the generate app command to scaffold the application. Finally you can package the application and build it using a single sencha build command.

Index

▓ E, F